How
Cities
Provide
Services

How Cities Provide Services

An Evaluation of Alternative Delivery Structures

Sidney Sonenblum, John J. Kirlin,
and John C. Ries

Ballinger Publishing Company • Cambridge, Massachusetts
A Subsidiary of J.B. Lippincott Company

 This book is printed on recycled paper.

Copyright © 1977 by Ballinger Publishing Company. All rights reserved. No part of this publication may be reproduced, stored in a retrieval system, or transmitted in any form or by any means, electronic mechanical photocopy, recording or otherwise, without the prior written consent of the publisher.

International Standard Book Number: 0-88410-439-7

Library of Congress Catalog Card Number: 77-2313

Printed in the United States of America

Library of Congress Cataloging in Publication Data

Sonenblum, Sidney, 1924–
  How Cities Provide Services

  Includes index.
  1. Municipal services—California. I. Kirlin, John J., joint author. II. Ries, John C., joint author. III. Title.
HD4606.C2S64   352'.0794   77-2313
ISBN 0-88410-439-7

Contents

List of Figures	ix
List of Tables	xi
Preface	xv
Introduction	xvii

Chapter One
Structures for Municipal Service Delivery … 1

Local Government Reform	1
The Reform Tradition and Structural Adaption	1
The New Reform	4
Alternative Ways For Providing Services	5
Service Structures and Modes	7
Modes of Service Delivery in California	7
Modes For Specific Services	9
City Types in California	11

Chapter Two
Selecting Service Delivery Structures … 15

Adaptive Behavior	15
Components of a General Model For Service Structure Selection	18
Available Alternative Structures	18

vi Contents

Considering Alternative Structures 27
Relation of Structure to Satisfaction 34
Reconsidering Structural Improvements 53
A General Model of Structure Selection 62

Chapter Three
A History of Contracting in L.A. County 71

Service Contracting 71
  Intergovernmental Cooperation 72
  Service Contracting as a Way of Doing Business 76
Incorporation, Contracting, and a Municipal County 79
Contract Pricing 87
Trends in Contracting 95
  County Department of Engineers 99
  Department of Roads 107
  The Los Angeles County Sheriff's Department 110

Chapter Four
Contracting of Municipal Services 117

The Effect of Contracting on City Budgets 117
  What Influences the Degree of Contracting? 118
  Does Contracting Affect Taxes? 124
  Does Contracting Affect Budget Expenditures? 125
The Effect of Contracting on Municipal Expenditures 128
  Effects of City Bureaucracy 130
  Effects of Special Districts 132
Contracting, City Budgets, and Municipal Services
  For Cities in L.A. County 136
  What Affects Contracting? 136
  How Does Contracting Affect Revenues and Taxes? 137
  How Does Contracting Affect Expenditures? 138
  What Affects Structural Competition? 138
Effects of Contracting on Specific Services 142
  Police 142
  Fire Protection 143
  Street Maintenance, Cleaning, and Lighting 146
  Other Services 147
Other Counties in California 148

Chapter Five
The Case of Police: Chief or Sheriff — 153

Police Contracting: Issues and Trends — 153
Some Statistical Comparisons of Police Service
   in Contract and Independent Cities — 156
Models of Police Performance — 160
   An Analysis of Similarity of Service Delivery — 162
   An Analysis of Patrol Manpower Levels — 165
   An Analysis of Expenditure Levels — 171
   Analysis of Difference in Output Levels — 174
An Integrated Analysis — 177
A Note on Crime and Arrest Data — 179

Appendix: Selected Methodological Issues — 183

Multiple Data Sources and Research Strategies — 184
The Citizen Survey — 188
   Scaling and Measurement of Attitudes — 188
   Salience and the Measurement of Attitudes — 191
   The Relationship Between Evaluations and Preferences
      in the Measurement of Attitudes — 193
Elite Interviews and Questionnaires — 194
   Exploratory Questionnaire — 204
   The Structural Incidence Questionnaire — 206
   The Police Services Questionnaire — 206
   Individual City Manager Interviews — 207
   Group City Manager Interviews — 208
   Other Interviews — 211
Modes of Service Delivery — 212
   Conceptualizing a Typology of Service Delivery Modes — 212
   Implementing the Typology in California — 216
   City Types in California — 226
The Econometric Analysis — 230
   Data Issues — 231
   Pooling Issues — 243
   Recursive Modeling Issues — 244
   Summary — 245

Bibliography — 247

Index — 265

About the Authors — 273

List of Figures

1-1	Effectiveness and Acceptability of Regional Service Delivery Approaches	3
1-2	Distribution of Modes for Service Delivery in California	8
1-3	Clusters of Twenty-six Municipal Services in California	10
1-4	Frequency of Modes and Producers in California Cities	11
1-5	Types of Cities in California According to Degree of City Government Involvement	13
1-6	Types of Cities in California According to Degree of City Government Control	14
2-1	March-Simon General Model of Adaptive Motivated Behavior	17
2-2	Service Selection as Adaptive Motivated Behavior	18
2-3	Alternative Structures to City Departments by Service Cluster	20
2-4	Selected Budget and Municipal Service Data	50
2-5	General Model For Selecting Municipal Service Structures	68

List of Tables

2-1	Type of Service Structure	19
2-2	Comparison of High and Low Expenditure Services	22
2-3	Relation of Service Structure to Service Cluster	23
2-4	Typology and Service Attributes	28
2-5	Frequency of Service Attributes Encouraging Structures Other Than City Departments, by Typology Categories	30
2-6	Preferred Service Structure	31
2-7	Correspondence Between Structural Preference and Actual Structural Selection	33
2-8	Reasons For Selecting Structure	35
2-9	Structure Effects on Performance Characteristics	36
2-10	Effects of Structure on Aspects of Decision Process	40
2-11	Managers' Views of Effects of Contracting on L.A. Region	42
2-12	Managers' Ratings of Service Performance by Alternative Structures	44
2-13	Consensus Index for Selected Characteristics	45
2-14	Consensus Indexes for City Departments, by Service	47
2-15	A Classification of California Cities	54
2-16	Disaggregation of Services Shown in County-City Agreements for 1973	56
2-17	Service Providers in Twenty-One Contract Cities	57
2-18	Expected Changes in Police Structure	60
2-19	Police Service Structures	61
2-20	Community and Service Characteristics Affecting Choice of Police Structure and Performance	63

xii List of Tables

2-21	Effects of Trade-offs between a City's Desire for Local Control and Service Delivery Structures	67
3-1	History of Patrol Car Rates	89
3-2	Summary of Service Agreement Trends	96
3-3	County Department and Special District Service Agreements	97
3-4	County-City Agreements for Selected Years	100
3-5	Cities with County Contracts	104
3-6	Estimated Contract Revenues, 1973/74	105
4-1	Mean Values for Selected Variables in Selected L.A. County Cities	120
4-2	Estimated Regressions for City Budgets in L.A. County, by Group—Step I: Contracting Equations	123
4-3	Estimated Regressions for City Budgets in L.A. County, by Group—Step II: Tax Rate and Revenue Equations	126
4-4	Estimated Regressions for City Budgets in L.A. County, by Group—Step III: City Expenditure Equations	129
4-5	Estimated Regressions for All Cities in L.A. County: Self-Provision Equations	131
4-6	Estimated Regressions for All Municipal Services in L.A. County: Step II: Tax Rate Equations	134
4-7	Estimated Regressions for All Municipal Services in L.A. County—Step III: City Expenditure Equations	135
4-8	Summary of Structural Competition	140
4-9	Estimated Regressions for Specific Service Expenditures in L.A. County—Step IVA: Excluding Employment Effects	144
4-10	Estimated Regressions for Specific Service Expenditures in L.A. County—Step IVB: Including Employment Effects	145
4-11	Mean Values for Selected Variables in California and Cities Outside L.A. County	149
4-12	Estimated Regressions for City Budgets in California and Cities Outside L.A. County	150
4-13	Estimated Regressions for Specific Service Expenditures in California and Cities Outside L.A. County: Including Employment Effects	151
5-1	Indicators Important for Assessing Police Performance	157
5-2	Description of Variables	158
5-3	Significance Test of Differences Between Means of Police Service Variables for Independent and Contract Cities	159
5-4	Significance Test of Difference in Variance of Police Service Variables for Contract and Independent Cities	163
5-5	Significance Test of Differences in Means and Variances of Variables for Unincorporated Areas and Contract Cities	164
5-6	Chi-Square Test of Crime Rate Differences	165

List of Tables xiii

5-7	Simple Correlation Coefficients Between Inputs and Outputs in Contract Cities	166
5-8	Comparison of County and City Police Salaries	168
5-9	Demand for Patrolmen Per Capita	170
5-10	Demand for Patrolmen Per Street Mile	172
5-11	Determinants of Police Expenditures Per Capita	173
5-12	Determinants of Property Offense Rates	176
5-13	Determinants of Violent Offense Rates	178
5-14	Crimes and Arrests in Contract and Independent Cities	180
A-1	Interview and Questionnaire Sample and Respondent Cities	195
A-2	Interview and Questionnaire Response Rates	202
A-3	Percentage Distribution of Provision Modes for Specific Services Among 84 California Cities	219
A-4	Summary of Distribution of Provision Modes	221
A-5	Expenditure Weighted Distribution of Services By Basic Mode	221
A-6	Finance, Planning, and Producer Actors in Basic Modes for Providing Services	222
A-7	Supplemental Modes of Service Provision	225
A-8	Comparison of Weighted and Unweighted Basic Modes of Provision	226
A-9	Percentage Distribution of Modes for All Services	227
A-10	Service Clusters, by Actor	229
A-11	Selected Data for Cities in Los Angeles County	232
A-12	Glossary of Variables	235
A-13	Mean Values for Selected Variables in Los Angeles County Cities	242

Preface

There is renewed debate in the halls of government, in newspapers and on campuses as to how cities do and should provide services to their residents. An important aspect of this debate concerns how the organization of local government—especially in metropolitan areas—relates to the cost and quality of municipal services. The authors' interest in these questions has been stimulated by the presence at our doorstep of a much celebrated, but relatively little studied, alternative to areawide government, namely, municipal service contracting, which is also known as the Lakewood Plan. Each of the 78 cities in Los Angeles County has at least one service contract with the county government. One-fifth of the cities provide over 40 percent of their services this way. With the help of a grant from the Research Applied to National Needs (RANN's) Division of the National Science Foundation, the authors undertook a comparison of municipal service contracting with other ways cities provide services in Los Angeles County and throughout the state of California. This book grew directly from and is based on the analyses and findings of that study, but it also goes well beyond the study.

We have accumulated many debts in preparing this manuscript and conducting the study upon which it is based. We are especially grateful for the company, the spirit of inquiry and collegiality, and the dedication of the professional and clerical staff which completed the original study: Donald Atwater, Theodore Bartell, Elizabeth Bennett, Paul Blustein, Phyllis Cadei, Reva Clayton, Mary Crawford, Clarissa Dong, Carl Hensler, Steven Mehay, Thomas Moule, Margaret Newhouse, Patricia Nicholas, Richard Ryan, Douglas Scott, Marilyn Schroeter, Ann Stevens and Brian Stipak. Among the many public officials who provided assistance and support, three must be mentioned by name: Vaughn Blankenship of the National Science Foundation, Clarence Leland of the Los Angeles County Chief Administrator's Office, and George Voight of the California Contract Cities Association. Finally, there was the splendid cooperation of city officials who responded to many questionnaires, the city and county officials who came to UCLA for group interviews, and the citizens who responded to our surveys. The message which this book carries is theirs. The quiet and unassuming contributions of city officials are improving the quality of city life. We are honored to be able to report and interpret their progress. We, of course, are solely responsible for the contents of this report.

Introduction

The primary purpose of this volume is to report on the findings of a research study[1] and present a model of the processes used by city officials in deciding whether and how to change existing structures or adopt new structures for providing municipal services. In the model presented, the concept of service structure is independent of the governmental jurisdiction; service structure is defined as a certain *pattern of relationships among governmental units* (and private firms, in some instances) rather than as a component of them. A city is a city is a city—no matter how it is organized—strong mayor, commission, council-manager, and so on. Its structure as a city has no necessary implications for the structures through which it delivers services to citizens. It can provide services through a variety of means: its own departments, by contracts with other units of government or with private firms, by overlapping jurisdiction with special districts, by issuing franchises to private firms, or by many combinations of each.

This reconceptualization of service structure is one of the most important products of our study. It can be used to classify service structures systematically and precisely; it can also be used to classify cities and services. Specifically, service structure is defined as a pattern of relationships among corporate actors (governmental and private) with respect to the three activities involved in providing a service, namely, planning it, producing and distributing it, and financing it. Obviously, one actor—a city for example—can perform all three, or two, or only one of these activities for different parts of the same service, for an entire service or for a set of services. Although the possible combination of public and private actors performing the three service activities is great, a limited set of

1. Sidney Sonenblum, John J. Kirlin, and J. C. Ries, *Providing Municipal Services: The Effects of Alternative Structures* (Los Angeles: UCLA Institute of Government and Public Affairs, 1975).

patterns emerges from an analysis of cities in California and an even more limited set predominates. And just as structures tend, in reality, to cluster around only a few alternatives, so also specific services tend to be associated with a limited number of structural alternatives, and cities tend to adopt a few distinguishable structural alternatives. The reconceptualization of service structure and the classification of structures, services and cities is reported in Chapter 1. Additional detail is provided in the Appendix.

The variety in service structures along with the patterns apparent in cities prompt an inquiry into the difference, if any, which service structure makes. The data readily available to pursue this inquiry for a reasonably large cross-section of California cities is modest at best. City revenue and service expenditure data are relatively easy to obtain along with some socioeconomic data for cities. However, service output measures are hard to come by and we limited ourselves to obtaining such data for the police service only. We also assembled historical information on the experience with contracting in Los Angeles County from administrative records and public documents. Information on the attitudes and perceptions of citizens and such officials as city managers, police chiefs and department heads was essential. We obtained it through a battery of questionnaire interviews and surveys. The design and an evaluation of these instruments is discussed in the Appendix. Analyzing and interrelating the various types of data produced an intriguing composite picture of the performance characteristics of different structures as well as hypotheses explaining why there are differences in the structure of cities and of services.

This integrated analysis of the several data sources was given coherence and meaning by a model of motivated adaptive behavior developed by James G. March and Herbert A. Simon.[2] The results of the integrated analysis are reported in Chapter 2. The underlying motivation for adopting new or otherwise revising existing service structures relates to how much inefficiency and financial burden a community is able and willing to bear for retaining varying degrees of control over the quality of municipal services. Different cities can and do make different trade-offs among control of quality, efficiency and financial burden.

The difficulties of making major structural changes for an entire service, however, are sufficiently great and the cost savings sufficiently uncertain as to provide incentives for those seeking to ease financial burdens to undertake a wide variety of structural tinkering. A single service may be broken down into several component parts, each having a different structure. In each case, the purpose is to reduce costs or increase efficiency without incurring too great a loss in local control of service quality.

Two policy issues emerge from this analysis. First, cities will not normally consider alternatives to city departments unless alternatives are available and

---

2. James G. March and Herbert A. Simon, *Organizations* (New York: Wiley, 1958), pp. 48-50.

known. Therefore, disseminating information on successful alternatives would be very useful. Second, cities will not abandon a department unless it is perceived to perform badly on the criteria of local control of service quality (departments are not abandoned solely because they are costly or inefficient). Therefore, structures need to be invented which lower costs without sacrificing local control.

Contracting as a means for providing municipal services is most extensive and most elaborate in Los Angeles County. The use of contracts expanded dramatically during the decade following the incorporation of Lakewood in 1954. By using contracts with the county and special district, many newly incorporated communities were able to keep their city property taxes low while gaining the benefits of incorporation. They achieved this by trading off some control over the quality of their services. Since the mid-sixties, the number of contracts between Los Angeles County and cities has stabilized. We do not expect to see them expand further because cities are experimenting with a wide variety of structural arrangements in an effort to invent ways of maintaining or increasing control over service quality while gaining some cost savings. The experience in Los Angeles County is recounted in Chapter 3.

The structure selected for providing a service makes a real difference. We found a direct relationship between the use of city department structures and the city's tax base. The wealthier the city, the higher its expenditures and the more likely it is to provide services through city departments, thereby maintaining complete control of service quality. The less affluent cities have smaller city budgets. The actual per capita expenditures for services tend to be lower. Additionally, a relatively large proportion of their services are provided through special districts which collect their own taxes and whose expenditures never show up in the city budget. These cities also happen to be the ones which contract for more of their services. They give up a measure of local control in the hope of gaining economy and reduced financial burden. In this they succeed, but they also purchase less service. These findings are based upon econometric analyses relating aggregate fiscal and administrative data to service structures for a number of California cities. The results of these analyses are summarized in Chapter 4, with further detail and a discussion of technical issues reported in the Appendix.

In the case of police services, where some output measures were available, we were able to undertake a more detailed analysis of the consequences of alternative structures for quality and other service attributes in Los Angeles county cities. We did so by developing regression models (for the year 1968/69) in which service structures and other variables were related to such factors as police expenditures, manpower, arrests and crimes. Cities with their own police departments spent more on police than cities which contracted for the service from the Los Angeles County Sheriff's Department, and also provided more patrol officers per capita. The lower expenditures and the fewer patrol officers in the contracting cities are almost totally the result of whether a city does or does not contract, and are not a result of other factors which might have such an effect. According to our analysis, contracting—taken by itself—does not significantly affect crime rates. However, the fewer number of patrol officers, which is associated with contracting, does seem to result in higher crime rates. Our analyses suggest that residents of a city that contracts generally get neither more nor less police service for their money than do residents of cities which have their own police department. However, city bureaucracies tend to exert pressures to expand city services. Cities that contract seem more able to resist these pressures and therefore have the opportunity to spend less money and to be provided with less police patrol service than cities having their own departments. In exchange for this opportunity they also give up a measure of local control over police services. The findings of this analyses are reported in Chapter 5.

Based on this analysis of California cities, there seems to be no doubt that service structure makes a big difference and selection of structures is one of the important decisions that communities make. Communities can and do choose different trade-offs between local control of service quality and financial burden. Different structural arrangements do perform differently for different services. Communities are showing more and more imagination in inventing structural arrangements that help to dampen rising service costs without, however, exacting unacceptable losses of community control of quality. It is our hope that those at the national and state levels of government who are in a position to influence the structure of local government will take note of these trends. There is no need to believe in panaceas—whether of the areawide variety or the decentralized variety. The reality of local governmental structure is much richer, more complex, and more promising. There is vitality and healthy ferment. Truly creative responses to the mounting costs of local government are being developed. These efforts need to be recognized, supported, and encouraged. It is our hope that this volume will bring the variety and experimentation currently going on in local government to the attention of both academicians and practitioners.

**How
Cities
Provide
Services**

 Chapter One

Structures For Municipal Service Delivery

LOCAL GOVERNMENT REFORM

The Reform Tradition and Structural Adaptations

From the very beginning, practitioners, scholars and reformers have claimed that efficiency, economy, responsiveness, civic virtue, and most, if not all, other blessings of "good" government could be realized, if only the "proper" governmental structures were adopted. Sadly, the definition of proper structures has changed over the years and is often in contention at any given time. The disagreement is as much over the definition of what makes good government as it is over the structural prerequisites of achieving it. For some activists, good government means honest government; for others, it means public services at least cost; for still others, it means people deciding what they want, whatever that may be and at whatever cost.

One of the oldest normative stances emphasized the paramount importance of citizen participation and its structural prerequisites. In today's argot, this position is expressed as "small is better." Its tap roots are the Aristotelian commitment to participation in the governance of the community as a condition of virtue, and the American Populist principle that power is evil and its only legitimate exercise is based on common participation and consent. This belief stood behind Thomas Jefferson's proposal that the country be divided into nearly autonomous wards, each to be like a tiny republic unto itself. This model for the structure of local government is based on the Greek polis, which combines the concepts of limited size, autonomy and citizen participation. It also provides much of the philosophical and moral underpinnings of contemporary proposals for neighborhood government, home rule and other forms of decentralization.

In the past fifty years, the undesirable implications of autonomous communities located within a metropolis have been pointed out. Paul Studenski, in a study for the National Municipal League in 1930, questioned Jefferson's ideal and defined the proliferation of small, independent governments as a problem because they were unable to provide the services demanded by their citizens. His solution was centralization: creation of a metropolis-wide government, an ideal to which many civic reformers are still committed. By the mid-1950s, studies of the New York and the St. Louis metropolitan areas had produced similar proposals for the creation of areal supergovernments and also laid the groundwork for alternative methods of dealing with the problems created by the proliferation of autonomous communities in the metropolis.

Students of government addressing the question of political participation in the polis pondered the low level of participation in municipal elections and concluded that citizens were basically satisfied with their local governments. Legitimate government required consent and only minimal participation. Then came traffic congestion, smog, water pollution, race riots, the civil rights movement, free speech movements—and the backlash. Political analysts reexamined low voter participation and began to arrive at a different conclusion: the reason citizens do not vote is that they feel their votes would not make any difference—they feel alienated. Local government appeared to be losing its base of legitimacy.

Despite these developments Americans have been increasingly populating the cities and suburbs of metropolitan areas. The management of affairs in these areas has assumed national importance. The provision of services, resolution of areawide problems, and management of societal conflicts are recognized as the predominant problems confronting metropolitan areas. Local governments are wrestling with these issues, as any observer at meetings of the National Conference of Mayors, National League of Cities, or International City Management Association can attest. Similarly, the states have increasingly recognized their role in the governance of metropolitan areas, not only through direct provision of services, but also through establishing regional units of government and serving as a middleman between the federal and local government. Included among the specific actions which states have taken are creating planning and development districts, authorizing regional councils, establishing areawide umbrella agencies, approving city-county consolidation, and passing enabling legislation which encourages local government cooperation, joint-powers agreements and contracting.

At the level of the national government, resolving the problems of cities and suburbs in metropolitan areas has been one of the highest domestic priorities. In a 1965 message to Congress on cities, President Johnson said, "In the remainder of this century—in less than forty years—urban population will double, city land will double, and we will have to build in our cities as much as all that we have built since the first colonists arrived on these shores." In justifying the establishment of the Department of Housing and Urban Development, he called upon local governments "to break old patterns—to begin to think, work and plan for the development of entire metropolitan areas." Both before the Johnson Administration and after, the federal government has appeared strongly committed to creating conditions which will foster initiative at the state and local level through which metropolitan areas can devise the mix of structures and programs suited to their needs. Among the important actions of the federal government are its A-95 review procedures; its encouragement of councils of government and other regional institutions; its areawide grant programs for encouraging development, environmental control, and public facilities construction; and its regulatory and planning legislation for land use, water quality, and air pollution.

Despite the continued commitment to reforming structure as a strategy for improving conditions in metropolitan areas, there is very little empirical evidence about how structure affects governmental performance. A recent, comprehensive review of experience with structural changes found only fragmentary analyses of their effects upon the performance of governments, and claimed that insufficient evidence is available to support empirically based choices among alternative structures for governance of metropolitan areas [B7].[1] For this reason, discussions of how changing governmental structure may affect the delivery of services, efficiency, or any other policy goal are too often conducted on the basis of ideology or axiomatic reasoning rather than evidence about their advantages and disadvantages. And because of this there is no assurance that reform brings improvements. For example, the Advisory Commission on Intergovernmental Relations identifies thirteen potentially important types of structural reforms; as shown in Figure 1-1 the effectiveness of these reforms is believed to be inversely related to their likelihood of adoption.

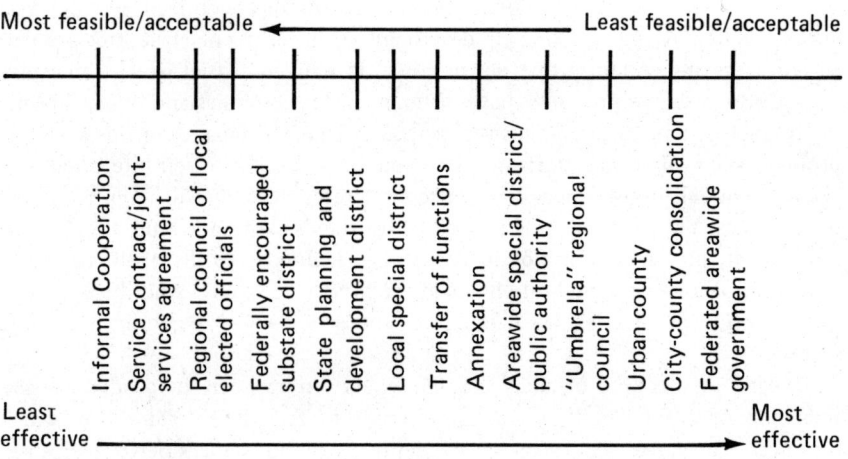

Figure 1-1. Effectiveness and Acceptability of Regional Service Delivery Approaches

1. References herein are enclosed in brackets, and refer the reader to specific sections of the bibliography.

The New Reform

The reform of government structure has traditionally focused on areal or jurisdictional considerations. The kind of question generally posed is, What government or system of governments can best deliver the variety of public services provided to a region? In recent years, however, there has been a movement away from this traditional focus.

The new reform movement has shifted the focus of analysis from governmental jurisdiction and its structure to specific services and the structures through which they are provided. At the very least, such a shift in focus improves the opportunity for measuring the performance of structures and thereby making more informed structural selection choices. However, to proceed in this manner it is necessary to develop a definition of structure which is independent of governmental jurisdictions. If such a definition can be devised, and the characteristics and consequences of alternative structures identified, then the problem of public service provision in metropolitan areas can be reformulated and made more tractable. Instead of asking the politically explosive question, How should the *governments* of metropolitan areas be organized in order to improve service provision?, one can ask, How can *service structures* be organized by governments in metropolitan areas so as to improve the quality and lower costs of public services? The problem of "proper" governmental organization (size and population of jurisdiction, council-manager, council-mayor, partisan or nonpartisan) can be largely separated out from questions of "proper" service organization. To make such a distinction is not to suggest the former is political and the latter is not. On the contrary, governmental structure and service structure, no matter how distinguished, are both political issues.

The new reform can be linked to two strands of theoretical and political developments. Along one line of development, government structures are perceived as having certain properties in common with industrial firms which produce distinguishable products, have different scale economies and organizational requirements, and different customers [B3]. The participants in this system—producers, consumers, and financiers of public services—are self-interested, not always rational, ill-informed, have different preferences, and differential access to resources. Yet all are seeking to achieve for themselves some kind of optimization which, in principle if not in content, is analogous to the profit or utility optimization of firms and households in the private economy. And the extent to which optimization is achieved measures the efficiency or performance of the system.

Integral to this kind of analysis is the separation between the production and financing of a service. It is not necessary that the same organization which produces the service also finance it. Under many circumstances performance can be improved if the structure which provides the service does indeed distinguish the production from the financing activity by having separate organizations perform each. From this perspective reform becomes a question of identifying those circumstances where performance would be improved by separating the production from the financing of a service.

A second line of development has emerged from the view that the multitude of overlapping jurisdictions and separate organizations involved with providing a service often result in unnecessary inefficiencies. Ony way to reduce these inefficiencies is through proper planning. Thus, in recent years planning has become equally important with production and finance as an essential activity in the provision of a service. The federal government, particularly, has emphasized the importance of planning in the provision of local services and has generally promoted, under the concept of comprehensive planning, the proliferation of regional organizations for the purpose of areawide planning and coordination. However, very often such planning agencies have been perceived by city officials as interfering with city government. The authority to plan may be of little importance if others have the authority to produce and finance.

The two lines of thought are thus, to some extent, in conflict: one suggesting that organizational specialization by activity in providing a particular service is ineffective because separating the planning from the operating activities generates conflict over authority and goals, while another line of development suggests that an organizational specialization which separates the producing and the financing activities is likely to improve overall efficiency in providing a service.

In spite of the uncertainties associated with structural performance, local governments are, to a considerable extent, involved with structural reform. However, it is rare that such reform is of the large-scale jurisdictional type associated with the reform tradition. Rather, the reform occurs on a small scale where changes are made in which organizations are responsible for particular activities of particular services. Thus, for example, a city might decide to transfer the production, financing, and planning of a particular component of a service—say a police laboratory—to some other organization than the city police department; or it might decide to give responsibility for a particular activity such as production of a service—say cleaning the streets—to some noncity organization, while retaining responsibility for the other activities such as paying for the street cleaning.

Such small-scale changes might be called structural adaptation rather than structural reform. Yet, whether adaptation or reform, it is essential that structures be so defined that the question of whether such changes improve performance in the provision of service can be considered.

ALTERNATIVE WAYS FOR PROVIDING SERVICES

Service Structures and Modes

Many different structures are used to deliver municipal services in the United States. In most places, city departments are the favored structure. In many places, contracting with other governments or private firms is an important alternative to city departments. City contracts with county government are particularly popular in Southern California.

Variations among cities in how services are provided is considerable. Special districts and county departments are used to provide particular services in some cities but not in others, making intercity financial comparisons almost impossible to evaluate. For a few services special authorities or other region-wide governmental structures are popular in some parts of the country but not in others.

Some cities encourage the franchising of private firms for service delivery while others prefer to engage in mutual aid or joint-powers agreements with their neighbors. The federal government increasingly assumes a responsibility to give local government grants and, directly or indirectly, to encourage regionalization of service delivery. The states pursue their own version of regionalization through substate districting, program coordination, and establishment of multi-jurisdictional umbrella organizations.

Until now there has been no systematic attempt to distinguish precisely among such different structures for providing municipal services. The boundaries, for example, between intergovernmental contracts, on the one hand, and grants, on the other, are not always very clear. These and other boundaries for service structures can be identified by specifying with precision the public or private corporate person (in our jargon, the actor) who performs each of the three central activities of service provision: planning, producing, and financing.[2] When the same corporate person (actor) performs all three of these activities for a service, as in the case of a typical department, we call that arrangement the *consolidated mode*. It is *consolidated* because the same actor performs each of the three activities necessary for service provision. It is a *mode* in order to help make the difference clear between our analytical constructs (modes) and the real-world organizations (structures) involved in providing services. A city department is a "structure" in common parlence. However, in our terms it is not necessarily a consolidated mode. It may be, if it performs all three service provision activities. If it does not, and some do not, then it is not a consolidated mode. Similarly, there may be other consolidated modes than the city department. For example, a special district structure may produce, plan, and finance a service, which in our terminology would be called a district consolidated mode. Clearly, precision requires a distinction between the pattern of relationships which define analytically distinguishable methods of providing services and the formal organizations of local government such as departments, bureaus, agencies, authorities, commissions, and districts.

There are three basic service modes in addition to the consolidated mode: (1)

---

2. The typology for service delivery modes developed in the course of this study is discussed in detail in the Appendix.

the contract mode—the actor who finances and plans the service does not produce it; (2) *the regulated mode*—the actor who plans a service does not finance or produce it; and (3) *the grant mode*—the actor who finances does not plan or produce the service. As indicated previously, the consolidated mode is very common in local government. A city (or county or special district, etc.) government finances the service through taxes (sometimes through user charges), produces it through city (or county or district) departments, and plans it through its internal decision-making mechanisms. If a city transfers production of the service to some other public or private entity (actor), but continues to plan and finance it, the service is then provided in a contract mode. If a city plans a service (setting rates and schedules for private firms engaged in residential trash collection or giving a franchise to a taxi company), but does not produce or finance it, the service is in a regulated mode. Finally, higher levels of government frequently assume responsibility for financing services they neither plan nor produce. In this instance, the service is in a grant mode.

This rather simple typology is suitable for analyzing individual services, groups of services, and cities. Some services tend to be provided via distinct and predictable modes. Other services vary in their mode from one city to the next. Cities tend to fall into certain patterned combinations of service modes. The typology, then, provides a basis for classifying service modes and cities which can be used for comparing cities that employ different alternatives. When better measures of service output are developed, the typology will provide a simple but quite precise differentiation among alternative arrangements for providing services, which can then be compared in terms of their performance. In the meantime the typology can be of great help in analyzing and understanding current patterns of service provision and identifying possible future trends.

Modes of Service Delivery in California

Descriptive information about 26 services was gathered from city managers in a sample of 84 California cities (half in Los Angeles County and half in other counties). Figure 1-2 summarizes how these 26 services are provided in the 84 cities in terms of modes of service delivery.

The consolidated mode accounts for almost three-fourths of all services delivered; the contract mode accounts for one-fifth; and the regulated and grant modes together account for less than one-tenth. These patterns hold for cities in Los Angeles County, in other counties, and for all cities in the state.

While the consolidated mode accounts for almost three-fourths of all municipal services delivered, consolidation by the *city* government accounts for only half. That is to say, although the city department is the single most important structure, one-half of municipal services are provided through other structures. And half of these other structures are consolidated modes.

The city finance variant of the contract mode accounts for about one-sixth of all services, and about half of these are contracts with the county as producer.

8 How Cities Provide Services

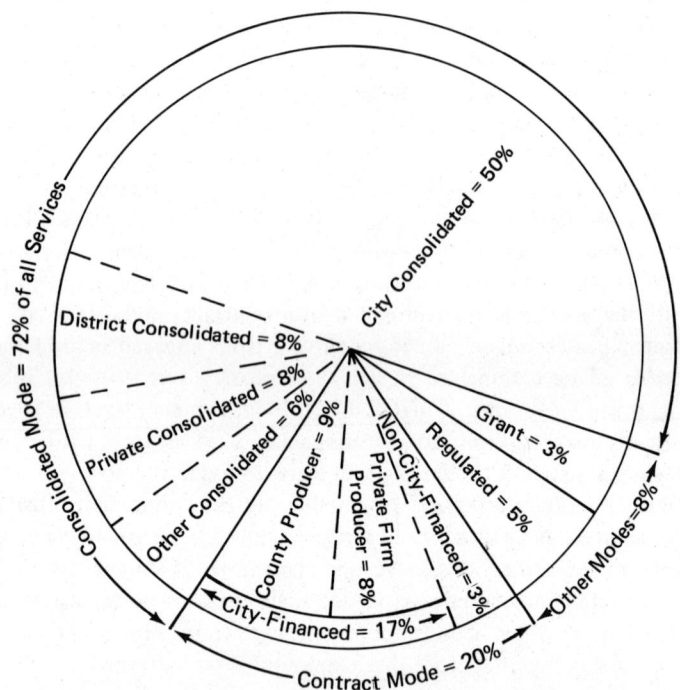

Figure 1-2. Distribution of Modes for Service Delivery in California

City government regulation accounts for two-thirds of the regulated modes, while city and county governments are each grant recipients in one-third of the grant modes.

Over fourth-fifths of all services are delivered through five specific modes: city consolidated (50 percent), district consolidated (8 percent), private consolidated (8 percent), city financed contract with county producers (9 percent), and city-financed contract with private producers (8 percent). This is true both when the level of service expenditures is not considered and when the specific services are weighted by their shares of city budget expenditures.

City governments finance two-thirds of all services and plan for about the same amount. However, they produce only half the services. The difference between the number of services which city governments produce and the number they finance arises primarily because of the availability of contracting. While it is clear that the city government is the most prevalent actor in municipal service provision, it also appears that there are other important actors involved in one-third of the financing and half of the production of municipal services.

District governments produce, finance, or plan about one-tenth of all service deliveries. Private firms also finance (that is, collect user fees) or plan about one-tenth of service deliveries, while because of contracting they produce about one-fifth of all services. The other important actor is county government, which produces about one-sixth of all services and equals the importance of private firms as a contract producer.

These percentages are about the same whether applied to cities in Los Angeles County or to other California cities. The only important regional differences are that in Los Angeles the county government is a relatively large producer under contract, while among cities in other counties private producers have a relatively large share of the contracts. Also, it appears that cities in Los Angeles County are more involved than other cities in regulating services that they do not produce.

According to our sample, about 30 percent of all services have more than one actor involved in a specific activity. This occurs partly because many services actually consist of components or subservices, each of which is provided through a different mode. It also occurs because city government very often is involved jointly with other governments in planning, even though it is not financing or producing a service. When these additional actors are treated as if they constituted supplemental modes of service delivery, then one-third of the 30 percent are consolidated, another third are regulated, and one-sixth are contract modes of service.

Modes for Specific Services

In spite of the variety of modes through which services are being delivered, specific services tend to be provided by one or two dominating modes. The twenty-six municipal services in this study fall into a small number of clusters, as shown in Figure 1-3.

One cluster of twelve services has been called the city core because they are almost always financed by city governments. Seven of the services in this cluster, which are particularly important and visible to city residents, are almost always provided through the consolidated mode with city departments as producers. They are called city production core services. The city production core includes planning, zoning, tree planting and trimming, parks and recreation, street signs and markings, street cleaning, and engineering services.

The other five of the city core services are largely public safety related and have been called the contract competition core because they tend to be provided not only through the consolidated mode but also through the contract mode. The contract competition core includes traffic patrol, general law enforcement, building and safety, street resurfacing, and traffic signal services.

Another cluster of fourteen services are not financed or produced by a large number (but not a majority of cases) of city governments. For this reason we have called them the city optional services. One group of nine optional services, tending to relate to the physical environment in the city, is often provided by special districts and has therefore been labeled the optional district competition.

10 How Cities Provide Services

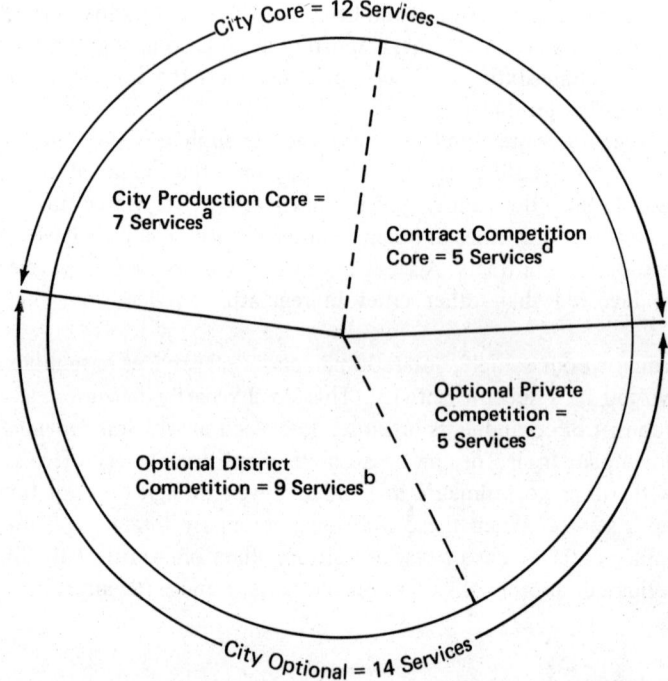

Figure 1-3. Cluster of Twenty-six Municipal Services in California

[a]City Production Core Services includes planning and zoning; tree planting and trimming; parks and recreation; street signs; street cleaning, and engineering services. The city consolidated mode accounts for 83 percent of deliveries from the City Production Core

[b]Optional District Completion Services includes fire protection; storm drains; noise pollution; sewer maintenance; street lighting; water distribution; libraries; and public transportation. The city mode accounts for 36 percent of their deliveries, while the district consolidated and regulated modes account for 24 percent.

[c]Optional Private Competition Services include animal regulation; residential refuse collection; ambulance service; business refuse collection and solid waste. City consolidated mode accounts for 12 percent of deliveries; private consolidated mode for 36 percent; and private contract mode for 14 percent.

[d]Contract Competition Core Services include traffic patrol; general law enforcement; building and safety; street resurfacing; and traffic signal maintenance. City consolidated mode accounts for 56 percent of deliveries and contract mode for 36 percent.

The district competition services include fire protection, storm drains, noise pollution, sewer maintenance, street lighting, water distribution, water-pollution abatement, libraries, and public transportation.

Another group of five services, often related to public health, has been called the optional private competition because it includes services which are very frequently produced by private firms through contract or consolidated modes. The private competition services include animal control, residential and business refuse collection, ambulance services, and solid-waste disposal.

Thus the consolidated and contract modes seem to dominate municipal service delivery in California. There are no services for which the regulated or grant modes are more important than the consolidated and contract modes. However, the regulated mode is relatively important for environment-related services such as refuse collection, solid-waste disposal, street lighting, and water pollution. And the grant mode is relatively important for capital-intensive services such as sewer maintenance, public transportation, water pollution, and storm drains.

CITY TYPES IN CALIFORNIA

Not only are particular services associated with specific modes across all cities in the state, but also particular cities tend to favor certain modes over others in their provision of municipal service.

For example, as shown in Figure 1-4, 33 of the 84 cities provided over three-quarters of their services through city departments or some other structure

Percent of Services	Modes			
	Consolidated Modes	*Contract Modes*	*Regulated Modes*	*Grant Modes*
75-100	33 Cities in Quartile	0 Cities	0 Cities	0 Cities
50-75	40 Cities in Quartile	4 Cities	0 Cities	0 Cities
25-50	11 Cities in Quartile	20 Cities	0 Cities	0 Cities
0-25	0 Cities in Quartile	60 Cities	84 Cities	84 Cities

Percent of Services	Producers			
	City Department	*County Department*	*Special District*	*Private Firm*
75-100	8 Cities in Quartile	0 Cities	0 Cities	0 Cities
50-75	40 Cities in Quartile	1 Cities	0 Cities	0 Cities
25-50	19 Cities in Quartile	21 Cities	5 Cities	19 Cities
0-25	17 Cities in Quartile	62 Cities	79 Cities	63 Cities

Figure 1-4. Frequency of Modes and Producers in California Cities

adopting the consolidated mode. An additional 40 cities use the consolidated mode for between one-half and three-quarters of their services. However, there are 60 cities which provide up to one-quarter of their services through contract, while another 20 cities provide between one-quarter and one-half of their services through the contract mode. Each of the 84 cities employs the regulated or grant modes for less than one-quarter of their services.

As shown in Figure 1-4 the most important producer of municipal services is the city department. Sixty percent of the cities use their own departments to produce over half of their services, while 20 percent are content with using departments for producing under one-quarter of their services. In 75 percent of the cities, less than one-quarter of the services are produced by county governments, special districts, or private firms. No city has more than half of its services produced by special districts or private firms, but one city does have over half its services produced by the county government.

These data indicate that cities differ substantially in the kinds of structures they use to provide municipal services. As indicated previously, services differ in the kinds of modes through which they are delivered and also group themselves into city core and city optional clusters according to the extent of city government involvement in their provision. By combining the three elements of city/structural differences, service/mode differences, and service/city involvement differences, five types of cities can be differentiated, as shown in Figure 1-5.

The city classification system is based on the mix of structures cities use to provide specific services. Most cities employ city departments more frequently than any other structure for most services. Therefore, classifying cities according to the structure most often used would provide only a gross classification in which most cities would be identified as city department cities. A more discriminating procedure is classifying cities according to the structures used relatively more often than in other cities.

Using this criterion of relative representation, one-third of the 84 cities in the sample are *self-provider cities*. These are the cities which use city departments relatively more than do other cities to provide both city core and city optional services. Another third are *production transfer cities*. These are the cities which, relatively more than other cities, employ some structure other than the city department to produce services while still participating in planning and financing the service. About one-quarter of these cities transfer production of the core services and about one-tenth transfer production of the optional services. The final third of the cities are *service transfer cities*. These are the cities which, relatively more than other cities, neither produce nor finance services, although they might be involved with some of their planning. Over one-quarter of these cities transfer the optional services, while less than one-tenth of the cities transfer any core services.

This classification arranges cities along a spectrum of city government involvement. The spectrum ranges from participation in each activity for all services;

Structures For Municipal Service Delivery 13

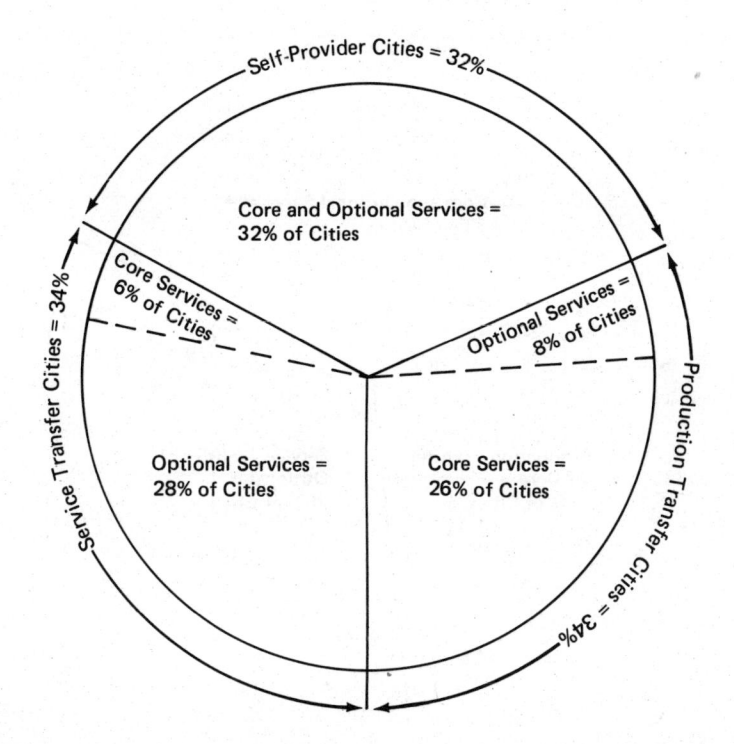

Figure 1-5. Types of Cities in California According to Degree of City Government Involvements.

goes on to participation in only the planning and financing activities for the core and the optional services; and ends with no city participation in any acitivites, except possibly planning for either the core or optional services.

The same classification also rearranges cities along a spectrum of city government control of service delivery, as shown in Figure 1-6. One type of city keeps control of the production, planning, and finance activities for core and optional services; this *city control* group is the same as the self-provider cities which account for 32 percent of all cities. Another type of city retains control over core services but gives up control of either production or both production and finance for the optional services. This *city control of core* group includes about 36 percent of the cities. A third type of city gives up control of either production or both production and finance of both core and optional services. This *non-city-control* group includes 32 percent of the cities.

By coupling measures of service performance with this city classification, we could arrive at meaningful generalizations to describe how performance differs among cities. For example, it is possible that self-provider or city control types of cities are seeking a high performance in terms of being responsive to citizens;

14 How Cities Provide Services

```
                    City Control = 32%

              Core and Optional Services =
                     32% of Cities

      Service Transfer of         Production Transfer of
      6% of Cities                Optional = 8% of Cities
                    Service Transfer of Core

  Non-city Council = 32%                              City Control of Core = 36%

           Production Transfer    Service Transfer of
           of Core =              Optional =
           26% of Cities          28% of Cities
```

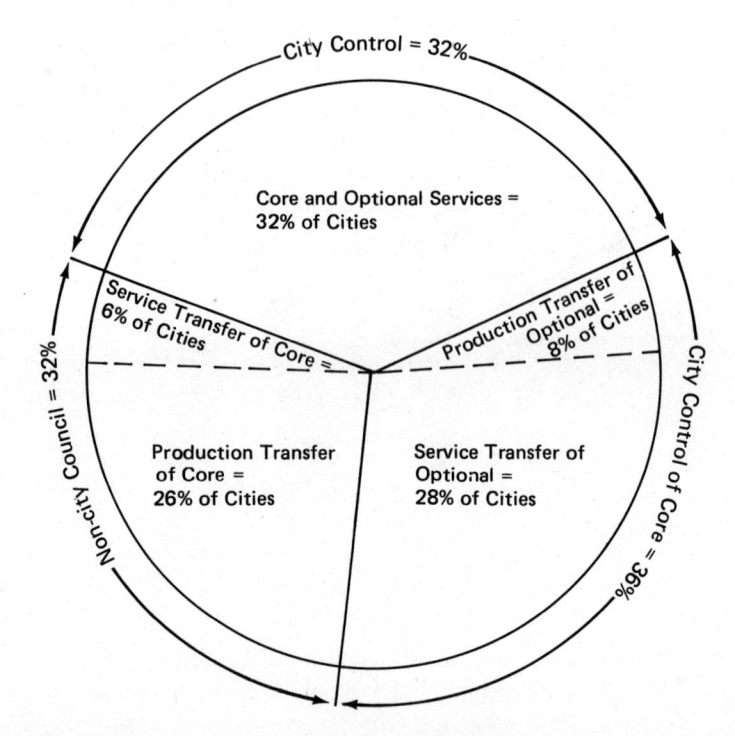

Figure 1-6. Types of Cities in California According to Degree of City Government Control

production transfer city types are seeking high levels of productivity; service transfer city types are emphasizing the reduction of property taxes; city control of core types are concerned with the level of quality of salient services; and non-city-control types are trying to limit the responsibilities of city government.

If such differential orientations are discovered it will become possible to obtain more subtle explanations of the changes in performance sought and likely to be achieved through various reform proposals.

Chapter Two

Selecting Service Delivery Structures

ADAPTIVE BEHAVIOR

It is not accidental that municipal services and cities themselves can be differentiated and grouped on the basis of their structures. Certain services are associated with specific structures because of the performance characteristics of the structures themselves. Similarly, the tendency for cities to group themselves into distinguishable structural patterns can be explained in terms of a city's preference for local control of services as well as the characteristics of service production and finance.

These findings are the starting point for an analysis of the decision process through which structures for municipal services are selected. Bear in mind, however, that city departments have long dominated municipal service delivery. Despite the proliferation of other structural arrangements, especially since the 1950s, a great majority of cities continue to provide most services through their own departments. And there are very good reasons why this is the case.

First, the very existence of a municipal bureaucracy acts to restrain serious consideration of structural arrangements which might compete with it. Second, it is often difficult to demonstrate that changing from an existing structure will result in perceptible improvement. Finally, citizens affect the process of selecting structures primarily at the time of incorporation, for it is then that the financial burden of cityhood can be most easily related to specific structural arrangements. After incorporation, citizen interest in issues of structure subsides.[1]

---

1. For example, since the inauguration of the Lakewood Plan in Los Angeles County (1954), every city incorporation study in that county has explored the cost implications of alternatives other than city departments for providing municipal services. Between 1956 and

16 How Cities Provide Services

According to a survey conducted during this study, only two-fifths of contract city residents even know that they are receiving services provided by contract; and with the possible exception of police services, citizen evaluations of services are generally unaffected by the structure through which the service is provided. It would seem, therefore, that citizens do not play a major direct role in matters of service structure once incorporation has taken place.

City Managers, elected officials, and senior municipal administrators appear to be the primary initiators of efforts to alter service delivery structures. Therefore, interviews with city managers and police chiefs provide one of the richest sources of data for understanding the process by which structures are selected. Their observations leave no doubt about the indirect role which citizens play as voters. City officials believe that citizens watch tax rates very carefully and punish elected officials who unnecessarily increase the municiapl tax burden. Caught between rising costs and perceived citizen opposition to tax increases (or the perceived need to maintain or improve services without raising costs), city officials are motivated to search for alternative structures, hoping thereby to avoid the dilemma.

The story told by the interviewed city officials about the conditions under which they consider alternatives to city departments is consistent with the models of adaptive motivated behavior found in organization theory. James G. March and Herbert A. Simon [B17] have developed a model, summarized in Figure 2-1, which relates search for alternatives to the level of satisfaction and also ties satisfaction to aspirations in the following way:

- The lower the satisfaction, the more the search for alternatives.
- The higher the payoff expected, the more the search.
- The higher the payoff expected, the higher the satisfaction.
- The higher the payoff expected, the higher the level of aspiration.
- The higher the level of aspiration, the lower the satisfaction.

This model is consistent with the account provided by city officials about structural selection decisions. Satisfaction with existing structural arrangements decreases either because of rising costs or demands for better services. Search for courses of action begins near the problem; that is, effort is devoted to increasing the performance or reducing the cost of the department providing the service. Only when these efforts fail are alternative structures considered, and then only if they are known and available. If no suitable alternatives are discovered, effort is likely to be directed once again toward improving existing arrangements. If

---

1965, twenty-eight of thirty-one communities which incorporated decided to contract with the county government for substantial shares of their municipal services, usually because of expected financial benefits. In only three of the cities did subsequent citizen interest eventually lead to a major revision in the structures which were selected at the time of incorporation.

Selecting Service Delivery Structures 17

```
                    ┌──────────────┐
            ┌──────→│ Satisfaction │←──────┐
            │       └──────┬───────┘       │
            │              │               │
            │              ▼               │
            │       ┌──────────────┐       │
            │       │    Search    │       │
        +   │   +   │     for      │       │  −
            │       │ Alternatives │       │
            │       └──────┬───────┘       │
            │              │               │
            │              +               │
            │              ▼               │
    ┌──────────────┐                ┌──────────────┐
    │   Expected   │───────────────→│   Level of   │
    │    Payoff    │                │  Aspiration  │
    └──────────────┘                └──────────────┘
```

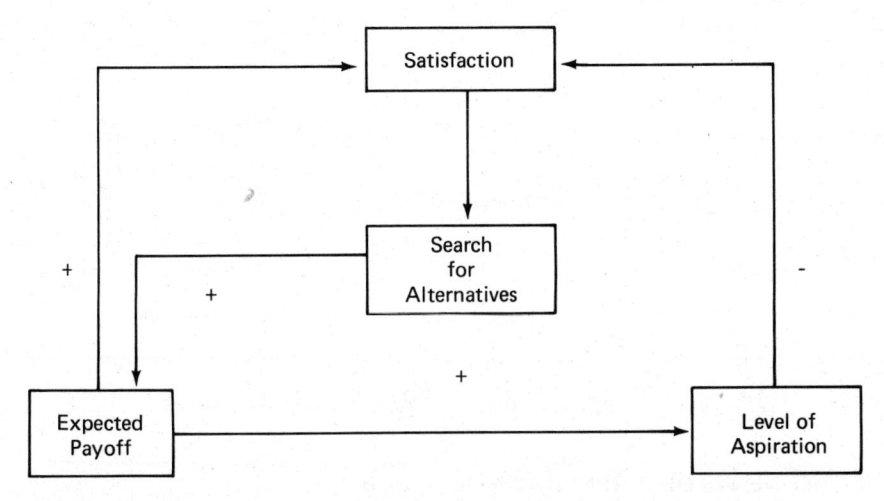

Figure 2-1. March-Simon General Model of Adaptive Motivated Behavior

these efforts do not result in a payoff sufficient to increase satisfaction, the level of aspiration will be lowered; this in turn reduces the motivation to continue the search for alternatives. When search efforts fail, city officials are faced with reducing service levels or increasing the tax burden. They are exceedingly reluctant to undertake the latter step, since it invites retaliation at election time. Figure 2-2 summarizes these general considerations which go into a decision about service structure.

The following section discusses in detail the three essential components of this decision-making process. First, search (that is, the consideration of new arrangements) is motivated, purposeful and problem-oriented. City officials seek improvements in response to financial pressure, often—but not invariably—accompanied by pressure for increased service. Second, search begins near the problem. City officials generally will not considered elaborate, complex, and ambitious reorganizations that will simultaneously cope with several municipal problems, including the one which prompted the search in the first place. On the contrary, they attempt to cope with the specific problem at hand, usually by making adjustments in existing structures. Finally, alternative structures must exist and be known to city officials before a decision to change structure can take place.

These elements emerge very clearly from the interviews and statistical analyses which describe the process of structural selection in Los Angeles County over the past few decades. A combination of increasing fiscal pressure, declining ability to improve the performance of existing structures, and an expanding range of alternative structures explains the history of contracting for municipal services in Los Angeles County and the ferment surrounding structural selection in California.

18 How Cities Provide Services

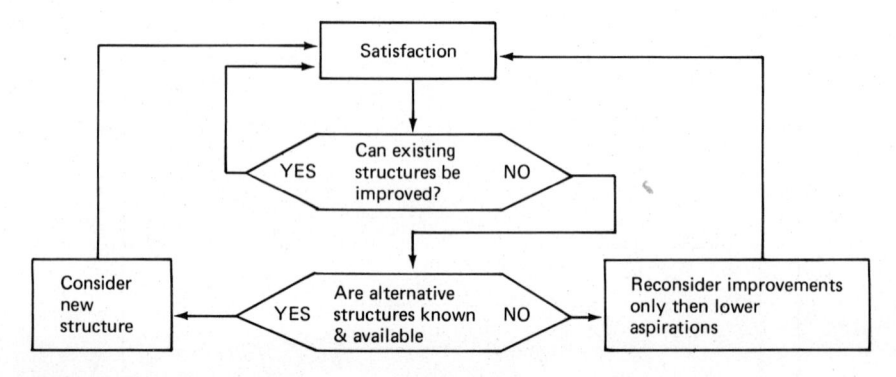

```
                    ┌──────────────┐
         ┌─────────▶│ Satisfaction │◀─────────┐
         │          └──────────────┘          │
         │                 ▲                  │
         │                 │                  │
         │         ┌───────────────┐          │
         │         │ Can existing  │          │
         │    YES  │ structures be │  NO      │
         │         │ improved?     │          │
         │         └───────────────┘          │
         │                 │                  │
         │                 ▼                  │
┌────────────┐    ┌────────────────┐   ┌──────────────────────┐
│ Consider   │    │ Are alternative│   │ Reconsider improvements│
│ new        │◀───│ structures known│──▶│ only then lower      │
│ structure  │YES │ & available    │NO │ aspirations          │
└────────────┘    └────────────────┘   └──────────────────────┘
```

Figure 2-2. Service Selection as Adaptive-Motivated Behavior

COMPONENTS OF A GENERAL MODEL FOR SERVICE STRUCTURE SELECTION

The adaptive model indicates how the process of search for structural alternatives begins. We now turn to developing a general model for the selection of a particular structure for a particular service by a particular city.

According to Figure 2-2, a model of structural choice must identify the activities which follow a decision that existing structures cannot be improved, but precede a decision that aspiration levels must be lowered. The first element of such a model is the availability of alternative structural arrangements for the services in question. The next component involves the extent to which municipal decision-makers (in this study, city managers) differentiate among structures, and how they evaluate any differences. Then comes an assessment of how various structures are perceived to perform for different services and how these performance differences influence the selection of structures. A final element of the model grows from the learning process which accompanies the consideration of alternatives, namely, achieving some of the benefits associated with different structures by creating new variations of existing structures which incorporate some of the desirable components of alternative structures.

Available Alternative Structures

Although most municipal services are provided through city departments, a more detailed examination of the structural typology indicates that services cluster into competing structures according to a fairly consistent pattern. Service clusters are first identified in terms of financing: by cities (core services), and by others (optional services). The core services are further separated into those produced and financed by city government (production core), and those not produced by city departments although financed by the city (contract competition core). The optional services are further separated into those that are, in many cases, produced and financed through special districts (district competition), and those that are produced by private firms (private competition). Table 2-1 groups services by these clusters and shows the percentage of cities in California that provide each service by city departments, contracting, or some other structure.

City departments in California provide half of all services and three-fourths of the core services. On the other hand, three-fourths of the optional services are

Table 2-1. Types of Service Structure

	Percentage of total service			Percentage of total operating expenditures (4)
Service clusters	City department (1)	Contract (2)	Other structure (3)	
Total typology services	48%	20%	32%	100.0%
City core services	71	24	5	55.5
City production core	83	13	4	21.0
Planning & zoning	96	4	0	1.0
Tree planting & trimming	87	10	3	2.0
Parks & recreation	85	4	11	12.0
Street signs	79	19	2	1.0
Street cleaning	76	20	4	2.5
Engineering	74	21	5	2.5
Contract competition core	56	38	6	34.5
Traffic patrol	70	29	1	8.0
General law enforcement	71	25	4	19.0
Building & safety	68	24	7	2.5
Street resurfacing	39	52	9	4.0
Traffic signal maintenance	35	53	11	1.0
City optional services	28	18	54	44.5
District competition	38	15	47	37.5
Fire protection	56	12	32	14.5
Storm drains	55	18	27	0.5
Noise pollution	50	7	43	0.0
Sewer maintenance	40	17	43	1.0
Street lighting	33	32	35	3.0
Water distribution	30	8	62	12.0
Libraries	30	18	52	6.5
Public transportation	6	8	86	0.0
Private competition	13	23	64	7.0
Animal	20	26	52	1.0
Resident refuse collection	15	20	65	3.0
Ambulance service	13	32	55	1.0
Business refuse collection	10	13	77	1.5
Solid waste	5	25	70	0.5

20 How Cities Provide Services

not provided by city departments. In the production core cluster, city departments provide four-fifths of all services, while almost all of the remainder is provided by contract. In the contract competition core cluster, only half of the services are provided by city departments, while the remainder is provided essentially by contract. So contracting increases as self-provision declines among city core services. Not only are core services rarely provided by some structure other than city department or contract, but also when core services are ranked by percentage of self-provision (col. 1 of Table 2-1), they are almost directly inverse to the percentage rank of contracting (col. 2). From these patterns one can infer that for the city core services, decisions to move away from self-provision are related to the availability of contracting structures. For the optional services, on the other hand, most of the alternatives to city departments come not from contracting but from other structures, particularly special districts and the private sector.

When special districts are available (as is the case for district competition optional services), then contracting is rarely selected as an alternative to city departments. It is chosen only one out of seven times, or about as often as it is selected for the production core services. On the other hand, districts are selected almost half of the time. Thus the reduced selection of city departments is balanced by the increased selection of special districts.

When the private sector provides the major alternative structures, city departments are selected only one time in seven. Part of this reduced use of city departments is balanced by increased contracting, but most is balanced by an increase in other structures. There is an inverse relation within the private competition service cluster between city department and other structures.

Figure 2-3 summarizes the relation between service clusters and structure alternatives. There is direct competition between city departments and contract

Service Cluster	Primary Alternatives to City Departments
Core	⟶ Contract
Optional	⟶ Special Districts
	⟶ Private Firms ⟵⟶ Contract

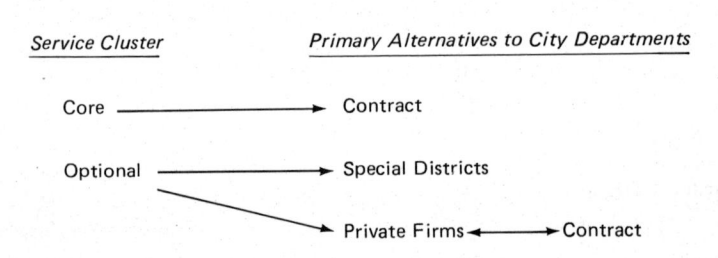

Figure 2-3. Alternative Structures to City Departments, by Service Cluster

structures only in the case of the city core services. And there is less competition for production core services than for the contract competition services. In the case of optional services, the relationships among alternatives become more complex. For the district competition services the city departments seem to be confronted by both contract and special district structures as alternatives, but mostly by special districts. However, there seems to be little competition between special district and contract structures. In the case of the private competition services, other (mostly private) structures seem to dominate, with about twice as much competition from contract as from city department structures.

Since different structural alternatives are selected for various classes of services, it is likely that there are particular service attributes which influence structural availability. The attributes to be considered are the level of service expenditures, service costs, price of service inputs, start-up costs, extent of service utilization, and degree of standardization of service quality.

Level of Service Expenditures. There are two reasons why a high level of service expenditures might lead to increasing the available structural alternatives. If the level of service expenditure is high, then the opportunity for substantial budget savings through cost reductions may arise, and this situation is likely to create incentives for alternatives to the city department structure to be made available. In addition, a high level of expenditures ordinarily means that a large number of employees are needed, so that managers and city councils seeking to avoid the personnel problems created by a large bureaucracy might prefer some structure other than city department.

On the other hand, the "big ticket" services might favor self-provision rather than alternative structures because such services are very visible and citizens prefer city departments in these instances. Furthermore, the bureaucracy in a large department—so the argument goes—has sufficient political strength to thwart efforts to reduce the size of employment or eliminate the department in favor of some other mode of service provision.

The data do not support either of these positions—that high expenditure levels encourage self-provision or that they encourage alternative structures. For example, Table 2-1, column 4 shows the estimated proportionate allocation of operating expenditures (excluding capital) among services.[2] There appears to be no systematic relation between level of expenditure and structure; that is, rising service expenditures are not systematically associated with the relative increase or decrease in importance of any structure.

Table 2-2 separates services into two groups—the six services which each account for at least 5 percent of total operating expenditures are the high-

2. These include not only city-financed expenditures but also other finance sources. The percents can be viewed as a budget allocation only if one assumes that the city government finances all the services—which is not the case in the typical city. In addition, a number of city services (about 25 percent of the city budget) are not included in these data.

22 How Cities Provide Services

Table 2-2. Comparison of High- and Low-Expenditure Services

| | Percentage of total operating expenditures || Percentage of all services provided through: |||
Services	Total	Per service	City department	Contract	Other structures
High-expenditure services[a]	67	12	57	16	27
Low-expenditure services	33	2	45	24	29

[a]The high-expenditure services (those that are at least 5 percent of total expenditures) include general law enforcement (19 percent), fire protection (14.5 percent), water distribution and pollution (12 percent), parks and recreation (12 percent), traffic patrol (8 percent), and libraries (6.5 percent).

expenditure services and the 18 other services comprise the low-expenditure group. City departments provide the high-expenditure services somewhat more frequently than they provide the low-expenditure services. Since city departments also dominate in the provision of production core services, one might expect the high-expenditures service to be in the production core. This is not the case.

Why is it, then, that city departments provide a somewhat higher proportion of high-expenditure services than other services? Part of the answer might be provided by a comparison of each of the high-expenditure services to its own service cluster, as shown in Table 2-3. The only high-expenditure service in the city production core is parks and recreation—a politically salient service. Traffic and general law enforcement patrol are in the contract competition core, while fire protection, water distribution, and libraries are in the district competition cluster, and there are no high-expenditure services in the private competition cluster. The police, fire, and recreation services, which comprise almost half of the budget, tend to utilize city departments relatively more than other services in their cluster. For example, city departments provide fire protection half of the time, but provide all district competition services only one-third of the time. Thus is would appear that even though there is resistance to placing high-expenditure services into the production core, there is a tendency to use city departments relatively more than other services in the same cluster. Consequently, level of expenditure does not by itself account for the selection of structure.

Service Costs. City departments are less likely to be adopted when there are lower cost alternatives which can take advantage of scale economies or opportunities for introducing productivity improvement.

Selecting Service Delivery Structures 23

Table 2-3. Relation of Service Structure to Service Cluster

	Percentage of services provided through city departments	Ratio of service to cluster
All services	48	–
Production core services	83	–
Parks and recreation	85	103
Contract competition services	56	–
Traffic patrol	70	125
General law enforcement	71	125
District competition services	38	–
Fire protection	56	150
Water distribution	30	80
Libraries	30	80

A single areawide producer is capable of producing at a lower cost than are a number of decentralized, smaller city departments if service production is associated with economies of scale. Such economies could lead to the adoption of either district structures or areawide producers under contract. Therefore, proponents of contracting generally go on to argue that not only does contracting offer the opportunity for lower costs than do city departments, it also allows cities to retain control over planning; the latter provides greater control over the quality and kind of service provided than would be the case under district provision. So contracting, it is claimed, provides a better mix of low costs and city control than is provided by other structures. This argument in favor of production as an areawide activity mixed with planning and financing as city government activities, tends to lead to the selection of a government producer (the county, for example) and is usually made in the case of the police service.

A second argument, however, leads to the selection of a private producer under contract. This argument says that if there are a number of alternative producers competing for business, each will seek to improve productivity and improve service quality in order to obtain that business. Since these incentives are not equally present when government is the producer, a city-financed contract with a private firm is probably the structure with lowest cost. This argument is often applied to refuse collection. Since city government as a customer is similar to any private firm or household as a customer, the city has the same control over the kind and quality of service it demands as does any customer in a private market. Indeed, the city may even be in a somewhat better position because to the extent that it is a large customer, it can push for beneficial terms in the contract and thereby share in the productivity improvements introduced by the producer. For example, some city governments that contract for refuse collection and bill households for the service gain net government revenues from this process of sharing in the producer's "profits."

Whether through contract or some other areawide structure, there is the potential for real resource economies as a result of larger-scale production. Such economies are related to some of the factors discussed below.

Prices of Service Inputs. The conventional argument about the price of inputs states that a large-scale producer can purchase needed equipment and materials at a lower price than can a small-scale producer. For example, libraries, water distribution, street resurfacing, and to some extent police services are relatively heavy purchasers of select materials and equipment. These are also services for which a relatively large number of cities choose county contract or district provision.

The advantages of large-scale purchase are not solely dependent on large-scale production. Increasingly cities are entering into joint-powers agreements for supplies and equipment purchases that enable them to retain city departments while obtaining some of the cost advantages of cooperative purchasing.

However, municipal services are preponderantly labor intensive, not material or equipment intensive. Therefore, major reductions in service costs are likely to depend on labor savings. Large-scale production does not seem to be associated with the payment of lower wage rates and employee benefits. For example, Los Angeles County government and the city of Los Angeles appear to pay higher money wages than smaller city governments in the area. Indeed, one of the expressed concerns of contracting cities is that smaller independent cities are in a position to pay lower wages than the county. However, this wage differential may be only apparent; that is, after adjustment for employee skill levels, the difference in wage payments between large-scale producer and small-scale producer may be reduced or eliminated entirely.

Employee cost differentials between the private and public sectors are probably more significant than the differential between large- and small-scale public producers. Government employers often have more constraints imposed on their hiring, firing, work rules, and wage practices than do private employers. Therefore, private employers can, in some instances, produce at substantially lower cost than can public employers. This could be part of the reason that relatively many cities choose to provide such labor-intensive services as animal control, refuse collection, traffic signal maintenance, and ambulance service through contract with private firms or entirely through the private sector. In addition, many city departments, in attempting to contain growth in costs, are seeking subservices that they can contract out to private producers, such as helicopter services by police departments. We expect that cities will increasingly seek to contract out for labor cost-saving subservices.

Start-up Costs. High start-up costs are sometimes cited as a reason for providing a service through a large-scale producer. Large-scale producers, with their more substantial financial base, are said to be in a position to adopt more advanced and efficient technologies than less financially secure producers. However, this is primarily a phenomenon of wealth and not of producer size. So although we find that wealthier communities prefer their own departments to contracting for services, the possibility that the wealthier communities can be either large or small means that selecting a structure with a large producer may or may not be sought to overcome high start-up costs.

The financial base of the city is particularly important in relation to departmental start-up cost, which takes its most dramatic form at the time of incorporation. Most of the newly incorporated cities in Los Angeles County, preferring to avoid the financial start-up costs associated with creating departments and bureaucracies, chose to contract with the county. Contracting with private producers would also avoid start-up costs, but for some services (such as police), private producers were not readily available, and probably county contracting seemed more reliable than private contracting for most services.

While start-up costs favor county contracting at the time of incorporation, it is less clear that they have a comparable effect as time goes on. For example, as Los Angeles County has offered new services for contract, the major contracting cities have not accepted these offers at a faster rate than have the independent cities. Thus, once a city has made arrangements for its basic services to be provided in a reliable fashion, it has more flexibility in the adoption or modification of structures for providing other services.

Capacity Utilization. An important avenue for the reduction of costs is higher capacity utilization of labor and equipment. In the production of goods (which can be kept in inventory), close to capacity production is feasible. However, in the production of services, peak load demands and the uncertainties associated with sudden crises often require the availability of labor and equipment that may be underutilized for a large part of the day or even longer.

City departments have the least flexibility in adjusting to fluctuating demands. Areawide producers, whether under contract or through district provision, have greater opportunity for making such adjustments, and by doing so can significantly reduce production costs. The services most amenable to such cost savings are those requiring back-up and those amenable to improved work-force scheduling.

Back up is a reserve force of labor and equipment available in an emergency to meet unexpected or fluctuating demand for a service. If this reserve force is literally in reserve, it will be underutilized for much of the time. If, however, it can be held in reserve for the sudden demands in some place or at some time while being fully utilized at all times in other places, costs can be saved.

Ordinarily, availability of this kind of reserve requires a fairly wide geographic area of demand for the service (although it need not be metropolitan-wide); for only within a wide area can work forces be easily shifted from places where they are less needed to places where they are urgently needed.

When fire protection is provided by a district, the back-up reserve offers the opportunity for lower costs than in city fire departments offering equal service. Since each city contributes to the support of the entire fire district, it is funding fire-fighting capabilities not only for itself but also for the other cities; that is, there are beneficial externalities.

Police protection is also a service characterized by a need for back-up. Back-up becomes available when the police service is provided through a single city or group of cities contracting with the county or through a police district. The police back-up is important not only to emergency situations, such as reassignment of forces to a suddenly crime-prone area, but is also important to more predictable fluctuations in demand, such as reassignment of forces to entertainment areas on Saturday nights.

When county police and district fire departments agree to provide their service to some locality, the back-up is implicit in the agreement. Ordinarily, a contract will not be arranged to provide police or fire services for some specific emergency, although in the case of some public works services this is precisely what is done. For example, a city suddenly confronted by a flood or a rock-slide that it does not have the capacity to handle will, at least in Los Angeles County, be likely to contract with the county engineers, who do have the back-up capacity. Cities will contract with the county even for nonemergency and predictable large jobs, such as street resurfacing, that are beyond the city department's capacity to handle. This type of specific job contract, which has long been important in public works services, is becoming increasingly important to other services as well.

Another way to increase capacity utilization is to improve the scheduling of a work force. For example, such services as refuse collection, street cleaning, or traffic signal maintenance often require a considerable amount of employee time simply to go from one work site to the next. Such transit down-time can be reduced by improved route scheduling. Often the down-time of equipment requiring maintenance and renovation can also be reduced through improved scheduling. Sometimes labor costs can be reduced by rescheduling of the labor input, such as the use of one-man police cars in certain places or times. The opportunities for improved scheduling are often, but not always, related to the size of the service area. Therefore, if an optimal service area size does not correspond to the city's size, it may be beneficial to the city to provide the service through a contract or district structure.

Standardized Service Quality. Some services have areawide consequences that encourage standardized service quality, for there are harmful externalities if inadequate provision in one city reduces service quality in other cities. For example, inadequate maintenance of traffic signals in a city is likely to slow traffic and increase accidents for commuters. Or inadequate maintenance of storm drains in one place can cause flooding in other places. Or limited recreational facilities in one community can lead to park overload in other communities.

One way to prevent such spillovers is to maintain a minimum level of service quality in each community. The professionalism of city managers or city department heads and governmental regulations are often, but not always, a guarantee that such a minimum quality will be provided. When it is not, demands are generated for metropolitan-wide standards assuring minimum qualities. Such demands are then sometimes the stimulus for changing from self-provision to district or county provision, where it becomes easier to enforce the standards. However, under areawide provision, minimal standards tend to become the general standard in the entire area and there is little opportunity for specific places to choose a higher quality of service. When such flexibility is sought, then metropolitan-wide contracting with the county could both assure minimum standards and leave open the opportunity for cities to obtain higher than minimal-quality service.

Overview of Service Attributes. Reasons have been given why high service costs, high input prices, high start-up costs, low degree of capacity utilization, and desire for standardization of service quality may each lead to a demand for structures other than city departments. Whether there is a connection between these service attributes and the selection of structures in the sample of cities can be examined by a matrix (Table 2-4), which displays services by cluster along the verticle axis and service attributes along the horizontal. The cells contain the authors' estimates as to whether the attribute is present (Yes) for each of the services. Since each service attribute is supposed to lead toward the selection of some structure *other than* city department, one would expect a higher incidence of other structures for services having the highest number of positive entries. Table 2-5 shows the frequency and percentage of distributions of positive entries by service cluster. The pattern expected on the basis of the conventional arguments (summarized in the preceding paragraphs) tends to emerge. Services in the city production core (provided by city department) have fewer positive responses than do services in other clusters. Differences among clusters exist, but are not distinctive enough to suggest why services are provided through various structures. From this analysis we conclude that the conventional arguments which seek to relate service attributes to structure only partially explain the actual selection in the sample of cities. To further explore the connection between service attributes and structures, we interviewed a sample of California city managers.

Considering Alternative Structures

Structural Preferences of City Managers. Twenty-six city managers were

Table 2-4. Typology and Service Attributes

	High service costs?	Economies of scale in input prices?	High start-up costs?	Large scale required for capacity utilization?	Standardized service quality desired?	Number of positive responses
City production core						
Planning and zoning	No	No	No	No	Yes	1
Tree planting & trimming	No	No	No	Yes	No	1
Parks & recreation	Yes	No	Yes	Yes	No	3
Street & signs	No	No	No	No	Yes	1
Street cleaning	No	Yes	Yes	Yes	No	3
Engineering	No	No	No	No	Yes	1
Contract Competition Core						
Traffic patrol	Yes	Some	Yes	Yes	Yes	5
General law enforcement	Yes	Some	Yes	Yes	Yes	5
Building & safety	No	No	No	Yes	Yes	2
Street resurfacing	No	Yes	Yes	Yes	Yes	4
Traffic signal maint.	No	No	No	Yes	Yes	2
District competition optional						
Fire protection	Yes	Yes	Yes	Yes	Yes	5
Storm drains	No	Yes	Yes	Yes	Yes	4
Noise pollution	No	No	No	No	Yes	1
Sewer maintenance	No	No	Yes	Yes	Yes	3
Street lighting	No	Yes	Yes	No	Yes	3

Table 2-4. continued

Is the service characterized by the attribute:

	High service costs?	Economies of scale in input prices?	High start-up costs?	Large required for capacity utilization?	Standardized service quality desired?	Number of positive responses
District competition optional						
Water distribution	No	Yes	Yes	Yes	Yes	4
Libraries	Yes	Yes	Yes	Yes	No	4
Public transportation	Yes	Yes	Yes	Yes	No	4
Private competition optional						
Animal control	No	No	No	Yes	Yes	2
Resident refuse	Yes	Yes	Yes	Yes	Yes	5
Ambulance service	No	Yes	No	Yes	Yes	3
Business refuse	Yes	Yes	Yes	Yes	Yes	5
Solid waste	No	Yes	Yes	Yes	Yes	4

Table 2-5. Frequency of Service Attributes Encouraging Structures Other Than City Departments, by Typology Categories

Typology categories	Total positive responses for all services in category	Total positive responses as a percentage of all responses
City production core	10	33%
Contract competition core	18	72
District competition optional	28	70
Private competition optional	19	76

interviewed: eleven from contract and fifteen from independent cities.[3] When asked to state how a list of services should ideally be provided in a city like the one they manage, city managers overwhelmingly favored city departments. Table 2-6 reports the managers' opinions about which structure ideally should provide various services, showing the structure most frequently chosen and the number of managers making that choice.

There is considerable consensus among city managers about what services are best provided through city departments. They are the preferred structure for seventeen of the twenty-seven services. Moreover, in the sixteen cases in which at least half the managers chose the same structure, city department was selected twelve times. There was a virtual consensus for city departments for six services;[4] a

---

3. Fourteen were from Los Angeles County cities, and 12 were from Northern California cities in the San Francisco Bay Area (Alameda County: 2; Contra Costa County: 3; Santa Clara County: 7).

After several abortive attempts to interview city managers individually, which foundered on the amount of detailed information requested and the difficulty of achieving uniformity in individual interviews, a structured group process was used as the interview setting. In this process four to six city managers were brought together for half a day. A senior staff member acted as the lead person, taking the group through each stage of the interview process, while other staff members (one for each interviewee) assisted the managers in completing the sections of the interview. A variety of data-collection techniques was used, including Milbrath-like card sorts, but the most common technique asked the manager to indicate, through checks or entires in matrices, which structure possessed which advantage or disadvantage, was best suited for particular services, and so on. At several points during the morning or afternoon, group discussion about questions being posed was stimulated. This served to change the pace, to give space for oral expression, and to allow managers to reflect upon the choices they were being asked to make, including hearing the views of others. Since the objective was elicitation of considered opinions about choices made in a political context of debate and power relationships, such open interchange is preferable to the secrecy more traditional to interviews privately soliciting attitudes.

4. There was virtual consensus that it is preferable for providing building and safety inspection, planning, parks, tree planting and trimming, zoning and subdivision, and recreation services through city departments. The only deviation from this pattern is found in the responses of some managers of contract cities in Southern California who prefer to have building and safety inspections contracted to county government.

Selecting Service Delivery Structures 31

Table 2-6. Preferred Service Structure

Specific services	Preferred Structure	Number of managers making choice
Preference for city department		
Virtual consensus		
Zoning & subdivision	City department	25
Planning	City department	21
Tree planting & trimming	City department	21
Building & safety inspection	City department	20
Parks	City department	20
Recreation	City department	20
Majority agreement		
Engineering planning & mapping	City department	18
Traffic safety & patrol	City department	18
Street signs & markings	City department	17
General law enforcement patrol	City department	16
Water distribution	City department	16
Plurality Preference		
Street cleaning & patching	City department	13
Sewer maintenance	City department	12
Sewer & storm drains	City department	12
Noise pollution abatement	City department	12
Street resurfacing	City department	12
Street lighting	City department	11
Preference for alternative structure		
Majority agreement		
Business refuse collection	Private franchise	15
Traffic signal maintenance	Private contract	14
Residential refuse collection	Private franchise	14
Solid waste disposal	County contract	13
Plurality preference		
Animal control & shelter	County contract	12
Libraries	County contract	10
Ambulance services	Private contract	8
Public transportation	Special district	8
Water pollution abatement	Regional government	8
Fire protection	City dept. & contract	8

majority of managers selected the department for five services;[5] and a plurality preferred the city department for six services.[6]

    5. A majority of managers prefer that street signs and markings, and engineering, planning, and mapping services be provided by city departments. A majority also would have general law enforcement patrol and traffic safety and patrol provided by city departments; however, a minority, exclusively contract city managers, would contract with county government.

    6. For six services, city department was the choice for only a plurality of managers, and a number of managers identified a specific alternative choice. Those services were (with the alternative structure following each service in parentheses): street cleaning and patching

However, there is much less agreement about the services for which other structures are appropriate. For ten services, city managers tended to prefer an alternative structure to the city department. In four of these, a majority agreed on a specific alternative.[7] The remaining six services had only a plurality of managers selecting some specific alternative.[8] Additionally, the distribution of manager views about ideal structures (Table 2-6) corresponds closely with the actual pattern of service structures (Table 2-1). The relationship between preferred and actual structures is summarized in Table 2-7. An index of manager agreement was developed which indicates the extent to which there is a consensus that the city department or some other structure is preferred. The index is constructed with reference to the consensus on a preference for the city department. Thus the highest index value indicates a virtual consensus of preference for the city department. As the index becomes smaller the consensus is reduced; and a high negative index would indicate a consensus of preference for some other structure than the city department. If the actual and preferred structures are in close correspondence, the highest index should correspond to the service cluster which most often adopts the city department structure; declines in the index would match reductions in the extent to which the city department is adopted. Table 2-7 demonstrates the close correspondence between preferred and actual structures, shown by the decline in the index as it moves from the

---

(contract with a private firm); sewer maintenance (county contract); street lighting (contract or franchise with a private firm); sewer and storm drain (county contract); noise pollution abatement (regional government); street resurfacing (contract with a private firm).

There was little difference in response between southern and northern managers or between contract and independent cities, so that these factors are not likely explanations for why a minority but still substantial number of managers did not prefer the city department. Apparently, other city characteristics or proclivities of the managers lie behind the lack of consensus.

7. The preferred structure for delivering traffic signal maintenance was contract with a private firm, but a number of managers preferred either a county contract or city department. For residential refuse collection, the most common choice was a franchise with a private firm, but some managers, particularly from independent cities, preferred a city department. Solid-waste disposal was believed to be best provided through county contract, and business refuse collection through a franchise with a private firm. For none of these services did any alternative garner five votes, and little pattern emerges in the distribution of other choices.

8. County contract was the primary choice for animal control and shelter and library services. There was a tendency for southern respondents to more frequently opt for private firm contracts as the second choice for animal control and shelter and for city departments as the second choice in providing libraries. Fire protection was assigned equally to city department and county contract, but there were also some managers choosing provision by a special district and directly by county government. Preferred structures for provision of ambulance services were widely distributed, with county contract and contract with private firm receiving most choices. Public transportation also elicited a wide range of choices, with the three most popular structures being special district, county government, and regional government. Similarly, water-pollution abatement was most commonly assigned to three structures: county contract, special district, and regional government.

city production, to contract competition, to district competition, to private competition clusters.

Reasons for Structural Preferences. Managers were asked in the group interviews to identify some of the reasons for structural choices they made. The reasons offered were generally the same at each group interview. Since no pre-identification of possible causal factors was made for this open-ended question, there apparently is a considerable degree of consensus among managers.

The city department structure is perceived as providing the city with local control over the service, and this is the major reason it is preferred by city managers. Control over the level of the service, control over the quality of the service, and control over responding to citizens were all important dimensions of local control. The preference for city departments among managers from Northern California was most likely to be based on control over level of services. Southern California managers tended to base their preference on control over quality of services. Control over responsiveness to citizens was equally important to both Northern and Southern California managers. However, community identity, which is sometimes related to responsiveness, was a significant factor only for managers of independent cities in Southern California.

A shorter list of reasons was volunteered for selecting county contract structures. Desirability of a service area larger than a city, the most frequently given reason, was mentioned only by independent city managers. Independent city managers also stressed economic factors, while contract city managers were likely to declare that local control of a particular service was unimportant.

Only a few reasons were given for selecting contract with a private firm. While there were almost no differences between northern and southern managers, there were differences between contract and independent city managers. Independent city managers were attracted to private contract as a way of decreasing personnel

Table 2-7. Correspondence Between Structural Preference and Actual Structural Selection

Service clusters	Index of manager agreement[a]
City production core	2.3
Contract competition core	1.2
District competition optional	.37
Private competition optional	-1.2

[a] A score of 3 = virtual consensus among managers that city department is the preferred structure (refer to Table 2-6 for definition of virtual consensus); 2 = majority agreement; 1 = plurality agreement; A score of (-1) = plurality agree that city department is *not* the appropriate structure for that service; and (-2) = a majority agree that city department is *not* appropriate.

problems and increasing quality control, while those from contract cities were attracted to the possibility of lower costs and reduced capital outlays.

For services which were assigned other structures than city department or contract (special district or regional government, for example) the rationale most commonly offered, especially by independent city managers, was the desirability of having the service provided to an area larger than that encompassed by city boundaries.

In addition to the open-ended question, managers were shown a pre-identified list of attributes characterizing services and providers of services, and were asked to indicate how these attributes affected their structural preferences. The results are summarized in Table 2-8.

The picture emerging from Table 2-8 is similar to the results of the open-ended question. City departments are preferred when local control over the service is desired. County contracting is chosen when the economies of providing the service encourage a larger provider. The remaining structures are elected much less frequently—and then most often as an alternative to county contracting—when some mode of provision other than city department is desired.

Except for the tendency of independent city managers to select city department structures more frequently than did other managers, there were few differences in preference that can be associated with the type of city where the manager is employed. In general, city departments were preferred when: a reliable provider was needed; there is close contact between city employees and the public; and the service is politically salient or difficult to monitor. Contract city managers were noticeably more likely to favor alternatives other than city departments (especially contracts with the county) when: capital start-up costs were high; extensive collective bargaining and hiring restrictions existed; more back-up forces were needed; comparable service levels were sought; spillovers were great; and scale economies were high. In services characterized by greater likelihood of fluctuating or unexpected needs, contract city managers favored county contracts and independent city managers favored contracts with private firms. Private contracts were preferred if many private providers were available and highly skilled personnel were needed.

Relation of Structure to Satisfaction

Managers not only perceive structures as having different characteristics, but there is considerable consensus among them about what these differences are. It is now important to determine whether or not these differences relate to performance, and the extent to which they influence the choice of structures. The following section begins with an effort to pinpoint the effects which different structures have on performance, and concludes with an assessment of the conditions under which one structure is preferred to another.

The Effects of Structure. During the course of the interviews, managers were asked to rank structures by nine performance characteristics and by their effects

Table 2-8. Reasons for Selecting Structure

	First choice of managers (number)[a]			Second choice of managers (number)[a]		
Attributes of Services and providers	City dept.	County contract	Private contract	City dept.	County contract	Private contract
Need for close citizen/ employee contact	25					
Great political saliency/ sensitivity	22					
Great interdependence with other services	15				7	
Great difficulty in monitoring performance	14				5	
Pressure to achieve minimum level of service	12				7	
Difficulty in measuring output	10				5	
Opportunity for decentralized delivery	9				7	
Great need for back-up		15		5		
Desire for comparable levels of service		14				
Great spillovers beyond the city		13				
High scale economies		12				
High capital start-up costs		9			6	
Need for small staff	9				8	8
Hiring restrictions		12		9		9
Availability of many providers			11			
Need for reliable provider	17					
Need for highly skilled personnel			15	6	7	
High equipment operating & maintenance costs						
Collective bargaining						
Extreme fluctuations in service need						

Source:
[a] In some cases the number of managers adds to more than 27. This is because some managers made more than one choice. For those attributes for which number of managers is not shown, no clustering of responses occurred.

on aspects of municipal decision-making. Also, because of the special concern for contracting, managers were asked to assess the regional impacts of contracting.

Performance Characteristics. Achievement of high levels of efficiency, quality of service, responsiveness to citizens, employee morale, citizen confidence, and control of quality are associated with a high level of performance, while a high per capita expenditure can be related to poor performance. Uniformity in the quality of service delivered to different areas is sometimes considered good, because it does not discriminate against poorer places, and sometimes considered bad, because it does not permit differentiating among the areas in terms of their particular needs. Similarly, if the effect of service delivery on property values is to raise them, the performance can be considered good; but if the effect is to lower property values, performance is bad.

Managers indicated which structure performed best and which structure performed worst for each characteristic. The results are shown in Table 2-9. In

Table 2-9. Structure Effects on Performance Characteristics

Number of managers responding as best performance

Characteristic	City dept.	County contract	Private contract	Franchise	Other structure	No effect	Depends on service
High efficiency	8	2	5	1			11
High per capita expenditure	9	2	4			2	10
High quality of service	16	1		1			8
High uniformity in delivery	9	8		3	3	1	6
High responsiveness	22						4
High employee morale	14	1				6	6
High citizen confidence	16	2	1			3	6
High quality control	21	2					3
High effect on property values	10	2				9	3

Number of managers responding as worst performance

Characteristic	City dept.	County contract	Private contract	Franchise	Other structure	No effect	Depends on service
High efficiency	3	6	1	1	2		
High per capita expenditure		7	2	3	2		
High quality of service	2	8	3	2	2		
High uniformity in delivery	5	2	3	1	3		
High responsiveness		8	5	4	3		
High employee morale		2	3	3	2		
High citizen confidence		5	7	2	1		
High quality control		7	4	2	3		
High effect on property values	1	3	6	3	1		

evaluating structures for the nine performance characteristics, city managers tended to rank city departments positively and other structures negatively. Over half of the managers ranked city departments as performing best for quality of service, responsiveness, citizen confidence, employee morale, and quality control.

Contracts with the county were evaluated poorly with respect to efficiency, responsiveness, per capita expenditures, quality of service, and control of quality. Only for achieving uniformity in services provided did best mentions outnumber worst for county contracts; and even here city departments received more best votes. Contracts with private firms were rated as efficient by some respondents but fared poorly on responsiveness, citizen confidence, and impact on property values.

Independent city managers accounted not only for many of the high ratings awarded city departments but also for more than half of the low department ratings. In addition, they accounted for many of the high ratings given county contracts and more than half of the low ratings. Contract city managers were less likely to assign low ratings to private contracts and franchises, although they were not more likely than independent city managers to rate them high.

In addition to these overall rankings for services in general, managers ranked the characteristics for 10 specific services, as follows.

General Law Enforcement: City managers felt that the city police department structure performs best according to most characteristics. Exceptions related to uniformity, where county contracts were equally preferred; and employee morale and property values, which quite a few managers believed are not sensitive to structure. Department structure was rated very high by all managers with respect to responsiveness, service quality, control of quality, and citizen confidence.

Residential Refuse Collection: In contrast to their views about law enforcement, city managers did not associate many of the positive characteristics with employing the city department structure for refuse collection. A majority associated greatest efficiency with franchise arrangements and private contract, while city departments were endorsed strongly for responsiveness and quality control. Generally, however, there was no strong consensus about structures and a relatively high incidence of responses indicating that there were no effects of structure on performance in residential refuse collection.

Street Cleaning and Patching: Once again, city managers most frequently selected city department as the structure they associated with positive performance for street cleaning and patching. A majority of them associated this structure with the highest efficiency, quality, responsiveness, citizen confidence, and quality control; but city street cleaning departments are also associated with the highest per capita expenditures. Quite a few managers felt that structure was not important with respect to citizen and council complaints, and the rest ranked the city department structure only slightly ahead of either private or county contracts in this regard. There was virtually no support for any structure except the city department and public or private contracts for providing street cleaning and patching services.

Fire Protection: The city fire department structure ranked high only in terms of responsiveness and ability to control quality. Half of the managers felt that a special district, rather than departments or contracts, was the most efficient provider of fire services. Fire districts were rated high in terms of quality and uniformity of service as well as efficiency. Furthermore, they were associated by the managers with lower per capita expenditures and fewer complaints. There were many responses indicating that structure has no effect on employee morale, citizen confidence, and property values.

Building and Safety Inspection: Managers more frequently selected city departments over county contracts as performing best for virtually all characteristics. County contracts, however, did compare favorably to city departments, in regard to per capita expenditures and uniformity of service. Managers apparently recognized only two viable structural alternatives for building and safety inspection: either city departments or county contracts. However, county contract was frequently indicated as the structure associated with the highest number of complaints from citizens and council members.

Planning: The managers tended to associate city planning departments with best performance for most characteristics. County contracts were selected most frequently as performing best in terms of per capita expenditures and uniformity, but many managers also felt that contracting of planning produces many complaints from both citizens and council members.

Traffic Signal Maintenance: The managers did not agree about the structure best suited for providing traffic signal maintenance. City departments received a majority endorsement only for responsiveness and a plurality for employee morale, citizen confidence, and quality control. County contracts, on the other hand, while not receiving majority support, did receive a plurality for uniformity and minimization of citizen and council complaints. Private contracts were viewed by a majority as the most efficient structure for traffic signal maintenance, and a plurality selected private contracts for their quality and low per capita expenditures. Private contracts were the second choice for uniformity, responsiveness, employee morale, citizen confidence, quality control, and minimization of citizen and council complaints. Private contracting is apparently viewed by managers as potentially competitive with city department structures.

Parks and Recreation: City managers overwhelmingly saw the parks and recreation department structure as performing best according to the various characteristics. However, a sizeable number of managers selected county contract or some other structure for uniformity in delivery of the parks and recreation service.

Zoning and Subdivision: The managers overwhelmingly associated positive performance in zoning and subdivision with city department structures. Once again, per capita costs and complaints tended to be associated with the city department structure, and county contracts received significant support only for uniformity.

Animal Control and Shelter: There was little agreement among the managers with respect to the structures associated with responsiveness, quality control, and citizen confidence in the delivery of animal control and shelter. County contracting was most frequently selected for uniformity and received considerable support for efficiency, service quality, and citizen confidence.

Aspects of the Decision Process. Who are the key actors and what are their interactions in the process of making decisions about service provision? Fifteen aspects of the behavior of the city council, the city manager, citizens, employees, and service providers were identified, and the managers were asked to indicate which structure most affected each of these aspects. The results are shown in Table 2-10. Their responses suggest that the managers interviewed saw the decision-making benefits of departmental structure as clearly outweighing its costs. Very few managers chose alternative structures over the city department because of their effects on the decision process.

Virtually all managers agreed that city departments permit the city council to exercise the greatest control over the allocation of the city budget and to have the greatest impact on ongoing service delivery decisions. Most managers believed that the city department structure also permits councils to exercise the greatest control over the level of city expenditures and affords them the greatest involvement in setting program objectives.

There was almost complete agreement about the effects of structure on managers themselves: the city department causes a manager to spend more time on personnel matters than does any other structure. But it also permits a manager the greatest exercise of his or her own personal managerial style.

Most managers believed that city departments provide citizens with the greatest opportunity for setting program objectives as well as the greatest impact on decisions involving ongoing services.

Virtually all managers believed that city department structure provides the greatest amount of planning in the city but also the greatest amount of collective bargaining with employees. Most managers also expressed the opinion that the greatest conflict during budget preparation is associated with the department structure. According to a majority of managers, the department structure also is associated with budgetary complexity and the most strained council-manager relations.

Managers in Southern California, as compared to northerners, were more likely to associate city department structure with highest council control over level of expenditures, allocation of the budget, and involvement in setting pro-

Table 2-10. Effect of Structure on Aspects of Decision Process

Aspects of Process	City Department	Contract with County	Contract with Private Firm	Franchise with Private Firm	Other Structure	No Structural Effect on Process	Effect Changes with Different Services
City Council							
Highest city council control over level of expenditures	19	2	3	1	0	1	1
Greatest city council discretion over allocation of expenditures	22	1	1	0	0	2	1
Most city council involvement in setting program objectives	19	2	2	0	0	3	1
Greatest city council impact on on-going service	25	0	1	0	0	0	0
City Managers							
Most city manager time spent on personnel problems	25	1	0	0	0	0	0
Most room for personal managerial style	24	0	0	0	0	2	0
Citizens							
Most citizen involvement in setting program objectives	19	0	0	0	0	4	3
Greatest citizen impact on on-going service delivery decisions	20	0	0	1	0	1	4

Number of City Managers Selecting Structure with Greatest Effect

Table 2-10. continued

	\multicolumn{6}{c}{Number of City Managers Selecting Structure with Greatest Effect}
Aspects of Process	City Depart-ment	Contract with County	Contract with Private Firm	Franchise with Private Firm	Other Structure	No Structural Effect on Process	Effect Changes with Different Services

Aspects of Process	City Department	Contract with County	Contract with Private Firm	Franchise with Private Firm	Other Structure	No Structural Effect on Process	Effect Changes with Different Services
Other Aspects							
Greatest amount of planning in city	23	1	0	0	1	2	0
Most strained relation between city manager and city council	14	4	3	1	0	4	0
Greatest amount of monitoring of service delivery	18	4	3	0	0	0	2
Greatest amount of collective bargaining	22	0	2	0	0	1	2
Greatest amount of conflict in preparing the budget	16	2	2	0	1	3	1
Greatest degree complexity in preparing the budget	15	3	4	0	1	3	1
Greatest ability to negotiate with providers	10	2	10	1	0	1	2

gram objectives. Independent city managers were more likely than contract city managers to associate city departments with highest council control over level of city expenditures, citizen involvement in setting program objectives, and city monitoring of services.

Managers in larger cities were more likely than their counterparts in smaller ones to associate city department structures with council control over budget allocations in setting program objectives and with budgetary complexity. More of them also associated contracts with private firms with highest council control over budget expenditure levels. Managers in smaller cities were more apt to view private contract arrangements as resulting in the greatest budgetary complexity. There were also more likely to say that citizen impact upon ongoing service delivery decisions depends upon the particular service.

Regional Impacts. Managers were asked whether county contracting, as compared with city departments, has had an effect on twelve important characteristics of the Los Angeles Region as a whole. Their views are summarized in Table 2-11. In general the managers felt that contracting results in greater similarities among the different places in the region.

Choice of Structure. Although patterns of agreement vary, managers seem to feel that structure does make a difference for service delivery. Furthermore, they seem to feel that this is true for most services. The picture that emerges from these interivews is that city departments are preferred when control over the service is desired. Where economies of scale, large start-up capital costs, or need for back-up services are important considerations, there is a preference for

Table 2-11. Managers' Views of Effects of Contracting on L.A. Region

Effect of Contracting	No. of Managers Agreeing
Standardization of minimum service levels	21
Increased incorporations	18
Increased professionalism	18
Increased areal uniformity of service distribution	18
Increased uniformity of wages	18
Increased service quality in low-income areas	17
Increased service costs	15
Increased federal aid	7
Increased acceptability of regional government	9
Decentralization of service delivery	11
Increased quality of service in region	10
Subsidization of areas that contract	10

county contracts. Similarly, in cases where service effects extend beyond city boundaries, county contracts are preferred. Other structures are selected much less frequently and most often as competitors to county contracts when some mode of provision other than the city department is desired.

We shall now consider structural selection from the perspectives of trade-offs among performance criteria, first as reported during manager interviews, then as implied by an aggregative statistical analysis. Finally we shall consider how these trade-offs might affect the variety of city structural patterns.

Performance Criteria Trade-Offs. The choice of structure appears to involve a trade-off among various performance characteristics. In order to test whether such trade-offs actually are occurring, the performance characteristics were grouped into three performance criteria: control, production, and finance. Control includes the following performance characteristics: control over the service quality; level of service quality provided; citizen confidence in who provides the service; and degree of responsiveness to citizen objectives. Production includes the performance characteristics of efficiency; uniformity in service quality; and employee morale. Finance includes expenditure per capita.

Table 2-12 summarizes the results of testing for trade-offs among performance criteria. The columns list the four most prevalent structures; the rows show the performance characteristics grouped into the three performance criteria. Then ten specific services, rated by managers during the interviews, are grouped into the four service clusters: city core, contract competition, district competition, and private competition.[9] These service clusters are then listed, under each performance characteristic, in order of decreasing local control over service provision. The numbers in the cells report the percent of all managers who rated the structure as providing the highest performance for all services falling within the indicated cluster.

Managers prefer city departments when local control is desired, but consider alternatives when department production and finance are costly. Therefore, we would expect managers to rank city departments high on performance for the city core services most often, and for the private competition services least often. Also we would expect managers to rank city departments higher for the control performance criteria then for the production or finance criteria.

Table 2-12 supports both these expectations. The percentage of managers who rate city departments as providing the highest performance for each of the control and production-related performance characteristics shows a pattern of

---

9. Planning, zoning, parks and recreation, and street cleaning are in the city production core; general law enforcement patrol, building and safety inspection, and traffic signal maintenance are in the contract competition core; fire protection is in the district competition core; and animal control and residential refuse collection are in the private competition core.

44   How Cities Provide Services

Table 2-12. Managers' Ratings of Service Performance by Alternative Structures

	Percent of managers selecting structure[a]			
Performance criteria	City department	County contract	Private contract	Special district
Control				
General quality				
City core production	80%			
Contract competition	60			
District competition	70			
Private competition	60			
Service quality				
City core production	80	–	–	–
Contract competition	60	10%	10%	–
District competition	40	20	–	30%
Private competition	50	10	30	–
Citizen confidence				
City core production	80		–	
Contract competition	70		–	
District competition	50		–	
Private competition	50		10	
Responsiveness				
City core production	100			
Contract competition	80			
District competition	90			
Private competition	75			
Production				
Efficiency				
City core production	80	–	–	–
Contract competition	50	20	20	50
District competition	30	20	–	–
Private competition	30	15	50	–
Uniformity				
City core production	40	30	–	–
Contract competition	30	50	10	–
District competition	30	30	–	40
Private competition	20	30	20	–
Employee morale				
City core production	50	–	–	–
Contract competition	40	10	–	–
District competition	30	–	–	20
Private competition	40	–	–	–
Finance				
Expenditure per capita				
City core production	60			
Contract competition	60	30		
District competition	70			
Private competition	70			

[a]Some managers selected structures not identified in this table.

Selecting Service Delivery Structures 45

decline from city core production services to contracting competition services to district competition to private competition services. Similarly, other structures are rated high by many managers only for the services that are not part of the city production core, and city departments rank higher for the local control criteria than for the production or finance criteria.

A city department consensus index was constructed in order to determine how sharply the managers differentiated among local control, production, and financial characteristics of structures. In Table 2-13 we have ranked the variety

Table 2-13. Consensus Index for Selected Characteristics

Service, decision, and response characteristics	Index value
Most citizen/employee contact	84
Greatest amount of time spent on personnel problems by manager	84
Most city council impact on service delivery	84
Most planning in city	78
Most opportunity for manager to employ own style	78
Most city council control over expenditure allocations	62
Greatest amount of collective bargaining	62
Most politically sensitive	60
Most citizen impact on service delivery	46
Most council involvement in decision-making	40
Most council control over expenditure levels	38
Most citizen involvement in decision-making	38
Most monitoring of service delivery	30
Most reliability for provider	30
Most interdependence with other services	30
Most conflict over city budget	22
Most budget complexity	16
Most manager/council conflict	8
Most need for equipment	8
Most difficulty in monitoring service	8
Most difficulty in measuring output	0
Most agreement on minimum service level	0
Most opportunity to negotiate with provider	−22
Most opportunity for decentralized delivery	−24
Most restrictions on hiring	−30
Small staff requirements	−30
Most fluctuations in demand for service	−38
Most collective bargaining	−46
Most need for skilled personnel	−54
Most available providers	−62
Most need for back-up	−62
Most opportunity for scale economies	−70
Most pursuit of comparable service levels in region	−86
Most spillovers to other jurisdictions	−100

of service, decision processes, and response characteristics in terms of their city department consensus index.[10] It appears that most of the characteristics that have a positive index are related to issues of local control; the characteristics with the highest negative indexes are related to issues of production; and the characteristics with small negative or positive values are varied, including some finance issues. Thus the expectation that the selection of city departments is related to achieving local control without an excessive production cost and finance burden is again supported.

A further test is provided on a service-by-service basis, as shown in Table 2-14.[11] For the first six services the consensus index (line 10) is positive, and they are labeled city department-efficient services. For these six services there is a declining consensus among the managers that city departments provide the highest efficiency. For the next three services there is a high degree of consensus that some structure other than the city department is the most efficient, and these are labeled city department-inefficient services. Fire protection is treated separately because it appears to be unlike the other services.

Line 9 is an index of the present incidence of service structure. It is positive (and declining) for the city department-efficient services and is negative for the city department-inefficient services. This indicates that the department structure is actually rejected in situations where it is inefficient.

The performance criteria of responsiveness, control, citizen confidence, service quality, and employee morale (lines 2-6) are fairly unambiguous indicators of local control. These criteria show positive and relatively high indexes for the city department-efficient services but low or negative indexes for other services. This indicates that local control is important in selecting the city department structure.

---

10. This measure takes on a value of 100 when all managers interviewed agree that a particular characteristic is most closely associated with the city department structure; it takes a value of minus 100 when all managers agree it is not associated with the city department; and it takes on a value of zero when the managers are split evenly. Hence the index shows the degree of consensus among managers—the higher the index the greater the consensus. Also the sign of the index indicates the structure about which there is consensus—a positive sign indicates a consensus for city departments; a negative sign indicates a consensus toward some other structure.

The consensus index is constructed by doubling the percentage of managers choosing the city department as first preference and subtracting 100. Thus, the manager interview data were reassembled so as to make high ratings and preferences for city departments the norm, and high ratings or preferences for other structures a deviation from the norm.

11. Lines 1-8 of Table 2-14 summarize the consensus of managers about the performance rating of city departments for eight specific characteristics. Line 9 gives the present incidence in California (expressed by an index whose construction is identical to the consensus index) of the use of city departments to provide the service. Line 10 is an index of consensus about whether the city department is the ideal structure for that service. Line 11 is an index of consensus about expected future increases of structures other than city departments for that service. The services are arrayed according to the consensus index for efficiency (line 1) in descending order from left to right, with the exception for the unusual case of fire, placed at the far right.

Table 2-14. Consensus Indexes for City Departments, by Service

	City Department-Efficient Services					City Department-Inefficient Services				
Service Characteristics	Zoning	Planning	Parks	Bldg. and safety	Law enforcement	Street cleaning	Animal control	Residential refuse	Traffic signal	Fire protection
High efficiency	92	54	46	46	24	16	-38	-76	-84	-46
High responsiveness	100	100	92	84	100	78	46	62	24	70
High control of quality	70	62	54	60	46	38	30	24	-16	38
High citizen confidence	78	46	78	54	54	8	8	8	-16	-8
High level of quality	96	38	78	62	78	32	-8	0	-62	-16
High employee morale	0	24	30	0	18	-16	-22	-30	-56	-46
Least uniformity of quality	-8	22	38	16	22	16	54	62	62	46
High per capita expenditures	30	8	30	0	24	30	38	24	16	46
Present incidence	92	92	70	36	42	52	-60	-70	-30	12
Ideal choice	62	62	54	54	24	0	-94	-54	-62	38
Future expectations	-30	-28	-8	-30	-24	-84	-70	-62	-84	-70

The uniformity of quality and per capita expenditure criteria (lines 7-8) are indicators of production and finance. These criteria have lower indexes for the city department-efficient services than for the other services. This suggests the importance of costs in the decision to use some structure other then city departments.

There is a relatively high but sharply decreasing consensus about whether the city department is the ideal structure for the city department-efficient services (line 10). Also there is a modest consensus that in the future these services will increasingly be provided through structures other than city departments. Thus one can say that city department-efficient services are now not only most frequently offered through city departments, but also that managers tend to view city departments high on the control criteria and low on the cost criteria for city department-efficient services. The city department-inefficient services are seldom provided through city departments; managers do not generally think they should be, do not tend to believe that city departments perform well on the control criteria, and have a high degree of consensus that in the future these services will increasingly be provided through structures other than city departments.

Fire protection is slightly above the average in the frequency with which it is provided through city departments, and there is only a moderate consensus in favor of city departments as the ideal structure for it. But there is a strong consensus among managers that it will be provided through other structures in the future.

The most important finding that emerges from these patterns is further confirmation that city departments can be differentiated from other structures in terms of their perceived performance. Second, the incidence with which services are actually provided through city departments and other structures is consistent with managers' performance ratings and preferences. Third, managers' expectations about future trends are consistent with their performance rankings.

The selection of service structures can be understood in terms of trade-offs among local control, production, and financial performance criteria. There seems to be a clear-cut preference for city department structures for services whose control-related characteristics are rated both positive and high and whose production- and finance-related characteristics are rated positive but moderate. It seems that managers select structures other than city departments when the department structure is perceived to perform badly for production-related criteria with no compensating advantages for control or finance.

A Statistical Test for Performance Trade-offs. The city manager interviews led to the conclusion that the choice of structure depends heavily on evaluations of local control, production and finance characteristics. In order to analyze whether quantitative data result in the same conclusion, a statistical model was developed to explain why cities in Los Angeles County contract, and to show the effects of contracting on tax rates and expenditures.[12]

Figure 2-4 compares selected variables for the three sets of cities in 1970. As compared with contracting cities, the self-provision cities have not only a significantly lower share of contracting in their budgets but also significantly higher city government property tax rates and expenditures per capita.[13] However, the contracting cities have significantly higher special district tax rates and special district expenditures than do the self-provision cities. The end result is that by combining the city government and special district budgets, the overall municipal service property tax rate of 2.3 percent is identical for contracting cities and self-provision cities. However, self-provision cities, because of their higher tax base, have a 40 percent higher average level of per capita expenditures for the total of municipal services than do contract cities—about $160 as compared to $115.

Thus, contracting cities tend to have a smaller tax base than do self-provision cities and to spend less on municipal services in general. Contracting cities generally have smaller city budget expenditures than do self-provision cities, but these lower budget expenditures are partially offset by higher special district expenditures.

The statistical model also shows that cities generally consider it desirable to maintain local control[14] over service delivery and, by keeping service expenditures low, to minimize the burden on the property taxpayer. The extent of contracting adopted by a city is determined by the trade-offs between these objectives. Cities differ in the trade-offs they make because they differ in their preferences for local control, in their commercial sales (which affect the tax base and therefore the affordable extent of local control), and in their assessed property values (which affect the tax burden imposed on homeowners and nonresidential landowners).

The extent of contracting in cities tends to increase when the value attached to local control goes down. But whatever the taste for local control, declining

12. This model, reported in detail in Chapter 4, was used to analyze structural selection by three classes of cities in California: "contracting cities," which are the 28 cities in Los Angeles County that contract with the county for at least 10 percent of their budgets but most of which contract for over 20 percent; "self-provision cities," which are the 44 cities in Los Angeles County that contract for less than 10 percent of their budgets but most of which contract for under 1 percent; and "non-L.A.-County cities," which are 42 cities sampled from five other counties in California.

13. Services provided through city departments and city contracts usually are funded through the city's budget. Often excluded from the budget are the many services funded and provided through other structures. We know that cities vary in the extent to which they use special districts and other structures as well as in the types of services they choose to fund outside the city budget. Therefore, it is possible that the relationships between contracting and budget expenditures or revenues are affected by the relationships between contracting and special districts.

14. The taste for local control is approximated by the median age of the population, which has been shown in other studies to be related to local control.

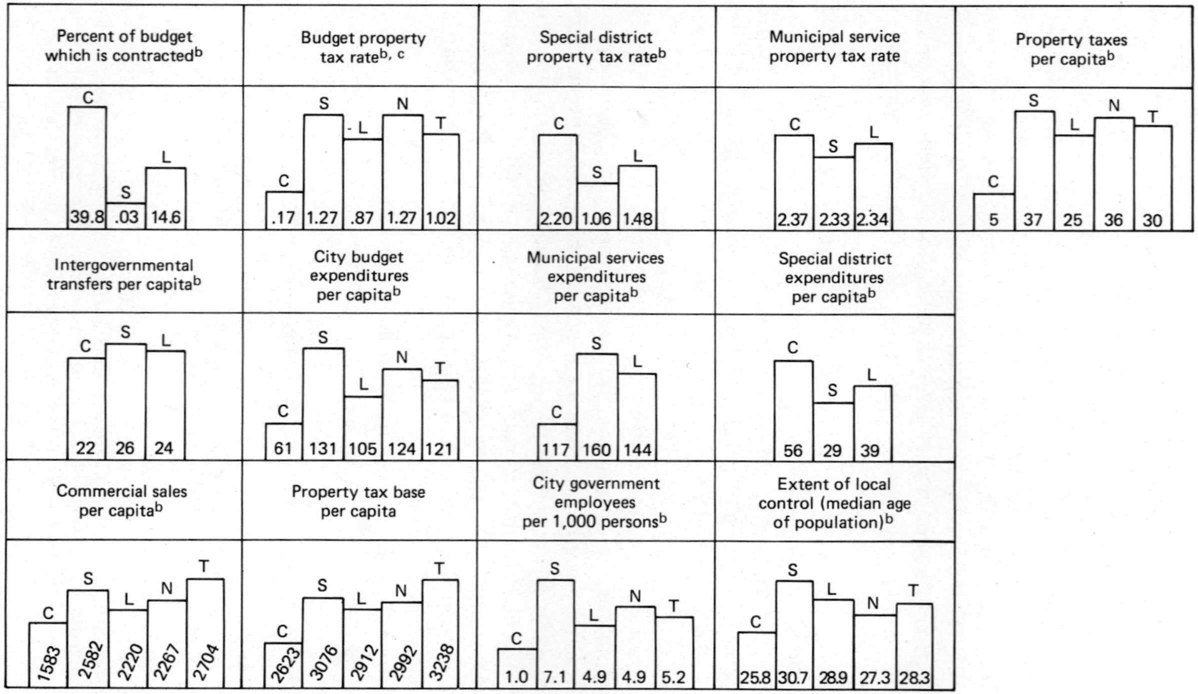

50 How Cities Provide Services

Figure 2-4. Selected Budget and Municipal Services Data: Contracting, Self-Provision and Non-L.A. County Cities[a]

[a]C = Contracting Cities; S = Self-Provision Cities; L = L.A. County Cities (C and S); N = Non-L.A. County Cities; T = California Cities.
[b]Difference between contracting and self-provision cities is significant at 0.05 level.
[c]Difference between L.A. County and non-L.A. County cities is significant at 0.05 level.

commercial sales appear to induce cities to increase their contracting because they cannot afford the added expenditure associated with achieving local control through the use of city departments.[15]

Since the decision to select contract structures is, in part, related to the city's tax base, we would expect that the extent of contracting in a city will affect its tax rates and revenues. And in fact, contracting cities have lower city property tax rates and lower property taxes per capita than do self-provision cities. Furthermore, so long as special district activities are not explicitly considered, increasing the extent of contracting results in a declining property tax rate as well as declining property tax revenues. When special district alternatives to city departments are made explicit, a different conclusion emerges. For among contracting cities, it is not increased contracting, but increased special district activities, which lower the city budget tax rate. However, the use of special districts does not lower city budget financing by as much as it increases special district financing, so that increasing the extent of contracting among contracting cities does not lower the overall municipal property tax rate.[16]

Increased contracting tends to lower city budget expenditures. Among contracting cities, for example, a 1 percent increase in the extent of contracting lowers budget expenditures by 0.5 percent. Increased contracting also leads to increased special district expenditures. But this increase is not enough to counterbalance the reduction in city budget expenditures due to contracting. On balance, the overall effect of increasing the extent of contracting is to lower municipal government expenditures, particularly among contracting cities.

The comparison of contracting cities with self-provision cities makes it clear that city departments are in competition with alternative providers—particularly contract and special district providers. Departments are rejected when the taste for local control is low; when they cannot be afforded because of a low commercial sales value; or, even when the non-residential property base is high, because

---

15. No matter what level of city revenues is provided by commercial sales, nonresidential propertyowners prefer to avoid bearing the added costs associated with local control. Therefore, a high nonresidential property tax base leads to an increase in the extent of contracting. However, residential propertyowners often are more willing than nonresidential owners to bear the extra tax burden associated with obtaining an added degree of control over the level and mix of service expenditures. Therefore, a high residential property base leads to a decrease in the extent of contracting and greater reliance on the use of city department structures.

16. Once a city decides to contract for a substantial amount of its services, further increases in contracting do not lower the overall municipal tax rate, even though they lower municipal expenditures. This is, in part, because increased contracting results in a smaller quantity of intergovernmental transfers, which could account for the lowering of budget and overall municipal expenditures without affecting the property tax rates. It also appears possible, although it has not been tested, that not only do lower residential property values result in increasing the extent of contracting, but increased contracting, in turn, leads to lowering residential property values. This also could account for increased contracting having the effect of lowering expenditures without lowering the property tax rate.

the higher base is used not to generate more taxes but to achieve the lower budget tax rates associated with contracting.

Cities that decide to increase contracting seem to decide, at the same time, to increase expenditures made through special districts. This means that expenditures through city departments are lower not only because there is contracting but also because there is a relatively high level of district expenditure. Cities that contract are not only contracting cities; they are, more generally, non-city-department cities. And to a large extent they are non-city-department cities because they choose to avoid adding to the financial burdens of property taxpayers. These findings are consistent with data provided by the city manager interviews, which also indicated that structural diversity varies from one city to the next.

Variety in City Structural Patterns. Both the city manager interviews and aggregative statistical analyses provide a comparable basis for explaining why different cities select different service structures. They do so because structures are perceived to have different performance characteristics and because cities weigh these characteristics differently. Managers prefer city departments when they do well on the performance characteristics relating to control, production, and finance. And, according to city managers, departments perform well on these characteristics for those services found in the city production cluster. For other services, departments still perform well on control characteristics, but performance drops off sharply on the production and finance characteristics. In the case of these other services, performance of district and contract structures is perceived to be substantially better on production characteristics.

The perceived differences in performance of various structures and the distribution of structures across cities suggests what is confirmed by the aggregative analysis—namely, that different cities make different trade-offs among categories of performance criteria. Some cities might select departments because the gains in local control of services outweigh the poor performance on production and financial criteria. Other cities might find local control less important and will seek to optimize quality and efficiency through contract or district structures.

In light of what managers have said about the performance of different structures for different services, a city which provides all services (both core and optional) through city departments is paying a high price to retain local control, because of the inefficient performance of the department structure for some services. In order to quantify the distribution of cities in the sample among different patterns of structural mixes, we developed a city type classification.[17]

17. The classification of city type is based on how the cities differ in the structures they use to provide the city core services and the optional services. For this purpose, it is sufficient to distinguish among the city department structure, the contract structure, and "all other structures," that is, all structures other than department and contract. The five city types are defined as follows (see also Table 2-15):

This classification groups cities according to the degree of control over service delivery that they choose to exercise.

Table 2-15 shows the distribution of California cities in terms of these city types. If the 84-city sample is representative, California cities are grouped in about equal proportions in three categories: those cities that relatively favor local control over all services, those cities that relatively favor local control of core services but not optional services, and those cities that are relatively willing to give up local control of optional and core services.

In addition, we can see that those cities that favor retaining control of core services but giving up control of optional services do so primarily through a total transfer of the optional services. All cities willing to give up some control of core services are also willing to give up control of optional services. However, most of these cities retain partial control of the core services by transferring only the production activity and retaining the finance activity, while the remainder transfer production of core services.

The city types can be further detailed by the type of activity which is transferred out. Thus, of the sample of cities in California about one-third are self-provision cities in the sense that they favor retention of production, finance, and planning activities; one-third are nondepartmental cities in the sense that they favor transferring the production activity; and one-third are transfer of service cities in the sense that relatively they favor transferring both production and finance activities.

Reconsidering Structural Improvements

Once a particular structure has been adopted by a city, the costs incurred in changing the structure are high. There are financial costs associated with making the transition, and these in some cases may exceed benefits that accrue from adopting a new structure for providing services. More important, however, is that

---

Local Control of All Services (1): Those cities that adopt city departments to provide both core and optional services at least as often as they are adopted by the average of all cities. Also these cities adopt other structures (i.e., neither department or contract) to provide optional services at a rate that is less than the average of all cities.

Production Transfer of Optional Services (2a): Those cities that use city departments to provide core services at least as much as the average of all cities, but provide optional services through city departments or "other structures" on less than an average basis.

Total Transfer of Optional Services (2b): Those cities that provide core services through city departments and optional services through "other structures" at least as much as the average of all cities.

Production Transfer of Core Services (3a): Those cities that provide at least the average of optional services through "other structures," while providing core services through city departments and "other structures" on less than an average basis and through contract structures on more than an average basis.

Total Transfer of Core Services (3b): Those cities that provide at least the average of optional services through "other structures" but provide core services through city departments on less than an average basis and through "other structures" on more than an average basis.

54 How Cities Provide Services

Table 2-15. A Classification of California Cities as Based on Control Over Services

City types[a]	Total	Percent of all cities in California		
		No activity transfer	Transfer of production	Transfer of production and finance
	100%	32%	34%	34%
1. Local control of all services	32	32		
2. Nonlocal control of optional services	36			
2a. Production transfer of optional services	8		8	
2b. Total transfer of optional services	28			28
3. Nonlocal control of all services	32			
3a. Production transfer of core services	26		26	
3b. Total transfer of core services	6			6

[a] City type definitions: see Note 17.
1. Cities which depend relatively on city departments to provide both core and optional services.
2. Cities which depend relatively on city departments to provide core services but not optional services; includes city types 2a. and 2b.
2a. Cities which depend relatively on city departments to provide core services and on the contract structure to provide optional services.
2b. Cities which depend relatively on city departments to provide core services but does not depend on either city departments or contracts to provide optional services.
3. Cities which depend relatively on structures other than city departments to provide services; includes 3a. and 3b.
3a. Cities which depend relatively on the contract structure to provide core services and on structures other than city department or contract to provide optional services.
3b. Cities which depend relatively on structures other than city department or contract to provide both core and optional services.

adopting a new structure is likely to impose costs on particular groups. So changing from a city department to a consolidated district structure may mean that the city manager or city council loses control over planning, and therefore over the quality of service provided.

Changing from a city department to a contract is likely to threaten the livelihood of city employees, who may completely resist the change or insist on being "folded in" to the contract arrangement. Often, if their security can be assured, employee wages and benefits increase under the contract structure. Similarly, changing from a contract with the county to a private contract represents a threat to county employees. Such a change provides little opportunity for county employees to be "folded in," although usually losses in contracts can be absorbed by the county without causing layoffs. However, if the county loses a substantial number of contracts at the same time, which may occur when there is a change in the contract price of service delivery, then a real threat is faced by county department heads who are seeking to efficiently provide services on an areawide basis.

Because interests are threatened when provision structures are changed, it is often advisable to make such changes at the fringes; that is, to seek improvements within an existing structure by adopting an alternative structure not for an entire service but for disaggregated, selected subservices that are particularly suited to a different provision arrangement.

Service disaggregation as a means for structural improvements will be discussed first for all services, and then a closer examination of the police service will be made.

Service Disaggregation as a Structural Improvement. Very often component parts of a service can be selected and each of the components provides through different structures. Table 2-16 illustrates the extent to which this is occurring in terms of service agreements between Los Angeles County and cities in the county. Three service areas are shown: roads, police, and engineering. These three services are disaggregated into twenty-six component parts. Moreover, varying percentages of these agreements are with noncontract cities which provide the bulk of their services through the city department structure. These data show not only disaggregation of services into component parts, but also that the components are provided via different structures.

Within contract cities a similar process of service disaggregation and adoption of a variety of structures for service components has occurred. Table 2-17 summarizes a 1972 survey of twenty-one cities conducted by the Contract Cities Association. These data show a pattern of service clusters being associated with particular structures. Moreover, the data show that the use of Los Angeles County as the service provider declined slightly in the 1967-1972 period, while provision through private firms and city departments increased considerably. In the years following incorporation, these cities, which had initially received the overwhelming majority of their services from Los Angeles County, have consistently moved toward adoption of other structures for particular services.

The total number of provider deliveries grew by 20 percent, with three-fifths of the increase attributable to city staff providers and two-fifths to private contracts. Because of the growth in number of providers without change in the number of services, it appears that alternatives to county contract are sought when a particular part of some service can be separated from the other parts and provided through a different means. It also appears that, when this separation happens, both city staff and private contract alternatives to county contract become attractive.

56 How Cities Provide Services

Table 2-16. Disaggregation of Services Shown in County-City Agreements for 1973

Service components	Number of service agreements	Percentage of total with non-contract cities
Roads		
Street maintenance & construction	28	11%
Bridge maintenance	35	46
Traffic signal maintenance	55	60
Street signs	21	10
Street sweeping	6	0
Street lighting maintenance	11	45
Subdivision engineering	26	4
Traffic striping and marks	31	23
Sheriff		
Helicopter	11	9
Law enforcement	30	7
County jail	77	62
Microfilm storage	16	81
Business license enforcement	25	4
Crossing guard	18	0
Motorcycle patrol	6	0
School safety	8	0
Community relations	5	0
Traffic law enforcement	27	0
Bicycle safety ped. off.	1	0
Engineering		
Building inspection	31	37
Industrial waste services	32	75
Sewer maintenance	3	100
Subdivision map check	71	79
Parcel map check	16	0
Master house map service	29	0
Engineering staff service	40	21

There was general agreement among respondents switching to private contact that private contractors were more efficient and less costly than county contract. Yet it should be noticed that, for those services for which cities adopted private contract, not only did they also retain county contract but they also added city staff. Apparently as complexities of service delivery expand, opportunities for division of labor emerge.[18]

---

18. The contract city managers indicated that they were inhibited from more extensive shifting to private contract because of the following [D37, p. 2]:
   a. The lack of private suppliers actively offering contract services to cities or orienting their operations toward this market for their services.
   b. The indecision on the part of many cities (both in their administrative staffs and city councils) to take the plunge away from the county despite the growing discontent with the county's spiraling overhead cost charges.

Selecting Service Delivery Structures 57

Table 2-17. Service Providers in Twenty-One Contract Cities, 1972 vs. 1967

		Number of Providers								
	Total		Private		City		County District		County Dept.	
Year	1972	1967	1972	1967	1972	1967	1972	1967	1972	1967
Private competition services	*373*	*289*	*91*	*44*	*129*	*79*	*0*	*0*	*153*	*166*
Street maintenance & const.	37	26	14	6	8	6	0	0	15	14
Street lighting maintenance	23	18	12	7	1	1	0	0	10	10
Street sweeping	21	17	11	5	7	3	0	0	3	9
Engineering staff services	28	19	9	3	6	3	0	0	13	13
Radar equip. maintenance	18	14	9	6	1	0	0	0	8	8
Tree trimming services	30	21	7	2	15	7	0	0	8	12
Traffic signal maintenance	22	17	7	1	1	1	0	0	14	15
Animal control	21	16	5	3	1	0	0	0	15	13
Park maintenance	22	18	4	2	16	10	0	0	2	6
Subdivision engineering	19	15	3	2	2	2	0	0	14	11
Planning & zoning	25	20	2	2	18	11	0	0	5	7
Recreation services	19	18	2	2	16	13	0	0	1	3
Tree planting & maintenance	24	19	2	1	18	10	0	0	4	8
Traffic striping	24	18	2	0	7	6	0	0	15	12
Noxious-weed abatement	19	17	1	1	4	2	0	0	14	14
Parcel map check	21	16	1	1	8	4	0	0	12	11
City competition services	*218*	*181*	*0*	*0*	*85*	*44*	*0*	*0*	*133*	*137*
Mapping	20	17	0	0	3	1	0	0	17	16
Personnel	19	16	0	0	17	14	0	0	2	2
Transient occupancy tax	13	8	0	0	7	3	0	0	6	5
Building inspection	20	17	0	0	4	2	0	0	16	15
Subdivision mapping	21	17	0	0	5	2	0	0	16	15
Street signing	22	17	0	0	9	5	0	0	13	12
Business license enforcement	24	19	0	0	12	6	0	0	12	13
Crossing guards	18	15	0	0	11	5	0	0	7	10

Table 2-17. continued

Number of Providers

Year	Total 1972	Total 1967	Private 1972	Private 1967	City 1972	City 1967	County District 1972	County District 1967	County Dept. 1972	County Dept. 1967
Motorcycle patrol	7	9	0	0	2	1	0	0	5	8
School safety	16	14	0	0	6	2	0	0	10	12
Community relations	16	15	0	0	6	2	0	0	10	13
Traffic law enforcement	22	17	0	0	3	1	0	0	19	16
District competition services	72	68	2	1	8	7	45	45	17	15
Lighting & lighting maint.	17	17	2	1	3	2	12	14	0	0
Library	18	18	0	0	2	2	16	16	0	0
Sewer maintenance	37	33	0	0	3	3	17	15	17	15
Sole county contract	60	54	0	0	3	3	0	0	57	51
School fire safety	12	12	0	0	2	2	0	0	10	10
Industrial waste	19	17	0	0	0	0	0	0	19	17
Weed abatement	15	13	0	0	0	0	0	0	15	13
Bridge maintenance	14	12	0	0	1	1	0	0	13	11
Total services	723	592	93	45	225	133	45	45	360	369

Source: California Contract Cities Association, *Analysis of California Contract Cities Services in Formation Log Survey*, mimeo n.d. pp. 4–7.

As is shown in Table 2-17, the services for which private contract and city staff have been adopted are generally services for which there are fairly clear indicators of output. Also, these services seem to require fairly simple technologies, which are susceptible to productivity improvements through more equipment usage.

The services for which city staff but not private contract have been adopted are essentially alternatives to county contract. These services tend to be politically salient and to be services for which private suppliers would generally not be available. The contract city managers gave no indication that city staff can provide these services more efficiently or at less cost than the county. These are the services for which some measure of local control is sought, even if cost savings are not achieved.

The services for which alternatives to the county (both contract and district) have not been adopted seem primarily to be maintenance types of activities, which are essentially the same in all areas of the county and which can be attended to on schedule wihtout impositions of unexpected demands on the work force. Thus for these services there seem to be no strong inducements to seek alternative providers.

Disaggregation in the Police Service. Further examples of the potential for disaggregation are found in views of police chiefs who were questioned about general aspects of police service provision and specific aspects of alternative delivery structures.[19] Thirteen chiefs were shown a list of specific structures and asked to indicate which of the structures they expected to increase or decrease in importance for providing police services. Their responses are shown in Table 2-18. It appears that about half the chiefs expected a greater diversity of structures for providing police services than currently exists. This includes net increases for self-provision, contracting, and other government structures. But the only overall consensus seems to be that structures utilizing intercity cooperative arrangements, including both joint-powers agreements and police service districts, will increase in importance.

In addition, the chiefs were asked to identify the structures currently being used in their cities, for a list of specific police services they were also asked to indicate the structure they considered to be the likely mode in the future as well as the structures they would prefer for their cities. The results are shown in

---

c. The ease and comfort and the lesser demands on administrative direction of continuing a tried and familiar relationship with the county.

d. The political orientation of our cities toward the county, including a sort of in-bred attitude that county services and contract services are synonymous.

19. Personal interviews were administered in group sessions with 13 police chiefs from medium-sized police departments. The chiefs were selected from three Southern California counties to obtain information about alternative structures for providing services, including those currently in use and candidates for future adoption.

Table 2-18. Expected Changes in Police Structure

Structure	Number of chiefs expecting: Increase	Decrease
City department	5	1
Contracting		
With county	6	2
With private firms	4	0
With others	0	0
Joint agreements		
Joint arrangements	6	0
Joint police service districts	8	1
Joint-powers agreement	13	0
Other governments		
County	4	1
State	5	3
Federal	2	2
Other	4	2
Private provision	1	2

Table 2-19, As would be expected in independent cities, most of the services are currently self-provided; only some specialized support services are not. While the police chiefs expected and preferred the basic and community services to continue to be self-provided, they also expected and preferred the general support services to shift to some form of joint agreement. However, although there was a preference for the undercover services to be provided through joint agreements, there was little expectation that this will happen.

The preferred structure tended to be either self-provision for most services currently and likely to be provided through city departments, or a shift to joint agreements for other services. Even the second-choice alternative tended to be either city departments or joint agreements. Contracting and private provision of police services were considered neither likely nor desirable by independent city police chiefs.

It appears that the chiefs were willing to give up or dilute their control over some police activities that are not considered central to their enforcement of the law. The chiefs apparently perceived an opportunity for cost saving and improved quality by joint provision of the general support services, just as they have already achieved cost savings by going outside the departments for specialized services. Also, the chiefs saw an advantage in joint agreements in the provision of the areawide services that require undercover operations, since in small departments police officers are likely to become known. However, control over the core of law enforcement—patrol, follow-up investigations, traffic, and licensing—was not willingly given up and is likely to remain with the city's police department.

Selecting Service Delivery Structures 61

Table 2-19. Police Service Structures

Disaggregated components of police services	Number of responses citing city department as being provider			Structure with plurality response[a]			Second-choice alternative to plurality[a]	
	Current	Likely	Preferred	Current	Likely	Preferred	Likely	Preferred
Basic services								
Patrol	13	11	9	CD	CD	CD		JA
Follow-up investigation	12	11	9	CD	CD	CD		JA
Undercover services								
Crime prevention	11	8	5	CD	CD	JA	JA	CD
Vice/narcotics	7	6	3	CD	CD	JA	JA	CD
Community services								
Traffic enforcement	13	12	6	CD	CD	CD		OG
Parking control	13	11	6	CD	CD	CD	OG	JA
Permits & licenses	10	7	6	CD	CD	CD	JA	OG
Noncrime youth program	6	7	4	CD	CD	JA		CD
General support								
Vehicle maintenance	10	8	4	CD	CD	JA		CD
Records & identification	9	3	1	CD	JA	JA		
Communication	8	3	0	CD	JA	JA		
Personnel	7	3	4	CD	JA	JA	CD	CD
General supply	6	2	3	CD	OG	CD	CD	OG
Specialized services								
Custodial	7	3	3	CD	JA	CP	CD	JA
Crime-related division	4	6	5	OG	CD	JA	OG	CD
Training	2	0	2	OG	OG	JA	JA	OG
Lab. analysis	0	1	1	CP	CP	CP	OG	JA

[a] CD = city department; JA = joint agreements; CP = county provided; OG = other government provides.

Two major categories of reasons for structural preference were mentioned frequently—local control and costs of production. It appears that the city department was more favored for basic and community police services because community control is important and the possibilities for cost savings due to economies of scale were presumed to be low. Joint arrangements were favored for general support services because the demand for community participation is low and economies of scale were presumed to be important. The chiefs repeatedly stressed the desire to retain local control in the cities receiving a service, and they felt that, in the case of support services and undercover activities, such control was greater through a joint arrangement than through provision by the county or some other agency.

Factors that are often mentioned as arguments for contracting—reduction of spillovers, uniformity of service levels, elimination of duplication—were not cited frequently by independent city police chiefs. Moreover, it does not appear that the chiefs' preferences were based on a shortsighted viewpoint. Indeed, their frequent choice of joint arrangements and their cited reasons for those choices indicated clearly that the chiefs were aware of areawide problems and favored a joint city rather than a contracting approach to their solution.

The police chiefs were asked to rate certain community and service characteristics in terms of the effects on performance along the dimensions of lowering the crime rate, reducing the response interval, and increasing efficiency. Chiefs were also asked which of these characteristics tended to favor the adoption of city department or other structures. The results are shown in Table 2-20. Factors that tend to favor high community control and result in high performance tend to lead to the adoption of city department structures. Factors associated with high production costs, but neutral toward performance, appear to result in a search for alternatives to city departments. These results are strikingly similar to those of the survey of city managers, who also tended to favor city departments when the need or desire for control was great, but tended to seek alternative structures when production costs and service expenditures were high.

A GENERAL MODEL OF STRUCTURE SELECTION

Service attributes, such as economies of scale, have characteristically been used to explain the choice of structures for the delivery of municipal services. However, substantial evidence exists to show that actual structural selections are based additionally upon the availability of alternative structures, the attributes of structures, and a city's willingness to relinquish control over the delivery of services.

A strong predilection toward service provision through city departments exists, being demonstrated in the actual incidence of structures used and in preferences expressed by city officials. The basis of this preference is the desire

Table 2-20. Community and Service Characteristics Affecting Choice of Police Structure and Performance (13 Responses)

Community and service characteristics	Structure chosen					Effect on performance measures						
	City depart-ment	County contract	Joint powers	No structure	Crime rate Lower	Crime rate Raise	Response interval Reduce	Response interval Increase	Efficiency Increase	Efficiency Decrease
High-control-high-performance factors										
High demand for local control	11	—	—	1	6	—	6	5	—	—
High citizen/employee contact	11	—	—	1	10	1	9	2	11	—
High community income	10	—	—	1	6	3	—	—	11	—
High provider reliability	9	—	2	1	10	—	9	4	12	—
High-cost-low-performance factors										
High residential density	6	1	—	3	1	10	4	8	3	10
Great diversity of population	5	—	—	5	1	9	—	—	3	8
High mobility of population	4	1	—	4	—	9	—	—	1	10
High fluctuation in need for service	3	2	1	3	—	8	5	7	3	9
High production-cost factors										
Consensus on minimum service needed	7	2	1	2	—	—	7	5	—	6
Difficulty in measuring performance	6	1	—	6	—	—	3	4	5	6
Importance of scale economies	3	2	2	1	5	3	11	1	5	5
Need for skilled personnel	2	2	2	3	5	4	4	4	8	—
Need for equipment	1	—	2	5	—	6	6	5	—	—
High start-up costs	1	6	2	2	—	—	—	—	—	—
Need for back-up	0	1	5	4	2	5	7	5	—	—

of city officials to control the quality of service delivery, which they overwhelmingly believe is best accomplished by city departments. Local control is the name of their game.

Structures other than city departments are chosen when cities are willing to trade off some degree of local control for production efficiencies or a shift in the financing base of the provision of a service. Fiscal exigency is the most common impetus to adoption of structures other than city departments.

The city officials who select service delivery structures are seeking alternative methods of service delivery that will achieve production improvements or shift fiscal burdens away from the city budget, while maintaining the maximum possible local control over delivery of the service. The period immediately after incorporation—generally a time both of fiscal concern and when there is no stake in already established city departments—is the point when adoption of alternatives to city departments is most frequent. Subsequent to these initial choices of structures, few fundamental changes in service delivery structures are made.

Once a structure for service provision is chosen, various factors make rejection of that structure and adoption of a new one difficult. Only in unusual circumstances do cities make these fundamental shifts, although they do occur and may increase in frequency as the fiscal strain on cities increases. More frequently a service is disaggregated so that some component part can be shifted to a new structure. This lowers the costs attendant to a structure change (such as collection of information on alternatives, overcoming any opposition to the change), and has the effect of delimiting the risk potential in any change to components of services.

Thus, the strategy cities adopt for changes in service delivery structures usually involves disaggregation of a service and the movement of a component of that service to a new structure. This strategy reduces risks to the cities and allows the identification of component parts of services for which local control is less important. Service attributes are important at this point, but so are the availability of alternative structures and the degree of local control the city preserves.

In the future, new structures will be sought that reap production improvements and relief of fiscal burden while maintaining more local control. The expectation of city managers that special districts encompassing several cities will be developed to provide police services is a good example of this strategy.

Our data indicate that there are differences in service attributes, available structural alternatives, and performance characteristics both among structures and among cities. An effort to model the decision process through which service structures are selected must incorporate all of these differences. We have considered four components of a general model for service selection: (1) the availability of alternative structures; (2) the characteristics of service structures; (3) the values associated with different performance characteristics; and (4) the possibility of gaining some of the values by adapting existing structures. The analysis indicates that new alternatives are likely to be considered only if tinkering with existing structures does not remove the dissatisfaction and if alternatives are available and known to city decision-makers. Among the reasons why existing (especially if they are city department) structures might not cope with the perceived problems no matter how much they are improved are: high service costs, scale economies, high start-up costs (especially for a new service), unused capacity, need for standardization of service among jurisdictions, service spillovers among jurisdictions, and hiring restrictions. Traditional theory uses these factors to account for the selection of alternatives to city departments. Evidence developed in the course of this study confirms that such service attributes may lead to consideration of alternatives to city departments, but do not account for either the decision to abandon departments or the alternative chosen.

We can account for the choice of specific alternative structures if we include as variables both the performance of different structures and community taste for local control. A city government seeking to select appropriate structures for service delivery needs criteria for comparing the performance of different structures. Our study indicates that there are three questions frequently asked by cities judging structural performance:

1. Is production at least as efficient as that provided by other structures?
2. Is the financial burden reasonable and will it be borne by appropriate persons?
3. Is control over service delivery kept in the hands of officials who are responsive to citizen needs?

There are a number of possible performance criteria that could be identified. However, the use of these three—production efficiency, financial burden, and service control—has several advantages. They are meaningful to the practitioners involved with selecting structures; they relate to the community benefit and can therefore be perceived as objectives or incentives for selecting structures; and they can be linked to the specific activities that define structures (that is, production, financing, and planning activities).

Achieving a high level of efficiency is an objective (and therefore an incentive in structural selection) because it provides a socially desirable resource allocation. Although broad measures of efficiency describing optimal resource use ordinarily are not available, some of the important dimensions of efficiency are described by the relation of inputs to outputs in the production process. Production efficiency is likely to differ systematically among structures because particular structures tend to favor certain types of technologies, to be more or less able to take advantage of scale economies, and to involve different types of persons in the production activity.

Holding down the financial burden associated with service delivery is a second objective. Although the financial burden is related to production efficiency, it is affected primarily by the level of service quality sought. Therefore a structure that provides the lowest financial burden is not necessarily a preferred structure. The financial burden is also judged by who bears the costs. Do those who receive the service pay for it? Do particular kinds of families bear an excessive share of the costs? Are the costs distributed appropriately between different groups of taxpayers? Although such questions are not easy to answer, they do enter into evaluations of government performance. The financial burden is likely to differ systematically among structures because particular structures tend to seek different levels of service quality and to prefer tapping different revenue sources for the financing activity.

The third objective is that some preferred set of actors be in control of the planning, producing, and financing of a service. The preferred actors may be different for each activity and alternative preferences may be held in various groups in the community. From the community perspective the preferred actors are those who establish service targets compatible with citizens' desires and who make certain that promised services are actually provided. Frequently there is a strong preference for city officials to have control over service delivery and, even more particularly, over the planning activity. Structures systematically differ in the amount of local control they provide because they differ in the mix of city government, other government, and private-sector involvement in service delivery.

Thus, structure is a term used to distinguish among methods for producing, planning, and financing the provision of municipal services. One structure is preferred over another because it has particular features that influence the degree of efficiency, burden, and local control associated with providing a service. It may not be possible within one structure to achieve simultaneously high levels of production efficiency, a low financial burden, and extensive local control. Therefore selection of an appropriate structure can involve complex considerations about the kinds of trade-offs a community is willing to make in order to achieve a desired end. This study indicates that cities are aware that such trade-offs must be made and that structural selection options are available.

Our analysis has emphasized the interrelationship of service attributes with structural performance characteristics and between service clusters and (city manager) estimates of the performances of different structures. Table 2-21 is a matrix that summarizes this complex three-way relationship by relating a city's willingness to forego local control of the provision of municipal services (as measured by the activities they have transferred to other units of government or private firms) to particular service clusters.

The trade-offs made by cities are captured in the three levels of desire for local control, displayed as columns. By arraying these choices against the four types of services, shown as rows, the complex trade-offs being made are captured and expectations about future choices generated.

Consider the possible sequence of choices over time for a city that becomes dissatisfied with its existing structures for service delivery. At any given time, a

Table 2-21. Effects of Trade-offs Between a City's Desire for Local Control and Service Delivery Structures[a]

Type of service	City's desire for local control		
	Control both core & optional services	Control core, but not optional services	Control neither core nor optional services
City production core	oo	oo	+
Contract competition core	oo	o	++
Special district competition optional	o	+	++
Private competition optional	o	+	++

[a]Within each cell, the symbols represent the likelihood of service provision structures other than city departments, as follows:
oo = very few structures other than city departments.
o = few structures other than city departments.
+ = a mix of city departments and other structures.
++ = many structures other than city departments.

city has already made choices placing it in one cell of the matrix and will have very few to very many structures other than city departments. With the exception of cities with revenue bases generated disproportionately by nonresidents (unusually large proportions of property tax revenues from nonresidential land uses, for example), as discovered in the aggregate statistical analyses described above, cities will prefer greater degrees of local control. Once experiencing dissatisfaction, initial efforts will be directed toward improvements within existing structure, and only if these efforts fail are alternative structures considered. In their consideration, cities will progress through the trade-offs indicated by the matrix from the bottom right to the upper left.

If local control is surrendered, it is more likely in the case of optional than for core services. In these trade-offs, cities seek to achieve either increased production efficiencies or relief from financial burden. Moreover, these choices occur within the constraints of available alternative structures. In general, the private competition structures available for optional services (such as franchise) offer the promise of both increased production efficiency and relief of financial burden upon the city budget. The special district structure can be characterized as offering similar promise. Contract structures, on the other hand, typically offer the possibility of increased production efficiency and a lesser degree of relief from financial burden, because the revenues to pay for the contracted services must still be raised by the city.

68 How Cities Provide Services

The elements of this decision process may also be summarized in the behavioral model of adaptive search behavior shown in Figure 2-5. The general model states that a new structural alternative will not even be considered unless the existing structure performs poorly on both production and local control criteria. If the existing structure either performs well on production criteria, or poorly on production criteria but well on local control criteria, efforts will be made to introduce improvements in the existing structure. At some point, if efforts to make improvements fail, aspiration levels will be lowered and the search for structural improvement will be abandoned. When an existing structure performs badly on both production and local control criteria, serious consideration will be given to alternative structures, providing they are available. The services for which such consideration will be given is determined by the community's taste for local control, and structures selected are determined by the service cluster involved. The expectations about benefits from the structural change affect both satisfaction and aspiration levels.

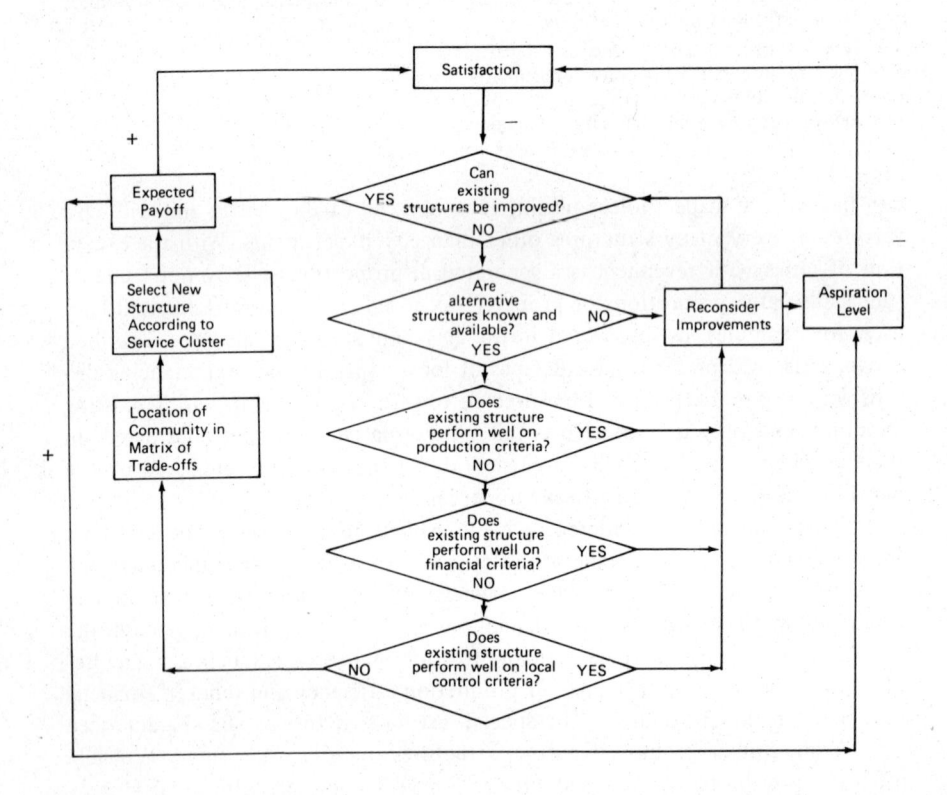

Figure 2-5. General Model for Selecting Municipal Service Structures

Selecting Service Delivery Structures 69

Two policy issues emerge from this model. First, alternatives to city departments will not even be considered if they are not available. Second, when cities abandon departmental structures it is primarily because they are perceived to perform badly on local control criteria—especially control of quality, responsiveness, and citizen confidence.

※ Chapter Three

A History of Contracting In L.A. County

SERVICE CONTRACTING:

The government of Los Angeles County is ready to provide a full array of municipal services to cities in the county. Any city that chooses to do so can contract with the county to provide services ranging from law enforcement to animal control, from planning to building inspection, from street maintenance to recreation. Each of the 78 cities in the county has at least one service agreement with the county government. About two-fifths of the cities have over 10 percent of their services provided by the county; one-fifth of the cities obtain over 40 percent of their services from the county.

Municipal service contracting—sometimes with the county, sometimes with private firms—is not peculiar to Los Angeles. It occurs throughout the country, relatively more in some places than in others and relatively more for some services than for others. Los Angeles contracting is unique only in the number of cities and municipal services involved and in the carefully thought-out procedures for delivering services through intergovernmental contractual arrangements.

Contracting in Los Angeles County is variously identified as *full-service contracting* (conveying the idea that all municipal services are available for contract) or as *contract service agreements* (a more businesslike label to convey the idea that a mutual decision between the county and cities is involved), or the more popular label, the *Lakewood Plan* (identifying the city which incorporated in 1954 and became the testing ground for full service contracting). In the preceding two chapters, the reasons why contracting has come to represent a major alternative to the city department structure were set forth. In this chapter the origins and development of the contract system in Los Angeles will be described and analyzed in more detail.

Service contracting is rooted in two different concepts of its purpose. The first is that contracting represents a form of intergovernmental cooperation that will improve urban governance; the second is that contracting is a way of doing business that will improve efficiency in the delivery of municipal services. Since improved urban governance does not depend only on improved efficiency in service delivery, there is a difference between these two concepts of contracting. Failure to distinguish between these two sets of objectives accounts for much of the disagreement about the performance of contracting. The county agencies, particularly L.A. County Sheriff's Department, tend to perceive contracting as a form of intergovernmental cooperation that will improve governance; the contracting cities tend to see contracting as an alternative way of producing services that is more efficient; and the independent cities view contracting as an alternative way of financing services that leads to inequities.

Intergovernmental Cooperation

That county officials perceive contracting as a form of intergovernmental cooperation is exemplified by the following statement of Arthur Will, who was L.A. County Administrative Officer in 1970 and who was involved with the design of the contract services plan at its conception:

> The County Contract Services Program, if studied from its beginning in 1907 to its present-day level, presents an example of the tremendous amount of intergovernmental cooperation and assistance that has been achieved in the Los Angeles metropolitan area. [D36, p. 1]
>
> Of direct benefit to the establishment of effective government in this county is the opportunity the program has provided to smaller cities to contract with a large sohpisticated governmental unit for high-quality municipal services through a uniform service delivery system that they may have been financially unable to secure for themselves. [D36, p. 8.]

Contracting is seen as a form of intergovernmental cooperation because it supposedly provides the opportunity for consolidation of service production while maintaining decentralization of delivery. As Wills points out, L.A. County directly provides health services, assessing, tax collecting, jail services, and, to a lesser extent, election services to all cities, after having provided them on a contractual basis. Each of these began as a contract service available to cities and then became consolidated under the county government. Additionally, the use of county-city joint-powers agreements to build hospital facilities and regional parks and joint use of governmental buildings were to a degree based on the mutual cooperation first demonstrated in the contract program. This is also true of the county-city cooperative purchasing programs, the county's training of paramedics, county fire departments, the partial consolidation of lifeguard and beach and cleaning services, and the complete consolidation of the air pollution control district and the Public Defender's Office.

A decade earlier, L.S. Hollinger, then County Administrative Officer and also an original designer of the contract services plan, noted the relationship between contracting and consolidation:

> From a practical standpoint functional consolidation is usually accomplished only when both governments involved believe that they will receive benefits that substantially outweigh disadvantages and/or when one jurisdiction has no practical alternative but to consolidate it. [D15, p. 1.]
>
> Another type of consolidation (in addition to functional consolidation) comes through county-city contracts where a city requests the county to provide certain municipal-type services within city boundaries which the city fully pays for. [D15, p. 2]
>
> The county provides municipal type services to the unincorporated area and to cities under contract while the various other cities provide their own services. Our studies indicate that it is in the area of municipal-type services which are being provided by several political jurisdictions that further efforts should be directed toward county-city consolidation. Those activities which should be studied with a view towards consolidation are as follows: libraries, parks and recreational facilities, animal regulation, planning, road construction and maintenance, building and safety services, fire protection, police protection, election services, licensing of charitable solicitors. [D15, p. 2.]

These potentially consolidated services were mostly being provided under contract. Clearly Hollinger is suggesting that contracting represents a step toward consolidation. Contracting and consolidation are seen as desirable because the L.A. County government is, to a large extent, a municipal government, and therefore duplication of municipal service delivery should be eliminated.

In 1950 the League of California Cities reported that in its judgment L.A. County government was essentially a municipal government for the unincorporated urban areas, since it provided to these places services that were ordinarily provided through city government. However, these services were not financed through taxes imposed on residents, as would be the case in municipal financing, but rather were financed through general countywide taxes. The league reported that about $10 million of county funds were being used to subsidize the unincorporated places, and almost half of this was a subsidy for police protection. Furthermore, unincorporated communities, recognizing this subsidy, were not incorporating.

The league demanded reform of city/county fiscal relations and the state legislation began to investigate. They found that although one-quarter of the Sheriff's budget was being spent exclusively in the unincorporated areas, much of the revenue to cover these costs was being collected from city residents. They found a similar situation in the case of health services. Two recommendations were made as a result of this investigation—one was consolidation and the other was not. For health services, the legislature recommended that the county government assume a countywide responsibility, thereby relieving the cities of this burden. By 1964 this recommendation was implemented. For the police service, however, the recommendation was not that the county government assume all law enforcement responsibilities but that the unincorporated area become a police district, or a set of police districts, with the authority to raise taxes for financing the law enforcement provided. This recommendation was not implemented, for in 1954 the introduction of the contract services plan intervened.

Under contracting, the county government could indeed implement its desire to be a complete municipal government. For now the county could provide municipal services not only to unincorporated areas but directly to municipalities as well. Also, under contracting a combination of consolidation and special district servicing is achieved, since consolidation is achieved through the widespread use of contracting in the county and districting is achieved because the cities that incorporated and became tax-raising jurisdictions in effect became the police districts that were initially recommended by the state legislature [E6].

Contracting and consolidation are not the only forms of intergovernmental cooperation. Joseph Zimmerman, in a nationwide study of intergovernmental agreements [B16], reports that three-fifths of the cities responding to his questionnaire indicated that they entered into either formal or informal agreements with other governmental units or private firms for the provision of services to city residents. The near-unanimous reason reported for entering into such agreements was to "take advantage of economies of scale," although it is not clear what is encompassed by this. Cities, and particularly the larger cities with between one-quarter and one-half million people, most commonly entered into service agreements with county government. Also, almost half the cities reported that they had service agreements with other cities, although probably a large share of these were informal agreements involving simply mutual-aid pacts or joint maintenance of highways and bridges.

In the nation as a whole, the services for which there are a relatively large number of intergovernmental agreements include planning and financing, health, law enforcement, fire protection, public works, and library services. Cities in the West, perhaps because of more available contracting opportunities, have substantially more intergovernmental agreements than cities in the East or South.

In spite of the variety of forms of agreement and differences among cities, Zimmerman concludes that all forms of intergovernmental cooperation essentially are a step toward functional consolidation:

> We may view the use of agreements for the provision of services as a limited and temporary form of functional consolidation, based on a partnership approach in which administration is centralized and policy making is decentralized. [B16, p. 88.]

John Kirlin [E6], however, claims that there are real differences among the various forms of intergovernmental cooperation because a different dynamic develops among the participants when cooperation takes one form rather than another. Kirlin's position is that intergovernmental cooperation creates a set of dependencies among the partners. With respect to contracting, and focusing on police contracting, Kirlin says that the Los Angeles Sheriff's Department (LASD) has become dependent upon contract law enforcement, if not for its survival, at least for maintenance of a reasonably high level of activity. Through an analysis based on organization theory, Kirlin claims that the LASD could be expected to seek a reduction in this dependency, which can be accomplished if the contract service is made so attractive to cities that other alternatives will not be considered. Kirlin says that the LASD has adopted several strategies precisely in order to reduce its dependency on contracting cities while maintaining its image as a countywide law-enforcement agency.

The first strategy is to keep the contract price low. Both contract cities and the LASD are interested in keeping prices to a minimum, the contract cities in order to save money and the LASD in order to preserve the contract relationship. As a consequence the LASD has consistently sought to establish minimal prices. There are several factors that assist in achieving low pricing. First, unlike other department heads the sheriff is an elected official and has a political base dependent on neither other county officials nor the independent cities in the county. Second, county budget procedures are such that there is no incentive for the LASD to recover the costs of policing from those places where the costs are incurred. Third, there is a tendency for some contract cities to purchase that amount of law enforcement which they can afford from the city revenues remaining after other service needs are met. If the remaining revenues are low, the price should also be low to meet a minimal level of service quality.

A second strategy adopted by the LASD is to change the internal structure of the department. Contracting has forced the sheriff to adopt a decentralized structure for delivery of the police service. This has been in response to both the desire for expanded local control on the part of the contract cities and the sheriff's desire for improved efficiency. The station house in a district has come to be viewed as the police department for cities in that district, and the station captain as the police chief. This has tended to increase the authority of station captains and to have shifted the consideration of how to deliver police services away from functional groupings (such as detectives vs. patrol) and more toward spatial or geographic groupings.

A third strategy has been to adjust policy about how the law-enforcement service is delivered. In response to the needs of contract cities and in order to keep the contract price low, the LASD has selectively adopted the use of one-man patrol cars, even though its preference has been for two-man cars; has established policing regions, in which several cities can join together to receive the police service as a region while jointly funding the service on the basis of cost-sharing formulas provided by the sheriff; has been willing to reduce the number of patrol units provided to a city and has never determined that these reductions bring the city below a minimum standard consistent with professional law enforcement; has changed its personnel policies so that there is a minimum one-year tour of duty in contract cities and has allowed contract cities a voice about which deputies are assigned to the city; and has introduced team policing and the neighborhood car plan in contract cities to provide closer contact between residents and law enforcement personnel.

By viewing contracting in terms of organizational response to stress, Kirlin has given us a sophisticated view of what influences the behavior of the county provider of contract services. But what about the receiver of these services, the contracting cities? And what about that "third party," the independent cities that feel they are involved in supporting the provision of services they do not receive? For a picture of these participants we should turn to the image of contracting as a business activity.

Service Contracting as a Way of Doing Business

When contracting is perceived as intergovernmental cooperation, included as benefits from the production under contract are not only the benefits of those who receive the service but also the benefits accruing to those who produce the service. Kirlin's illustration indicates clearly that the interests of the LASD police bureaucracy as much as the interests of the financers of the service are involved in deciding the quantity of law enforcement. Ordinarily when providers are in this position they manage to secure a larger allocation of resources to their purposes then they would obtain under more competitive conditions. Lyle Fitch [B8] identifies this process as allocation efficiency, which he distinguishes from production efficiency. Production efficiency is concerned with the question of whether one producer can provide some output at a lower level of resource use (that is, lower cost) than some other producer. It is production efficiency that is of concern when contracting is viewed as a way of doing business. Thus, when contracting is seen as a form of intergovernmental cooperation, the focus is on allocation efficiency and the resources made available to the service; but when contracting is viewed as a way of doing business, the focus is on production efficiency and who shall be the producer of the service.

If producers are to be selected on the basis of their production efficiency, then a clear definition of what constitutes the output of a service is necessary. Yet it is a characteristic of public services that their outputs are difficult to define and even more difficult to measure. It is partly because of the difficulties associated with specifying the nature of service output that city governments prefer to provide services through their own departments. That is, being unable to specify their service needs in advance, they choose to retain control over service production. Yet contracting does exist, including contracting of services whose outputs are only vaguely perceived.

Cities deciding to contract have avoided the issue of output measurement because they have been able to view service contracting in the same way as they view materials procurement; that is, as a purchase of inputs. What is procured through contracting is not, for example, some amount of crime prevention, but rather some number of patrol cars; not some level of street cleanliness, but rather some number of street sweepers; not some quality of building inspection, but rather the man-hours devoted to the inspection activity. So even though service contracting relates to the purchase of a service delivered to the final consumer, it is viewed as if it were procurement contracting, which relates to the purchase of inputs into the production process.

Several consequences flow from this view. The first is that if the basis for contracting is related to input procurement, then one of the ways to improve contracting can be through introducing performance contracting; that is, by introducing more objective standards of performance and improving the monitoring process of contracting cities. And, indeed, many contracting cities are advocating precisely this innovation.

A second consequence is that services tend to be thought of less in terms of their aggregated effects and more in terms of specific components or activities: not the police service, but laboratory analysis or record-keeping; not the street service, but median line or traffic signal maintenance. As such components or subservices become smaller in scope, they also tend to become procurement-type items, which are measurable and definable. As a result, the prices of different vendors, providing comparable subservices can be compared, and a provider can be selected on the basis of comparative costs. This also is happening as cities increasingly seek to find the least costly means of obtaining particular subservices.

A third consequence of viewing contracting as a kind of input procurement is that judgments about the effectiveness of contracting as compared with alternatives need not be based on quantitative information but rather can be derived from general economic principles relating to the theory of the firm. From such a perspective, whether contracting is judged to be more efficient than some alternative structure depends on the extent to which there are present economies of scale, competition, and transaction costs. For example, the following sorts of arguments can be made.

Two kinds of economies of scale need to be distinguished. The first relates to the size of the jurisdiction required for effective planning, production, and financing of a service. Often these activities can be more effectively performed through a large-scale jurisdiction rather than being fragmented among smaller jurisdictions. When this is the case, the principle of "fiscal equivalance" indicates that the optimal way of providing the service should be through the larger jurisdiction [B11]. However, it need not be the case that the same-sized jurisdiction is optimally effective for each of the planning, production, and finance activities; when it is believed that smaller jurisdictions are effective for planning and finance, and that larger jurisdictions are effective for production, contracting—and particularly contracting with the county—is perceived as an efficient way of doing business.

A second kind of scale economy relates to the use of specialized resources. If a producer has a number of customers, it very often can utilize specialized resources, such as particular skills or equipment that it would not otherwise be able to employ. Such specialization may or may not be associated with the economies resulting from jurisdictional scale. Often, however, the specialization is not available to smaller cities. When this occurs, contracting with a producer that can assemble many contracts and many clients becomes a method for obtaining the benefits of efficient, specialized resources. Often such specialized resources are available to private rather than government producers, and as a consequence private rather than county contracting becomes the preferred way of doing business.

Another argument in favor of private contracting is that private firms operate under conditions of competition and are therefore necessarily more efficient than either city or county production of a service. If it is believed that competition does produce efficiency, then contracting is certainly a way for cities to benefit from competition as well as to induce more competition. However, for competition to result in efficiency, several other things must also be happening. For example, competition can be guaranteed to be efficient only if the customer really knows what he or she is buying and can, therefore, differentiate among products. We have already seen that this is often not the case for public services. Also, it sometimes happens that competition and economies of scale are incompatible, since large-scale operation may bring about either public or private monopolies. In addition, there is nothing to prevent government agencies from competing for customers and thereby contributing to efficiency.

The argument over competition usually states that private firms are more efficient than government agencies because employees place their objectives above the goal of being efficient in production; in this view, the civil service is dysfunctional, collective bargaining in the public sector is threatening, public employees resist productivity improvements, and the public budgetary process creates no incentives for efficiency. Private contracting is then perceived as a way for cities to do business that will avoid these problems.

Private contracting is also seen as efficient because it reduces the administrative burden or transaction costs associated with providing the service. For example, if each city produces its own services, each also must do its own monitoring, which might result in high costs as compared with contracting. Similarly, the city manager and other officials spend a considerable amount of time on personnel issues, which would be reduced with contracting. The city council and city departments are often in conflict about to whom and how services should be provided, which inhibits planning and slows down improvements.

However, there are also reasons to expect that private contracting increases rather than reduces transaction costs. For example, contracting, as the city managers indicated in Chapter 2, can increase transaction costs because of the burdens associated with obtaining contracts and coordinating activities with the bureaucracy. Also, private contractors often feel the necessity to make political contributions, which would increase contract costs. Contracting also opens up opportunities and inducements for graft, and the mere suspicion of such corruption could lead to the public's rejection of contracting.

Another important issue is the impact of contracting on technological innovation. Cities are sometimes less innovative than private firms. This is partly because, without profits to reinvest in their operations, they are characteristically short of funds; and pressed by day-to-day operations, they can give little thought to inventing basic improvements. However, private firms are not exempt from these disadvantages. In addition, private firms ordinarily know relatively little about the needs of municipalities and consequently about the kinds of improvements that might make municipal service delivery more effective.

In summary, from the perspective of those who perceive contracting as an improved way of doing business, contracting, whether with the county or with private firms, provides the proper incentives for successful performance. It is performance, not contracting, that is the objective of seeking improved ways for governments to do business. Contracting is only one among several alternatives, and as Lyle Fitch [B8] notes, the alternatives must be compared in order to weigh the advantages against the disadvantages, for specific services and particular communities.

INCORPORATION, CONTRACTING AND A MUNICIPAL COUNTY

L.A. County government has traditionally struggled to maintain or expend its role in delivering public services. As the importance of municipal-type services increased, the county government became invovled in conflict with cities over issues of domain in response to the issue of to which county residents county government should provide what services, and had problems over issues of subsidy in reference to the issue of to what extent, if any, cities should share in the support of services they do not receive.

Contracting can therefore be perceived in the context of the historical and changing relationships between county and city governments—that is, as a response at a particular period of time to the issues of domain and subsidy that confront a county government seeking to be a truly municipal county. An understanding of the origins and development of contracting can therefore be improved if we examine the history of city incorporation in L.A. County. Five historical periods can be distinguished: (1) the pre-urban; (2) the urbanizing; (3) the suburbanizing; (4) the contracting incorporations; and (5) the maturation periods.

Los Angeles was the first city to incorporate in the county, which it did in 1850. Thirty-five years passed before Pasadena and Santa Monica became the second and third cities in the county. Then, within five years of this pre-urban period, five more cities incorporated. The trend toward urbanizing L.A. County had begun.

The urbanizing period for the county lasted until the 1930s. Between 1897 and 1930 there were 45 incorporations in the county, while the population in the county increased from 150,000 to 2.21 million. The population in the cities grew even faster, not only because of incorporations and internal growth, but also because of annexation. So while less than 75 percent of the county population was living in cities at the turn of the century, by 1930 the cities contained 85 percent of the people.

The issues that are still being struggled with emerged during this early period of urbanization. County government expanded as it provided municipal-type services to the residents of the unincorporated areas. Because of this, there was little opposition to the city incorporations, since the county government would probably have found it difficult to meet the growing service demands of cities as well. Indeed, the county even provided some services to cities under contract.

In a report reviewing the history of contracting, Chief Administration Officer Arthur Will [D36] noted that L.A. County's first service agreement with a municipality involved tax assessment and collection with the then city of Lordsberg (now called La Verne) in 1907, and by 1950 all but three cities—Arcadia, Long Beach, and Pasadena—had entered into such agreements. In 1938 the Regional Planning Commission of L.A. County provided advisory zoning services to the city of San Gabriel. During the thirties and forties the county entered into agreements, on a limited basis, for the issuance of building permits and inspection, animal regulation, personnel services, zoning and planning services, and street and highway construction and maintenance. Also during this period the county road department developed a variety of contracts with smaller cities. Some contracts were for specific projects only, while others covered general roadwork set up on a continuing basis. By 1950, 16 cities were utilizing the county road department for general roadwork, installation and maintenance of traffic signals, or painting traffic stripes. By 1953 the county contract program included about 450 service agreements with 45 cities [D36, pp. 2, 3].

The earliest contracts, for tax assessment, had been authorized by state legislation passed in 1895. A fuller range of services was authorized by 1914 amendments to the California Constitution, which enabled charter counties to provide municipal services to cities on a contract basis. A change in the California Code in 1915 permitted transfer of municipal functions by chartered cities to the county, and in 1953 this right was extended to general-law cities as well.

Thus, the issue of domain during the first third of the twentieth century was apparently not critical. The same, however, cannot be said of the subsidy issue. Financing of county services to unincorporated places came through the county's general fund, which was supported by tax payments of all county residents. The cities, therefore, complained that their residents were supporting the provision of county services while receiving no benefits. These complaints were probably justified. Because of the subsidy, county government would not have reason to oppose new incorporations, for thereby the subsidy could be more spread out.

It was on this foundation that the suburbanization period for L.A. County began. Between 1930 and 1954, population in the county more than doubled. But what is more interesting is that a disproportionate share of the growth took place in the unincorporated areas. By 1954 the unincorporated areas constituted almost one-quarter of the county's population, as compared with one-sixth in 1930. The growing population of the unincorporated area was essentially an urban population, requiring a full array of municipal services from the county. Thus, to the extent that cities were indeed subsidizing unincorporated areas, the subsidization was becoming increasingly onerous because of these population shifts. Yet to the extent that incorporation took place, the growth in county government would slow down. County officials began to actively discourage new incorporations, arguing that unincorporated areas were receiving levels of service comparable to those in cities, but for less cost. There was only one new incorporation during the entire 1930-1954 period.

The period of growth of suburbanization began with a portent of things to come. In 1931 the mayor of Los Angeles indicated that the city was tired of supporting unincorporated areas and suggested that the city be constituted as a separate city/county jurisdiction. The subsidy issue was now in the open. Proposals and investigations abounded.

The county and the cities were essentially seeing, or at least talking about, different sides of the coin. The county was arguing that efficiency could be achieved with county provision of services without a loss of local control. Thus, in 1934 the county proposed county centralization of service delivery with the cities determining their own policies about the level and quality of the services to be received. The cities, on the other hand, were interested not in questions of efficiency but questions of finance. They claimed that because of the subsidy the purported county efficiency was more apparent than real. The "unofficial cities,"—the urbanized unincorporated areas—should incorporate, or barring that, special taxing districts should be established to assess these areas their full costs.

In 1949 a city/county committee of the League of California Cities was established essentially for the purpose of protesting against the subsidies being received by unincorporated areas. As would be expected, very little cooperation was forthcoming either from the unincorporated areas or from the county. As a result the league moved up to the state level to plead its case. The County Supervisors Association, pushed by L.A. County, responded by starting its own lobbying of the state legislature.

The legislature, typically, did not want to become involved with what it considered to be local government disputes. It was left to the League of California Cities and the county supervisors to negotiate their own solution. Two bargaining positions were available. The league wanted state legislation forbidding county general funds from being spent for services in unincorporated areas unless the residents paid for them. The county supervisors wanted broader sales-tax powers for the county in unincorporated areas. But neither the league nor the supervisors was willing to trade support for the other group's proposals when the issue came to the legislature in 1951. Therefore, state action was not taken. But some compromise clearly was required. The compromise that emerged, and became legislation in 1953, was to make it permissible—but not mandatory—for the county board of supervisors to create community service areas as a means for making higher service levels available to and funded by unincorporated areas.

The issue was compromised but not resolved. The county was still using general funds for the support of unincorporated area services. These areas were still not incorporating, and subsidy remained, as did the tensions between county government and the cities.

Meanwhile, the county government began to rethink its position on new incorporations. The population growth was causing many communities to seek incorporation as a means for control of land use, including residential exclusionary policies. Also, some of these communities felt that incorporation would allow them to lower their property taxes and some felt a dissatisfaction with the services they were receiving from the county.

The county officials began to feel that they probably could not stop a new wave of incorporations. Indeed, it would be better to make an ally of these communities by facilitating their incorporation, particularly since they would likely join the opposition if they were to be annexed by existing cities. So in 1954 a city-county coordinator position was created in the County Administrator's Office to assist communities in studying the feasibility of incorporation.

Around this time there was an ideal opportunity for the county to explore and forge new cooperative relationships with communities that were seeking incorporation, for there was in progress an incorporation/annexation battle between the city of Long Beach and the unincorporated community of Lakewood. From this battle came not only a new city of Lakewood but a new form of intergovernmental cooperation—full service contracting.

The city of Long Beach had encircled what was then the Montana Ranch property with a shoestring annexation in the late 1920s, designed to block other municipalities from annexing the property. No attempt was made to add the territory to Long Beach until the area became the site of a huge housing development two decades later. Between 1950 and 1954 this new area of Lakewood exploded to a city of over 75,000. Particulatly attractive as annexation bait for Long Beach was the huge Lakewood Shopping Center.

The residents of the burgeoning area were split on the issue of annexing to

Long Beach, and during 1953 Lakewood was divided into seven areas for purposes of holding annexation elections. In four of the areas, where older residents predominated, annexation passed. The other three were populated largely by World War II veterans and their families, who had no particular allegiance to Long Beach.

Community and business leaders of the "free area"—which was still threatened by annexation to Long Beach—had several reasons for wanting to maintain Lakewood's independence. They feared that the city of Long Beach would be unresponsive to Lakewood's local needs, that the services would be inadequate, and that Lakewood would lose its identity. The anti-annexation group began to consider incorporation as a defensive move against annexation.

An alliance was then formed among: (1) the Lakewood business and civil leaders; (2) the Lakewood utility companies, particularly the Lakewood Water and Power Company and Southern California Gas Company, who stood to lose their Lakewood franchise if the area were annexed to Long Beach municipal utility companies; and (3) the county officials, incluidng County Counsel Harold Kennedy, Assistant Chief Administrative Officer John Leach, future County Administrative Officers C.S. Hollinger and Arthur Will, Fire Chief Keith Klinger, and Under Sheriff Peter Pitchess. These county officials were officially neutral on the question of annexation, but they encouraged Lakewood leaders to incorporate under a contract services plan that would entail a continuance of county services to the area. Lee Hollopeter, president of the Lakewood Water and Power Company, acted as an informal leader for the Lakewood group negotiating with the county.

Discussion of the idea of incorporating Lakewood and contracting with the county for most municipal services began in 1950. A 1951 report of the Lakewood Taxpayers Association noted that "the county was not reluctant to contract for all services; however, they did not commit themselves as we were not at that time undertaking an incorporation campaign" [cited in D34, p. 147]. In 1953, County Supervisor Legg made the first announcement of the possibility of incorporating a city with virtually no employees and issued a report indicating that a contract services agreement between cities and the county would be legal. An incorporation campaign was mounted, largely on the basis of the argument that there would be no rise in local taxes to provide for initial municipal costs, since the county would simply continue to provide the services it had been providing before but under contracts paid for largely by state revenues that would become available upon incorporation.

The voters of Lakewood passed incorporation by a 3-to-2 margin in March 1954. Harry Goerlick, City Administrator of Lakewood in the late 1950s, later conceded in an interview that the incorporation was not really a movement of the people but was sponsored by a core of leaders who successfully got out the vote on election day. [D38].

Two years of experience with the contract services plan was enough to demonstrate its worth. The period of contracting incorporations began, and it lasted for a decade. Between 1956 and 1965 there were thirty-one incorporations, and all but three (Downey, La Verne, and Bell Gardens) contracted with the county for a significant share of their services.

Ten of the newly incorporated cities indicated that they had incorporated for reasons of home rule and control of land use; six to avoid annexation; eleven to gain a tax advantage for property owners; and four because they were dissatisfied with the county services. Incentives for incorporation were strengthened in 1958 by the Bradley-Burns Tax Act, which allowed a one-cent increment to the sales tax to be returned to the city where it was collected. Thus, unincorporated communities would not obtain these revenues, which would go to the county instead. However, the process of incorporation was later slowed down by the Local Agency Formation Commissions that were formed throughout the state during the mid-1960s.

Approximately one-third of the new cities incorporated so they could control decisions affecting economic activities or a life-style associated with high socioeconomic status. The communities of Industry, Commerce, Irwindale, and Santa Fe Springs were all dominated by large industrial and commercial enterprises, which banded together to prevent annexation to neighboring cities with property taxes. Dairy Valley (now Cerritos) incorporated to protect agricultural land from subdivision encroachment or inclusion in a larger municipality which, Dairy Valley leaders feared, might outlaw dairy farming as a health hazard. Bradbury, Rolling Hills Estates, Hidden Hills, and Walnut, all estate-type residential communities, feared that annexation might alter the semirural, exclusive character of the areas. In Baldwin Park, Bell Gardens, and La Puente, residents were dissatisfied with county delivery of a number of services and believed they would have greater control if they incorporated. In Bellflower, Baldwin Park, Lawndale, La Puente, Norwalk, and Paramount, government costs were the issue, and a popular incorporation slogan was "representation without taxation," an objective that could be achieved by the combination of inexpensive county contract services and state subventions (through Bradley-Burns) to pay for these services.

In all cities, incorporation leaders stressed that contracting with the county for municipal services would eliminate the rise in local taxes usually associated with establishing a new city, and they were fairly accurate. In 1970, 21 of the newly incorporated cities had no property tax, a claim that none of the cities incorporated before 1954 could make. None of the contracting cities had a property tax rate reaching a dollar per hundred, and, on the average, contracting cities as a group had a tax rate one-third the average of other cities.

From the perspective of the new cities, contracting was clearly a success. From the perspective of the county it was also a success, for the county continued to provide services to most of those communities, which had been receiving county services prior to incorporation. Since county provision of municipal services, including contracting, was not a new instrument, what was the design emerging from the Lakewood incorporation that made contracting so attractive? It is often suggested that the unique aspect of the contract services plan is that it is full service contracting. That is, a city can, if it chooses, obtain *all* its services from the county. For example, Arthur Will has noted that the concept of a contract city developed with the incorporation of Lakewood. "Rather than selectively contracting for specific services when needed as 'independent cities' had previously done, the city of Lakewood chose instead to receive on a continuing basis a majority of its basic municipal services from the county" [D36, p. 2].

But only one city (Hidden Hills) has actually made the full service choice, and only five cities contract for over half of their budget expenditures (see Table A-11 Appendix). Thus, while the concept of full service is appealing, it is probably not critical.

What is critical is the county's willingness, and indeed the sheriff's eagerness, to provide police services to cities. The opportunity for communities to have their own city government without having to have their own police department proved almost irresistible to most of the newly incorporated cities. As has been noted earlier, the contract services plan in effect provided an opportunity for the unincorporated community to become a city and a police district.

It is also true that cities wanted their own police departments would not become contracting cities. For example, the citizens of Downey, which did incorporate in 1956 without contracting, were particularly aroused against the L.A. County Sheriff's Department. In spite of the then high crime rate in the unincorporated community of Downey, the LASD was covering the area with only two patrol cars. This was seen as inadequate service by citizens, who therefore sought incorporation partly in order to have their own police department [D31]. Another illustration is the city of Signal Hill, incorporated since 1924, which contracted for police services in 1959 as a result of conflict between the city council and a succession of city department police chiefs. However, from the day that sheriff's deputies began patroling the city, citizen complaints mounted, as did felony arrests and traffic fines. By the end of 1959, the council members who had supported police contracting were recalled, and soon thereafter a local police department was reinstated [D31].

Thus, once communities were assured of police protection, incorporation became attractive. But for contracting to become attractive, one more element was needed. This was the element of relating police contracting to the sheriff's legal responsibility for providing countywide law enforcement. Two things were thereby accomplished. First, the sheriff became a strong proponent of contracting because it provided a vehicle for meeting his legal responsibility and professional adherence to the principle of areawide law enforcement. Second, it provided the rationale for minimizing the costs of contracting for law enforcement. For if the sheriff is required to provide police protection to the entire county, contracting cities—as a matter of principle—should be charged only for that protection they receive, which is in addition to what must otherwise be provided. In the initial contracts with Lakewood, this additional amount was considered about equal to the fines and forfeitures collected by the local municipality.

So the principle was established that contracting charges should relate only to the services provided that are above some minimum. This principle was applicable essentially only to law enforcement for which the minimum could be interpreted as a legal responsibility. But if this principle is made the basis for contract charges, financial subsidies are inevitable. The contract services plan could be seen, as it was by many, as a tactic allowing for the continuation of subsidies; but now the subsidies flowed not from cities to unincorporated areas, but rather from independent cities to unincorporated areas and contract cities.

It could not be expected that the contract service plan would solve the subsidy issue. Even as late as 1970, the county administrative officer reported, "On the basis of all countywide local tax collections, a tax inequity exists to the extent that the unincorporated area of the county is being subsidized approximately $5 million by that portion of the county represented by the incorporated cities" [D16, p. 12]. What the contract services plan did do, however, was to enable a more precise definition of the underlying issue. Thus, the continuing controversy over contract price could from then on be placed in the context of how much of the full cost of police protection should not be charged because it is implicit in the sheriff's countywide responsibility. The advantage of such a focus is that it shifts the price and subsidy negotiations from issues of principle or philosophy to issues of accounting—that is, it becomes more amenable to resolution through negotiation. For example, the 1964 grand jury reported:

> The crux of the problem encountered in determining what the rate should be for contract law enforcement services revolves around the point that the Sheriff has overall county-wide responsibility for general law enforcement which, although reduced by a city's incorporation, is not eliminated. Because it is not possible to precisely define or specifically pinpoint the exact extent of the Sheriff's statutory responsibilities, it is similarly impossible to compute a single true indisputable cost for the law enforcement services which the Sheriff renders. [Cited in E1, p. 15.]

Over the twenty years of the contract services plan, such resolution has been forthcoming, essentially by agreement to severely limit the extent of sheriff's activities that would be excluded from the contract price. As the lawenforcement contract price escalated because of this, contracting cities became increasingly concerned about the charges; during the same time interval the county officials, with the exception of LASD, became more inclined to favor a fuller cost pricing. So by the middle of the 1960s a period of maturation had set in during which further net growth in contracting was relatively small and there were withdrawals as well as additions to the number of contracts, and more increases in independent city contracts than in those for contracting cities.

It seems that now, after a decade of maturation, the contract service plan is moving into another phase, a phase that is likely to be characterized by the increasing insistence of contracting cities on expanding the scope of their own participation in service delivery; insistence on improved county performance, as defined by the cities, for the payments that are made; and search for alternatives to contracting that are more suited to their needs.

It is by no means certain that the contract services plan can continue under such pressures, for—although the issues of subsidy may no longer generate the passions of yesterday—the issues of domain are becoming increasingly significant. The county government is again investigating the potential for countywide consolidation of services, and the L.A. County Sheriff's Department is investigating the potential for delivery of law-enforcement services through police districts. It may yet turn out that the contract service plan has been transitory and that new structures will emerge or that old structures will become more intensively utilized.

CONTRACT PRICING

Essentially the same procedures for setting contract prices are followed for each of the county contract services. The county auditor publishes an annual price list for services that the county offers for contract. The prices are based on a formula that, following state law, includes recovery of "additional" county costs associated with providing the service. These additional costs include direct salaries and wages, employee benefits, divisional and departmental overhead, services and supplies, applicable county overhead (which is defined by law), and liability insurance.

On the basis of these cost items the contract price for all services except police is stated in terms of an hourly charge per type of employee used to provide the service. This charge, of course, includes not only the salary component but the other listed items as well. For law enforcement and traffic patrol the charge is stated not in terms of an hourly rate but rather in terms of an annual rate for one- and two-man traffic and patrol cars.

Since pricing is now based on a specific formula, it is essentially beyond the control of the county department, and even to a large extent beyond the control of other county agencies, including the county administrative officer and board of supervisors. Because the prices are not negotiated with individual cities or even set by the county departments, the county claims that it does not seek or solicit contract business. A list of services and their associated hourly unit prices is published, and a contract will be entered into with any city interest in purchasing the services at these prices.

Although pricing may be beyond the county's control, this is not the case for the quality of the service provided and, at least in the case of law enforcement, the level of service made available. Although the terms of contracts vary with the requirements of particular services, each contract contains language that unequivocally reserves responsibility for service quality to the county department. For example, in the case of street maintenance the contract reads, "... ordinary maintenance and repair of streets within the City shall be performed without demand and such streets shall be maintained and repaired in the same manner, to the same extent, and kept in a similar condition of suitability as similarly situated County highways." In the case of animal control the wording is: "... the rendition of such services, the standard of performance and other matters incidental to the performance of such services and the control of personnel so employed, shall remain in the County." In the case of law enforcement, the agreement reads: "It is hereby agreed that the minimum level of basic law enforcement service shall be determined by the County." While cities may choose any or all of the following services—traffic enforcement, license inspection and enforcement, street-crossing guards, school safety officers, community relations, and helicopter patrol—the activities and equipment that constitute these services are determined by the Sheriff's Department.

In all instances except law enforcement, the county performs the services that are contracted for and bills the city for the costs associated with the performance. In some instances man-hours needed to perform a service will be estimated in advance, but if the actual work time exceeds the estimate, cities are billed accordingly. In the case of law enforcement, the number of service units (one- or two-man patrol cars) and their associated costs are agreed upon in advance. If back-up forces are needed in the course of a year, the city is not charged for them (conversely, if patrol cars are taken from the city to back up forces in another city or in unincorporated areas, the billing to the city is not reduced).

Although pricing is now based on a straightforward formula leaving very little room for discretion or negotiation, this has not always been the case. The history of contract pricing is an exciting chapter in the story of intergovernmental relations in L.A. County. It is essentially a history of police pricing based on annual patrol car rates, which are shown in Table 3-1. Also, this history confirms the Kirlin thesis [E6] that the county, and particularly the Los Angeles Sheriff's Department, will seek minimal contract prices in order to reduce dependencies on contract cities.

The story begins in 1954, when the sheriff agreed to provide the same level of law enforcement to the city that he had previously provided to the unincorporated area in exchange for retaining all fines and forfeitures. In private correspondence, John Leach, then assistant county administrative officer, agreed that these revenues did not cover costs. However, Leach claimed the county could do no better, for it was the sheriff's legal responsibility to provide law enforcement to any area that did not have its own police service. Thus, the

Table 3-1. History of Patrol Car Rates ($000)

Year	Rate
1958/59	$ 78.4
59/60	78.4
60/61	78.4
61/62	78.4
62/63	93.9
63/64	95.8
64/65	101.9
65/66	104.3
66/67	107.3
67/68	113.1
68/69	119.5
69/70	139.1
70/71	230.0
71/72	252.8
72/73	269.1

Source: Booz-Allen and Hamilton. "Determination of Law Enforcement Contractual Costs," 1971 Los Angeles, p. 18.

sheriff would be legally obliged to provide the police service to Lakewood, even at no charge. The fines and forfeitures thus represented a concession by the city of Lakewood, which it did not have to make [D30].

Seeking to avoid the appearance of promoting of subsidy, the county in 1957 adopted a price formula that included the direct salaries and other employee benefits of the patrol officers in the contract city, the costs of the patrol cars and other supplies and equipment, and a limited amount of support and supervision expense. Added to these figures was a factor representing a prorated share of 50 percent of the general county overhead. The contract cities were not charged 100 percent of the overhead, on the theory that contracts are mutually beneficial to the cities and to the county. The exclusion of half the general county overhead and most of the L.A. Sheriff's Department overhead was based on the principle that this was a reasonable estimate of the costs associated with the areawide statutory responsibilities of the sheriff. Since this formula was devised not by the sheriff but by the county administrative officer and the county auditor/controller, it would seem that not only the sheriff but also other county officials had an interest in keeping the contract price low.

The L.A. County Grand Jury reviewed the costing formula and decided that, aside from some need for improved accounting procedures, the formula was essentially equitable. The price set by this formula was about $78,000 per patrol car and remained in effect until 1962. At that time the grand jury set a new rate of $94,000, which was based on a compromise solution. On the one hand, the grand jury rejected the argument that since the basic policing in contract cities did not add costs to the LASD, the cities should be charged only for those services additional to the basic policing; on the other hand, it accepted the argument that since the sheriff had areawide responsibilities, which should be supported by all the areas in the county, these costs should not be in the contract price. The Solomon-like solution was to charge a price that, as reported in the *L.A. Times* (11/27/62), reflected "the extra service it causes the Sheriff to render as opposed to the normal service he would render if the municipality elected to have its own departments." Thus, the grand jury acknowledged that there is "normal staffing"—that is, overhead needs in the area station—and that the sheriff should not give "credit" to contract cities simply because their residents as taxpayers of L.A. County were also supporting other activities of the sheriff. Except for the 1965 grand jury decision that the contract city should be charged on the basis of 100 percent general county overhead, the 1962 concept was in effect until 1969.

In 1969 the Shoup-Rosett study [E13] indicated that a subsidy was indeed being received by contract cities and that this was the case even if an "equitable" price was based on marginal rather than full cost charges. This prompted the 1969 grand jury to recommend that the county reassess its methods of computing law-enforcement contract costs.

The grand jury asked the accounting firm of Peat, Marwick, and Mitchell to review the rate procedures, and that firm developed five alternative methods for calculating costs [E16]:

1. Include only direct salaries and fringe benefits, supplies, automobile services, and general county overhead—all of which at that time cost $130,000.
2. Add to the first figure the costs of patrol division overhead, which brought the cost to $168,000.
3. Add to the second figure the cost of station detectives, which raised costs to $199,000.
4. Add to the third figure the department overhead, which brought the cost to $216,000.
5. Add to the fourth figure the technical services division and the remaining detective staff, which brought the total costs to $303,000.

The first cost formula is essentially a marginal cost figure covering the direct field operation in the contract city, while the fifth formula represents a full cost figure. The difference bewteen the full and marginal cost is the indirect cost exclusive of general county overhead. The indirect costs can be separated into two components: (1) those associated with the station house overhead represent headquarters staff support and are included in the second and third formulas; and (2) those associated with the countywide police department overhead represent headquarters operational support and are included in the fourth and fifth formulas.

Peat, Marwick, and Mitchell thus, in effect, recommended three bases for determining contract prices: (1) marginal (city) costing; (2) station house (regional) costing; (3) and departmental (county) costing. The county administrative officer recommended station house costing. The principle of deducting from the price the "normal staffing" requirements was about to be discarded. Reaction could be expected from both the L.A. Sheriff's Department and contract cities.

The sheriff reacted with a proposal that can only be described as an offer to set up a separate county police department for contract cities. The basis for this proposal was a 1969 grand jury decision, which said that the Sky Knight Program, which provides law-enforcement patrol by helicopter, was distinguished from other sheriff functions because the contract cities provided the helicopters and funded all nonpersonnel costs of the program, such as maintenance and insurance. Therefore, the cities were not required to pay an overhead charge on top of the personnel costs. Building on this principle, the sheriff proposed that the cities buy or lease the necessary vehicles and automotive equipment, lease space in the sheriff's station, and provide necessary materials and equipment; and that the captain of the station house, as well as whatever lieutenants and sergeants were needed, be assigned directly to the cities and paid directly by the cities. The sheriff claimed that if all this were done, the county could not impose an overhead charge:

> Employee costs per se would not carry an overhead factor. There would be no more overall supervision involved than is the case with any independent police department. Services provided by the cities on their own would obviously require no supervision above the station level and therefore would not be subject to any general county overhead. [E9, p. 4.]

Shortly thereafter the sheriff made a new proposal, which deleted the recommendation that the cities provide their own vehicles, equipment, and materials, but retained the concept of regionalization. Under the regionalization concept, the station house would provide police service to the region as a whole, and the cities would share the costs. This, according to the sheriff, would minimize costs. The sheriff claimed that, while the grand jury recommendation to shift the basis of pricing from marginal costing to station house costing would result in a price increase of 65 percent, regionalizing would keep the price increase down to about 10 percent. These cost reductions would occur, according to the sheriff, because the deployment of personnel would become more efficient by eliminating parallel patrolling and the need to go out of the way to patrol an isolated section of a city that could be covered by the car of an adjacent city in the region. Thus the LASD, rather than continuing to attack the overhead payments, ended by supporting the principle of station house costing, but minimized its effects on pricing by using regionalization to reduce costs.

The contract cities' immediate reaction to the pricing formula change was to consider the alternatives to county contracting that were available and to commission the firm of Booz, Allen, and Hamilton to make its own study of equitable pricing for contract law enforcement. Four alternatives were considered in the study done by the contract cities association, none of which seemed appealing [E10]: (1) Police districts, it was felt, could not create an equitable tax structure, since cities with a high property base and little need for services would subsidize other cities in the district. (2) Contracting with other cities was believed feasible for very small cities located close to medium-size or larger cities, providing that the small cities were willing to give up control over matters of police policy. (3) Shared services, in which several cities share a police department, would be difficult to bring about because of the absence of an equitable cost allocation formula and mechanism for sharing in policy decisions. (4) Independent police departments, it was felt, could probably not now be organized in cities contracting for their police services.

Since attractive delivery alternatives were not available to the contract cities, they turned to Booz, Allen, and Hamilton to find an equitable and cheaper cost alternative to station house costing. Matching Peat, Marwick, and Mitchell in their ingenuity, Booz, Allen, and Hamilton also came up with five alternatives [E1]:

1. Patrol car plus selected support services, which was essentially the then-current system based on a patrol unit combining field cars and station detectives.
2. Individual service units, which separated station detectives from general law and traffic patrol units so that each service could be individually priced.
3. Basic service plus add-ons, which allowed full costing for the basic level of police service and marginal costing for additional units.
4. Contract city allocation, which allocated the full costs of the contract system on the basis of city characteristics.
5. Competitive pricing, which would not be related to LASD cost but would rather be some proportion of the costs that would be incurred by an independent police department to provide the service.

Booz, Allen, and Hamilton then rejected alternative 1 because it did not provide contract cities with any control over the number of station detectives assigned and they could not determine a way of relating the level of detective service to the price paid. Alternative 4 was rejected because it was impossible to relate level of service to price and it would be difficult for the city to establish its own desired level of service. Alternative 5 was rejected because Booz, Allen, and Hamilton doubted its legality and could find no reasonable way of implementing it.

The final choice was between alternatives 2 and 3. Alternative 3 was rejected because of the difficulties associated with defining "basic" units and "additional" units of service. Thus by a process of elimination, alternative 2 was found to be most equitable. Alternative 2 is most equitable because it allows each city to select the "package" of service it needs and pay on the basis of the costs of each component of the package.

Thus, much to the dismay of the contract cities and the LASD, Booz, Allen, and Hamilton concluded that the concept of marginal cost is inappropriate for determining the price of contracting police services, and also that a prorated general county overhead rate should be included in the price. Marginal costing was rejected because the contract program is not marginal to the LASD; it accounts for 48 percent of the case load and 31 percent of the population, and utilizes 36 percent of general law patrol and traffic cars of the Sheriff's Department. Also, it was felt that the costs of supplying police services to unincorporated areas should not be different from the costs of supplying a service unit to a contract city, and attempts to price marginally would merely shift the overhead costs to the unincorporated areas.

Applying a general county overhead rate was considered appropriate, first because it includes charges for services utilized by the sheriff and necessary to his operation even though not itemized in his budget; second because independent city police agencies must pay for these same kinds of services; and third because, since the county overhead would be paid by contract cities only on charges for police services other than those supplied to all jurisdictions in the county, these charges are in effect a fee for services provided specifically to the contract city and not payment for services provided on a countywide basis.

The L.A. Sheriff's Department response to the Booz, Allen, and Hamilton recommendation was a report to the L.A. County Board of Supervisors, *Law Enforcement for Los Angeles County: A Blueprint for the Future* [E11]. The LASD criticized Booz, Allen, and Hamilton for basing their recommendation on accounting rather than legal foundations; that is, the firm considered only the costs of providing the police service but did not in their formula account for the legal responsibility of the LASD to provide areawide law enforcement services, including needed support to independent city police departments. In its report the LASD notes: "Law enforcement, like all other facets of society, is evolving, and it must continue to do so; there is simply no other alternative. Contract law enforcement is a stage in that evolutionary process" [E11, p. 10]. To facilitate the process, the LASD recommends a four-phase development to complete regionalization of the police service.

The first phase has been the contracting phase. "Your Board overtly spawned the concept of regional law enforcement in 1954 when the City of Lakewood contracted for its basic governmental services." However, "the confrontation over costs of the contractual program has become a catalyst of disunity which could rapidly harden into insoluble conflict." Therefore, during the remainder of the first phase, it is essential to adopt an appropriate pricing system to "...hold the line while we move forward in drafting Los Angeles County's blueprint for the future" [E11, p. 2].

In the second phase, legislation will set up special police service districts, which every city may join at its own option. "The Sheriff shall determine the minimum level of basic law enforcement service to be provided to the district while the Board shall determine the amount to be levied upon property within the district to support the cost of basic law enforcement services within the district" [E11, p. 3]. In addition, special zones would be created within a district to provide to cities desiring it a higher level of law enforcement than the basic level.

The third phase would be a specific recognition by the L.A. County Board of Supervisors of the concept of regional law enforcement. "In effect we are already performing the functions of a regional law enforcement agency. All that is needed is for your Board to establish them as matters of policy" [E11, p. 7].

The final phase would then "progress to the ultimate level of efficiency—total regionalization" [E11, p. 8]:

It is necessary for city governments to think of themselves as part of a larger entity and to consider the good of that entity as a whole, rather than be concerned with only their individual areas. They must realize that their cities are not islands, nor are they surrounded by impregnable walls but that their well-being depends on the well-being of the County as a whole, particularly when considering the objectives of law enforcement. [E11, p. 39.]

In their response to the Booz, Allen, and Hamilton report, the contract cities adopted a short-run tactic rather than the sheriff's long-run strategy. Joining with the independent cities, they lobbied for passage of legislation in 1972, which would first identify certain county services as being countywide and therefore not to be included in the overhead component of contract price; and second would identify county services provided to unincorporated areas that were in excess of the countywide service and levy a tax on unincorporated areas in the event that the second-phase service costs exceeded revenues. Thus contract cities would have their contract price reduced because overhead would be reduced, and the independent cities would have the perennial problem of subsidies resolved. Only the unincorporated areas would be unhappy, which is probably not unrelated to the death of this bill in committee.

The contract cities' next step was support of the Gonsalvez Bill, which passed the legislature in 1972 but was vetoed by the governor. Then in 1973 the bill was reintroduced, was signed by the governor, and became law effective in January 1974.

The bill essentially brought about a reduction in the contract price by excluding certain countywide costs from overhead. The principle established in the bill is that the county may charge only the "additional" costs incurred in furnishing contract services, and may not include fixed or continuing costs of county government. The county estimated that, as a consequence of the bill, it would lose $1.2 million of revenue, 96 percent of which would be associated with the police service [D36, p. 4].

The independent cities were opposed to the bill, and so was the county. Except for the LASD, the county government, which had in the past favored minimal pricing, was now in favor of full cost pricing. The county's objection to the Gonsalvez formula is that it established a legal definition of what could be included in the contract price and limited the ability of the county to follow good accounting practices that would set rates above the legal definition.

The county, however, then said that it would continue to provide the contract services in spite of its loss in revenue because it would not be recovering production costs. The county's acceptance of this position was based on its willingness to see in contracting a form of intergovernmental cooperation that would benefit the county as a whole:

> Recognition that the state has now determined the charging formula and to continue the provision of present contract servcies to all cities without disruption to an effective service delivery system may be the one way to resolve a long standing controversy over contract service rates. [D36, p. 6.]

TRENDS IN CONTRACTING

According to Arthur Will [D36, p. 27]: "... by 1953, the County Contract Program had grown to the point where approximately 450 service agreements were in effect with the then 45 cities." Our estimates show that by 1973 the county had 1,300 service agreements with 78 cities. Table 3-2 traces this growth in service contracts.

By 1957 the incorporation of Lakewood and four other cities accounted for 200 contracts with the county. However, since there was apparently a decline in contracts with other cities, the net growth between 1953 and 1957 was about 100 contracts. In this early period of full-service contracting, the independent cities accounted for 60 percent of the county's service contracts. By 1966, with the rapid incorporation of 28 cities, there were 1,100 contracts in effect. There was an increase of 700 contract agreements during this contracting incorporation period (1953-1966), and essentially all of the increase took place in contract cities. The independent cities in 1966 accounted for less than half of the total contracts in effect. During the maturation period (1966-1973) there was a further increase of only 100 contracts, and 70 percent of this increase occurred in the independent cities. It seems clear that the contract service plan has essentially stabilized, at least as measured by number of service contracts.

As is shown in Table 3-3, six departments—Sheriff, Engineering, Roads, Health, Hospitals, and the Registrar/Recorder—accounted for four-fifths of the service contracts of 1973. These same departments accounted for over four-

Table 3-2. Summary of Service Agreement Trends

		Number of contracts			Service agreement contracts plus special districts		
Service agreement phases	Year	In all cities	In contract cities	In non-contract cities	In all cities	In contract cities	In non-contract cities
End of suburbanization period	1953	400[a]		400	450		450
Beginning of contracting incorporation period	1957	492	203	290	576	248	330
End of contracting incorporation period	1966	1097	672	425	1215	756	459
End of maturation period	1973	1196	702	494	1319	787	532
Growth during:							
New incorporation period	1953-1966	697	672	25	765	756	9
Maturation period	1966-1973	99	30	69	104	31	73

[a]Estimated by assuming there were 50 special district agreements.

Table 3-3. County Department and Special District Service Agreements

Departments and Services	1957 Number	1957 %	1966 Number	1966 %	1973 Number	1973 %	1957-1966 Total	1957-1966 Contract cities	1957-1966 Non-contract cities	1966-1973 Total	1966-1973 Contract cities	1966-1973 Non-contract cities
County departments total	492	100	1097	100	1196	100	605	469	136	99	30	69
Sheriff	83	17	213	19	224	18	130	125	5	11	3	8
Engineering	91	18	192	18	222	18	101	89	12	30	15	15
Roads	110	22	196	18	213	18	86	105	-19	17	-19	36
Health	53	11	151	14	125	10	98	37	61	-26	1	-27
Hospitals	35	7	99	9	108	9	64	27	37	9	5	4
Registrar	36	7	76	7	77	6	40	27	13	1	2	-1
Other	84	18	170	15	227	19	86	59	27	57	23	34
Special districts total	84	100	118	100	123	100	34	39	-5	5	1	4
Fire district	14	16	29	25	38	31	15	14	1	9	2	7
Library district	36	43	43	36	43	35	7	9	-2	0	2	-2
Other districts	34	41	46	39	42	34	12	16	-4	-4	-3	-1

98 How Cities Provide Services

fifths of the growth during the contracting incorporation period, but for less than half of the growth during the maturation period.

About one-fifth of the total increase in contracts during the contracting incorporation period was for the Sheriff's Department services, almost all of it in contract cities. Contract cities also substantially increased their roads services contracts, while other cities on balance reduced their road contracts. The increase in independent city health and hospital agreements was double the contract city increase. The increase in special district agreements between 1957 and 1966 took place in contract cities, with independent cities showing a net decline.

Engineering was the only department showing an important increase in the number of contracts during the maturation period, and the increase occurred in both contract and independent cities. The L.A. Sheriff's Department showed a small increase, as did hospital contracts. The Roads Department, on balance, showed a net increase that consisted of a decline in contract city agreements counterbalanced by an increase for independent cities. Health contracts in non-contract cities also showed a decline, while special district agreements remained essentially the same during the interval.

Table 3-4 shows the trends in contracts for each specific service; those services for which over half the cities had contracts in 1973 are listed there. These dozen services have consistently accounted for over half of all service contracts. They accounted for about half of the contract increases during the contracting incorporation period and for two-thirds of the increase during the maturation period.

For relatively few services there were actual contract declines during the 1957-1966 period, traffic signal maintenance and bridge maintenance in independent cities being the only important exceptions. During the maturation period, however, important contract declines were registered for rodent control in independent cities; for disaster and law enforcement, street lighting maintenance, street sweeping, and business license issuance in contract cities.

Table 3-5 shows that each city, whether it is a contract or independent city, has had at least one service contract with the county in each of the years listed. Many of the independent cities, as well as the contract cities, have at least one service contract with the County Registrar, Engineers, District Attorney, Animal Control, Health, Hospitals, Roads, and Sheriff's Departments. Relatively few of either the contract or independent cities have contracts with the County Agricultural Commissioner, Fire Department, Mental Health Department, and Treasurer. Although a number of the contract cities have contracts with the Parks and Recreation Department and the Regional Planning Commission, there are relatively few independent cities with such contracts. Similarly, while there are only a few contracts with the Personnel or Library Departments in contract cities, there are a number of independent cities that do have them. It appears that contract and independent cities are essentially similar in terms of the county departments with which they have some contracts; where they differ, as shown in Table 3-4, is that the number of contracts in the independent cities is small compared with that in the contract cities.

The estimated county revenue from contracts in 1973 was $19.5 million, as shown in Table 3-6. This results in an average revenue per contract of $16,000. Seventy percent of the total revenues comes from contracts with the Sheriff's Department, which average about $61,000 per contract. Another 24 percent of the contract revenues comes from the County Roads and Engineering Departments. With 95 percent of the revenues coming from law enforcement, roads, and engineering, it is clear that these are the only important contract services, even though they constitute only half of the service contracts with cities.

For each of these services, the county department is willing to make available, under contract to cities, any of the activities it performs in unincorporated areas. For each of the services, the price is set by the county controller, and there is no deviation from this price. In order to better meet the needs of contract cities, service delivery is made on a decentralized basis—typically through a regional office—and usually the department designates one person in each region to act as liaison with contract cities. Some departments maintain offices in the cities where they provide services and also designate one person in the department's central office to act as contract coordinator. These arrangements, evolved in response to demands by contracting cities, are said to significantly facilitate communications.

At least one member of the L.A. County Board of Supervisors views himself as playing the role of special representative on behalf of the contract cities within his district. The City-County Coordinator's Office, staffed with three professionals, plays an important linking role. Originally assigned the duties of informing incorporating municipalities of available service arrangements and coordinating contracting policy with contract cities, this Coordinator's Office presently devotes most of its time to contract renewals, problems relating to contracts, answering general information requests from all cities, coordinating intercity relations, and undertaking related studies.

All of these accommodations to the needs of contract cities are the result of seeking to provide a high quality of services to the cities. All of these accommodations are consistent with the thesis that departments reduce their dependency on contract cities by making available a service quality at a price that could not be matched by alternative providers. These similarities in the delivery processes for the three important contract services are placed in perspective in the following, more detailed, discussions of how the departments provide each of the services.

County Department of Engineers

The county building codes must, by law, be adopted by the cities. However, enforcement can be done either by the county or by the city, at the city's option. The County Department of Engineers has contracted with cities since

Table 3-4. County-City Agreements for Selected Years

Department	Total number of service agreements 1957	1961	1966	1970	1973	Percentage of total service agreements for non-Contract cities 1957	1961	1966	1970	1973	Change in number of contracts 1957-1966 Contract cities	Non-contract cities	1966-1973 Contract cities	Non-contract cities
Health														
City health ord.	53	33	151	124	125	79	88	68	60	61	37	61	1	−27
Mobile home inspection	53		73	74	75	79		63	61	61	16	4	2	
Rodent control		33	47	50	50		88	62	60	60	18	29	2	1
			31					90			3	28	−3	−28
Hospitals														
City prisoners	35	56	99	104	108	66	57	61	59	59	27	37	5	4
Emergency ambulance	35	56	35	37	41			66	62	63	12	23	3	3
			64	67	67	66	57	58	57	57	15	14	2	1
Mental Health			11	1	1			100	100	100		1	0	0
Library														
Reciprocal library services	1		9	13	13	100		100	100	100	0	8	0	4
	1		9	13	13	100		100	100	100	0	8	0	4
Parks & recreation														
Park maintenance	15	16	25	29	33	40	6	4	3	12	15	−5	5	3
Tree trimming			2	4	6			0	25	16	2		3	1
Recreation	12	16	20	19	22	25	6	5	0	14	10	−2	0	2
Tree planting & maint.	3		3	1	1	100		0	0	0	3	−3	−2	
				5	4								4	
Personnel														
Personnel staff services	12	12	15	23	27	100	100	93	78	74	1	2	6	6
	12	12	15	23	27	100	100	93	78	74	1	2	6	6
Regional Planning Commiss.														
Planning & zoning	11	22	20	19	23	18	9	10	5	17	9	0	1	2
	11	22	20	19	23	18	9	10	5	17	9	0	1	2
Registrar & recorder														
Election services	32	72	76	77	77	100	68	64	62	62	27	13	2	−1
	32	72	76	77	77	100	68	64	62	62	27	13	2	−1
Roads														
Street maint. & const.	110	179	196	217	213	44	17	15	35	31	105	−19	−19	38
Bridge maintenance	15	26	24	29	28	26	15	8	10	11	11	−2	3	1
	23	22	28	34	35	52	5	14	38	46	13	−8	−3	12

Table 3-4. continued

Departments	Total number of service agreements 1957	1961	1966	1970	1973	Percentage of total service agreements for non-Contract cities 1957	1961	1966	1970	1973	Change in number of contracts 1957–1966 Contract cities	Non-contract cities	1966–1973 Contract cities	Non-contract cities
Traffic signal maint.	35	30	33	58	55	69	30	30	62	60	12	−14	−1	23
Street signs		21	22	20	21		14	5	5	10	21	1	−2	1
Street sweeping	14	18	15	7	6	21	11	0	0	0	4	−3	−9	0
Street lighting maint.		14	19	11	11		21	16	45	45	5	3	−10	2
Subdivision engineering	7	24	25	26	26	0	13	8	4	4	16	2	2	−1
Traffic striping and marks.	16	24	30	32	31	3	21	23	22	23	11	2	1	0
Sheriff														
Total with county jail	83	143	213	210	224	63	40	25	30	29	123	5	3	8
Total without county jail	34	73	140	134	147	38	15	6	13	12	108	−5	1	9
Helicopter				13	11				23	9			10	1
Law enforcement	13	25	29	29	30	8	4	7	3	7	15	1	1	0
County jail	49	70	73	76	77	80	66	63	62	62	15	7	2	2
Microfilm storage	8		7	16	16	10		71	81	81	2	−3		8
Business license enf.	4	15	19	21	25	50	7	5	0	4	16	−1	3	0
Crossing guard	6	8	15	16	18	33	38	0	0	0	11	−2	2	0
Motorcycle patrol		7	8	5	6		29	0	0	0	8		1	
School safety			8	8	8			0	0	0	8		0	
Community relations					5					0			5	
Traffic law enforce.	3	18	27	26	27	0	22	4	0	0	23	1	1	−1
Bicycle safety ped. off.					1					0				
Disaster law enforcement			27					7	0	0	25	2	−25	2
Treasurer														
Bond collecting		9	11	6	6		11	9	17	50	10	1	−7	2
Transient occupancy				3	4				33	50			2	2
Business license issuance		9	11	3	2		11	9	0	50	10	1	−1	1
													−10	−1
Water Supply	1					0					−1			

A History of Contracting in L.A. County 101

102   How Cities Provide Services

Table 3-4. continued

Departments	Total number of service agreements				Percentage of total service agreements for non-Contract cities					Change in number of contracts					
										1957-1966		1966-1973	
	1957	1961	1966	1970	1973	1957	1961	1966	1970	1973	Contract cities	Non-contract cities	Contract cities	Non-contract cities
Civil Defense	3					33					-2	-1		
Animal control														
Animal control services	17	35	38	39	42	30	34	34	36	40	13	8	0	4
Animal shelter services	17	35	38	39	38	30	34	34	36	37	13	8	-1	1
					4					75				3
Communications				11	18			0	0	11			16	2
Electronic equip. maint.				11	18			0	0	11			16	2
Engineering														
Building inspection services	91	184	192	213	222	37	35	35	40	62	89	12	17	18
Industrial waste services	19	30	30	30	31	19	17	17	23	37	13	-2	0	1
Sewer maintenance	4	28	30	31	32	22	19	27	29	75	21	5	3	-1
Subdivision map check	1	9	2	2	3	67	50	50	89	100	1	0	0	1
Parcel map check	53	66	71	71	71	65	62	63	65	79	15	3	1	1
				14	16	50	57						8	8
Master house map service		27	25	27	29	10	4	8	9	21	23	2	3	1
Engineering staff service	14	29	34	38	40	28	24	21	21		16	4	2	4
District attorney														
City prosecution	24	38	45	52	57	29	37	40	44	49	10	11	2	10
Preservation of rights	18	38	45	52	57	17	37	40	44	49	15	12	2	10
	6										-5	-1		
Agriculture commissioner			2	1	1			0	0	0	2		-1	
Noxious weed abatement			2	1	1			0	0	0	2		-1	
Fire														
Weed abatement			5	4	6			20	75	50	4	1	-1	2
School fire safety officer			2	3	3			50	100	100	1	1	-1	2
			3	1	3						3			
Special district (non-contract)	84	119	118	120	123	46	33	29	27	31	39	-5	1	4
Fire	14	26	29	33	38	14	12	10	15	26	14	1	2	7

Table 3-4. continued

Departments	Total number of service agreements					Percentage of total service agreements for non-Contract cities					Change in number of contracts			
											1957-1966		1966-1973	
	1957	1961	1966	1970	1973	1957	1961	1966	1970	1973	Contract cities	Non-contract cities	Contract cities	Non-contract cities
Library	36	41	43	44	43	67	49	51	45	47	9	-2	2	-2
Lighting	14	44	15	14	14	29	36	7	14	21	4	-3	-3	2
Sewer maintenance	12	27	30	29	28	42	26	23	17	18	16	2	0	-2
Parks & recreation	6	11	1			33	36	100			-4	-1		-1
Water works maintenance	2					100						-2		
Total Contracts														
Including special districts	576	918	1215	1262	1319	57	38	38	39	40	222	31	129	75
Excluding special districts	492	799	1097	1142	1196	59	39	38	41	41	176	28	134	71

Source: L.A. County, "Services Provided by the County of Los Angeles to Cities 'Dot Chart.'" Mimeo, selected years Chief Administrative officer. County of Los Angeles, CA.

Table 3-5. Cities with County Contracts

	Total					Contract cities					Non-contract cities				
	1957	1961	1966	1970	1973	1957	1961	1966	1970	1973	1957	1961	1966	1970	1973
Number of cities in L.A County	60	73	76	77	78	13	26	29	30	31	47	47	47	47	47
Number of cities with a contract	60	73	76	77	78	13	26	29	30	31	47	47	47	47	47
Cities with contracts, by department															
Animal control	17	35	38	39	42	12	23	25	25	25	5	12	13	14	17
Communications				11	18				11	16					2
Engineering	57	68	72	74	74	11	25	27	29	30	46	43	45	45	44
District attorney	18	38	45	52	57	12	24	27	29	29	6	14	18	23	28
Agric. commissioner			2	1	1			2	1	1					
Fire			5	4	6		4	4	1	3			1	3	3
Health	53	33	73	74	75	11	4	27	29	29	42	29	46	45	46
Hospitals	35	56	71	70	72	12	24	27	29	30	23	32	44	41	42
Mental health			1	1	1								1	1	1
Library	1	9	9	13	13						1	9	9	13	13
Parks and recreation	12	16	20	21	24	9	15	19	19	21	2	1	1	2	3
Personnel	12	12	15	23	27			1	5	7	12	12	14	18	20
Regional plan. commiss.	11	22	20	19	23	9	20	18	18	19	2	2	2	1	4
Registrar/recorder	36	72	76	77	77		25	29	30	30	36	47	47	47	47
Roads	42	38	43	63	64	11	25	27	29	30	31	13	16	34	34
Sheriff	49	70	75	76	77	12	25	28	29	30	37	45	47	47	47
Treasurer		9	11	5	6		8	10	4	4		1	1	1	2
Cities with a special district agreement	36	51	34	51	36	28	29	27	25	12	25	25	7	26	24

Source: Table 3-4.

Table 3-6. Estimated Contract Revenues, Fiscal 1973-1974

Revenues by department	Estimated revenues ($000)	Percent of total revenues contracts	Average revenue per contract
Total	$19,366		$16,192
Departments			
Sheriff	13,750	71%	61,383
Roads	3,223	16	15,131
Engineering	1,650	8	7,432
Hospitals	452	2	4,185
Parks and recreation	130	1	3,939
Reg. plan. commiss.	48		2,086
Personnel	45	3	1,666
Registrar	21		273
District attorney	23		404
Other	389		1,888

Source: [A12, p. 187]
Will, Arthur V. "Report Concerning the County Contract Services Program," Los Angeles County Chief Administrative Officer, 1974 (mimeo).

the mid-1930s for the enforcement of the building laws. With the advent of the contract services plan, county engineering services offered to the city expanded in scope, both in the variety of tasks performed and in the number of cities involved.

The tasks fall into four main categories: (1) the enforcement of local ordinances affecting private construction and related activities in the development and improvement of private property; (2) property rehabilitation for the upgrading of substandard buildings on private property; (3) general engineering, including the design of sewers, storm drains, surveys, appraisals, right-of-way acquisition, and inspection for municipal improvements; and (4) the administration of special assessment districts formed under the provisions of the Street and Highway Code.

More specifically, services to contract cities include the following: In the Building and Safety Division, services include building inspection and plan checking, with additional duties such as business license, code, field work, and property rehabilitation. Of the $1.6 million of 1973 revenues the county engineer generated through contract, $1.3 million came from these services. Other services are provided through the Construction Division, where inspection of sewers, storm drains, and capital projects takes place. The Design Division prepares drainage reports and designs storm drains. In the Project Planning and Pollution Control Division, there is plan checking, permit processing, and inspection. The Mapping Division does house numbering, map maintenance, and appraisal work. The Sanitation Division offers industrial-waste inspection and various other inspection activities. The Survey Division does all necessary surveying. Finally, the Business Management Division processes monies collected and bills the cities; it also bills for other public works, such as rubbish collection, sewer charges, and so on.

The contract price is set in order to cover costs for the work done. The county controller establishes an hourly rate for each type of occupation; this rate includes the wage rate plus an overhead component. No negotiation of price is allowed to take place between cities and the county. Although the county refuses to negotiate price, there is rarely any complaint from the contract cities about the price set. However, independent cities sometimes claim that the hourly rate is too low and that, as a consequence they are compelled to bear part of the costs through their tax payments.

The majority of the costs of engineering and inspecting services are defrayed by the fees paid for the service by citizens. The county performs the necessary services and then bills the city for the cost, which is based on the occupational hourly rates and man-hours of input. The cities establish the fee schedule, while the county collects the fees from residents. Since the city fees are generally higher than the county costs, the cities usually obtain a net revenue from this process. These net revenues are ordinarily derived from building and safety inspection services but not from property rehabilitation or code enforcement.

Even when a city adopts the same fee schedule that the county sets, the city tends to obtain a net revenue, for the county sets its own fee schedules so that, on an overall basis, it neither makes a profit nor loses money. However, the Department of Engineers tends to place its high-productivity workers in the contract cities, probably because it tries to please the contract cities particularly. Since the fees set in the cities are based on an average rate of productivity while the actual work done is at a higher-than-average rate of productivity, the contract cities obtain a net revenue.

In order to provide a better service, the Engineering Department, under the authorization of the L.A. County Board of Supervisors, has established a regionalized service delivery system. In addition to the central office, the county engineer now maintains seven regional offices. In each region there is a regional engineer who is the county engineer's deputy and official representative to the contract cities. Ordinarily the contract cities appoint the county engineer as the city engineer, and the engineer assumes all the responsibilities of such an office. The regional engineers take these responsibilities seriously and are particularly sensitive to the needs of the city and responsive to the requests of the city managers.

Since the contract price is based on hourly rates, there is no need for specification of the work to be done. The contracts are not specific about the quality of service or the terms of the performance. The department claims that it provides the same quality of service to contract cities as it does in unincorporated places. However, the contract cities generally obtain a higher quality of work simply because of the higher level of skills of the personnel assigned to them.

The county department is occasionally willing to take ad hoc jobs from the cities. But it will do so only if the regional engineer feels that it is consistent with the city's needs. The department claims it neither uses such occasions to expand its activities nor uses the contracting process to keep departmental employment high. For example, the county will not bid on any projects to obtain the business. In spite of these claims, however, the department is willing to encourage cities to contract, because through contracting it can achieve a higher level of professionalization and quality of service in the metropolitan area. The department claims that it has an advantage over small cities in providing engineering services because it has available all of the skills needed to perform these services, while the small cities do not have the capacity to retain the necessary array of skills. Thus, economies of scale resulting from specialization enable contracting to provide cities with a higher level of service than they would otherwise be able to obtain.

Department of Roads

With the advent of the contract services plan, what had been county roads suddenly became city roads. When the roads were county roads, they could be made to correspond to well-defined district boundaries; now that they are city roads, the boundary lines are highly irregular, which necessitated a change in management procedures. The department responded by setting up a section for the sole purpose of coordinating city programs and establishing the position of road services representative to serve as liaison. Even though the department had been providing road services to cities since 1912, this was the beginning of the system that currently provides over 200 contracts between the cities and the County Roads Department, involving over $3 million of revenues and at least one contract in all but 10 of the 78 cities in L.A. County. Less than 30 of these contracts are agreements for utilization of total capabilities for the County Roads Department. Most of the contracts relate to specific services, such as traffic signal maintenance at some particular intersection. Singular ad hoc service contracts are a rule, rather than an exception, in the County Roads Department.

The department provides engineering services for planning and analyzing present and future street needs and the capacity to design, advertise, and supervise improvements of highway or local streets and also to repair and maintain the streets. The maintenance of streets includes sweeping, patching, cleaning, drainage facilities, soil sterilization for weed abatement, and storm damage cleanup. Maintenance crews are available 24 hours a day, 7 days a week, and the maintenance activities are routine activities under the control of a road maintenance superintendent.

Routine activities such as street widening; installation of curbs, gutters, and sidewalks; resurfacing and seal coating of streets; and installation and repair of street names and signs falls within the authority of the maintenance district engineer, who is responsible for street maintenance in the entire district of which a contract city is a part.

Additional activities include installation and maintenance of traffic signals, pavement marking, curb markings, signs, traffic striping, and underground power systems for streetlights. These activities fall within the Traffic and Lighting Division, with traffic engineers available to act as consultants and advisors to the contracting city.

Contract work of the County Roads Department falls into three categories: (1) engineering; (2) construction; and (3) maintenance, of which the last is the most important to the city's citizens. Engineering includes most of the usual public-works activities except sewer, water, and buildings and safety, which are handled by Department of Engineers. Included are capital improvement engineering for streets, bridges, and traffic signal installations. These are investment activities that require advance planning and scheduling to be fitted into the department's work load, whether they originate with contract cities or in other places. Also, there are day-to-day activities that require an immediate engineering response, including the issuance of permits to property owners, contractors, and utility companies involving engineering designs, street cuts for underground utilities, house moving, and the like. Subdivision plan checking and inspection of street construction and street drainage is also a daily departmental function, and is much in demand as a contract service. Most of the engineering work in such situations is borne by the subdivider and not by the city. In addition, traffic engineering services are provided that cover many activities, including signal design, speed-limit posting, parking and standing prohibition, traffic striping, and so on. Very often the county traffic engineers who work in the cities serve as consultants in the city's traffic commission.

The second area of contract work is construction projects. Very often a city needs a construction project involving streets, traffic signals, or street safety lighting. Usually a city advertises the project and then awards the contract to a private company. The county becomes involved in preparing the plans and specifications, providing the surveying and construction engineering and the laboratory testing, advising who should get the award, coordinating the project, and making the final inspections of the construction work as well as monthly estimates for city progress payments.

The third area of contract work involves street maintenance, which includes periodic repair, street sweeping, occasional resurfacing/resealing, weed abatement, traffic striping and marking, traffic signs and street name signs, repair and sweeping of alleys, inspection and repair of bridges, storm cleanup, and special services provided on city-owned property, including construction and maintenance work in city parks and city hall sites. Residents are acutely aware of the needs for street maintenance, particularly when adequate maintenance is not provided. City officials are aware not only of these needs but also of the seasonal characteristics of maintenance requirements, which affect the procedures for delivering the service as well as its costs. Streets periodically require repair and sweeping; however, resurfacing and resealing are only occasional needs according to age and condition of the streets. Weed abatement is a regular program; traffic striping and marking also has a fairly regular pattern, except in unusual weather conditions. On the other hand, traffic sign and street sign replacement is generally due to accidents and vandalism. While alleys require regular repair and sweeping, bridges are subject only to annual inspection and occasional repair. Storm cleanups are a major maintenance function, particularly during unusual winters when the threat to property is greater than that with which most cities are prepared to cope. In such cases the county provides services even in most cities that are not covered by contractual agreement.

Under the contract system, the city pays only for the services it requests and uses and the level of service is solely a city determination. The county sets the fees, just as in other services, by establishing an hourly rate for the service provided that is based on the labor input plus a proportionate overhead charge.

Decentralization in service provision is adopted, and the county roads commissioner in many cities is appointed as the city's superintendent of streets. The road maintenance superintendent is the key person in the field, is in contact with the city manager or other city personnel, and is responsible for the work done. The superintendent also recommends to the city the work that should be done in the coming year and costs it out for the city. The road maintenance superintendent is therefore the one who makes budget recommendations. If the city feels that it cannot afford the recommended work, it simply establishes a lower level of service, which is agreed upon with the county. The Roads Department invoices the cities on either a monthly or quarterly basis; occasionally, on special projects, billing is done at the end of the project. The charges shown on the invoice are separated into categories of labor, equipment, and material so that the separate components of cost can be clearly identified.

Cities usually pay for the work done on roads out of gasoline tax subventions from the state rather than out of their general fund revenues. Funds are allocated to each city by the state under provision of Sections 2106 and 2107 of the Street and Highways Code. These funds are directly related to the number of gallons of gasoline sold. Additionally, the county allocates gas tax funds to cities as based on the ratio of master plan mileage and population of the various cities within L.A. County. Under this aid-to-cities program, funds can be used for construction and maintenance of select system streets only. Section 2106 funds also can be used only for the select system of streets. Funds from Section 2107 may be used for any street purpose.

The revenues to be made available are easy to estimate, and cities tend to spend all of these revenues, but no more. It appears that the amount of work estimated by the county and city as being needed is likely to be the same as the work that can be supported by these estimated revenues.

The County Roads Department does not overtly solicit business to expand its contract activities. However, it does not hesitate to advertise that there is available to any city that wants it the full resources of a 2000-person department

110 How Cities Provide Services

possessing engineering skills, construction know-how, and the necessary specialized equipment for any particular job or that it has the means of willingness to rapidly provide services to any place that has experienced such catastrophic events as storm damage, fire, or landslide. In addition, there is a policy of providing free services for a year to newly incorporated cities, which is seen as an inducement to the cities to contract with the county.

In spite of these various efforts, the County Roads Department has been losing contract business. This is essentially because the Roads Department is more expensive than are private contractors in providing similar services to the cities. This is particularly the case for street sweeping and traffic signal maintenance, which have been the activities most in decline.

The Los Angeles County Sheriff's Department

The L.A. Sheriff's Department and the four city police departments of Los Angeles, Long Beach, Pasadena, and Santa Monica serve about 85 percent of the county population, while the forty-four independent police departments serve the remaining 15 percent. Because of such fragmentation, many people believe that consolidation or coordination would probably improve efficiency. For example, Booz, Allen, and Hamilton, after investigating the various kinds of policing functions as provided throughout the county, came to the conclusions that responsibility for police functions currently overlaps in many areas between the sheriff and city police agencies and that a great deal of duplication exists in the services offered by the Los Angeles County Sheriff's Department, the Los Angeles City Police Department, and many of the independent city police agencies [E1].

Because the sheriff does have a broad statutory authority for providing countywide law enforcement services, he has considerable discretion in determining the services to be offered by his department on a countywide basis. Therefore, many people believe that the LASD is ideally suited to assume the major responsibility for providing countywide coordination or consolidation.

Others argue, however, that a statutory authority is not a statutory responsibility, and that therefore there is not a legal basis for consolidation of county policing through LASD. For example, the Booz, Allen, and Hamilton conclusions about the legal basis for policing in L.A. County were that existing legal guidelines do not permit a clear delineation of responsibility for providing police service, but rather indicate a large amount of overlapping responsibilities and that the few statutory countywide responsibilities of the sheriff include only prisoner transportation, booking, custody and security of presentenced prisoners, provision of bailiffs, serving of civil and criminal processes, law enforcement in cities where the city has failed to enforce the law, and civil defense coordination.

According to the sheriff, the Los Angeles City Police Department and the LASD have already consolidated various activities, including automation of booking and the arrestee information system, a mutual booking form, consolidated prisoner transportation to arraignment court, and integrated bail procedures [E11]. In addition to these kinds of consolidated services, the sheriff claims to provide the following services on a regionwide basis to contract and independent cities alike: the Scientific Services Bureau, which provides laboratory services; the Training Bureau, which provides training for all agencies wishing to participate; the Research and Development Bureau, which develops new theories and concepts to promote professionalism in law enforcement; the Special Enforcement Bureau, which functions as a tactical unit to handle unusual situations; and the Aero Bureau, which investigates aircraft accidents and runs the Sky Knight program. The sheriff says that because of such activities the city of Los Angeles is the largest beneficiary of LASD services, and that many of the smaller police departments could not function without these services:

> The continued existence and efficiency of many of them are insured in part by the fact that we have a strong countywide law enforcement service provided by the Sheriff, not only through headquarters but through local stations throughout the county. [E11, p. 23.]

According to the sheriff, what contracting accomplishes is, first, coordination and integration of the police function within the county, so that it is "a binding cohesive force to permeate law enforcement throughout the county." Second by virtue of its size, the Sheriff's Department permits smaller cities to have their independent police departments, for, "without a countywide agency upon which to depend in times of emergency, many of these smaller departments which operate with what they consider to be normal levels of personnel and equipment would be unable to provide an adequate level of service." Third, even if contract law enforcement were terminated, the sheriff says, "the L.A. Sheriff's Department would not be appreciably reduced in size; but it will no longer continue to grow with the County, its regionalizing function will be rendered ineffective, and law enforcement here—and ultimately the people living here—will be the worse for it" [E11, p. 38.]

Even before the contract services plan, the LASD activities included operation of the county jail system, performance of civil functions for the superior court, policing of the unincorporated areas of the county, and some provision of policing services to cities within the county. The traditional policing functions included aid and assistance to cities in the investigation of major offenses, narcotics and vice offense enforcement, support for the patrol of major disturbances and riots, records, communications, identification support services, and administrative management assistance to cities unable to cope with problems at hand. The department also provided training and technical assistance to a number of cities. However, traffic control in unincorporated areas was considered to be the primary responsibility of the California Highway Patrol.

Thus the L.A. Sheriff's Department was the principal police agency in the unincorporated areas. Ordinarily, as incorporations occurred, the cities would assume primary responsibility for policing, which would limit the sheriff's responsibilities in these previously unincorporated areas. Under contract law enforcement, however, the LASD can take responsibility for providing the same level of basic police service to contract cities as to unincorporated areas, and in addition can assume responsibility for the traffic function. These basic services include the field patrol function; investigation support; staff support activities, including records, communications, technical services, and temporary custody; and essential administrative support. The contract system also provides for purchase of additional field patrol; traffic enforcement; accident investigation; and specialized functions, such as community or school safety patrol. Thus, with the advent of the contract system, the LASD assumed all the characteristics of a municipal police agency.

The L.A. Sheriff's Department is a municipal police agency not only in the sense that it provides municipal-type law enforcement services, but also in the sense that it provides these services to cities. According to its own estimates, the LASD claims that, of all of the services it renders to the county, 38 percent go to contract cities, 18 percent to noncontract cities, and 44 percent to unincorporated areas. If the patrol units are excluded from these totals, the proportions are 24, 42, and 34 percent respectively [E11, p. 98].

Booz, Allen, and Hamilton, in evaluating similar figures, concluded that contracting is an integral part of the LASD. The sheriff says that this is not so, since the independent cities and the unincorporated areas of the county receive by far the greatest percentage of LASD services. Furthermore, the sheriff maintains that contracting is not integral to the operations of his department, because if for any reason there should be a reduction in contracting, there would not be a reduction in LASD work force:

> Certainly no trained officer will be dropped from the Sheriff's Department because of a reduction in contract service levels. If this is true, personnel being used for contract law enforcement at the present will undoubtedly either be used for unincorporated area patrol or countywide law enforcement activity including back-up services for city police departments. [E11, p. 20.]

This judgment is probably correct, since usually, when there is consolidation of a function, the personnel performing that function are not released but rather are transferred to other duties. For example, when the Los Angeles City Police Department transferred the function of freeway patrol to the California Highway Patrol, this released 200 city police officers who were not fired but rather assigned to other duties.

The sheriff thus sees contracting not as integral to the L.A. Sheriff's Department but as an important form of consolidated law enforcement. Some of the contract cities, however, perceive contracting as integral to the LASD, although they also perceive a number of disadvantages to consolidated law enforcement. For example, after evaluating alternative ways for providing the police service, Temple City, which is a contracting city, noted:

> The prime police mission is to act as the enforcement area of the criminal justice system by protecting persons and property through advancing order and justice under democratic law. The means include authority, services, and other inputs with the basic element being the patrol force. Other department activities have the primary purpose of supporting patrol operations. By recognizing this distinction between basic patrol services and supportive service we can explore alternate ways of providing municipal law enforcement without adversely affecting the prime police mission and improving local control. That is, the supportive activities can be consolidated and/or coordinated while reserving the important responsibility or providing necessary patrol service to each local government. [E14, p. 31.]

The three alternatives actually suggested by Temple City include a consolidated law enforcement department with another city, a cooperative department utilizing shared technical services, and a functional city department. In the consolidated department, all technical and administrative services, down to the police function at the patrol level, would be shared. At the patrol point, each city would determine the number of patrol officers it needed. This consolidated approach retains a degree of local control, since it involves local officials in policy determination on an equal basis with other cities. The cooperative department utilizes shared technical services and facilities, but assigns each city the responsibility of its own administration. As compared with contracting, the sharing of costs results in a reduction of costs, while local control is increased. The functional department is essentially a city police department, which would have higher costs and greater local control than contracting. After a review of the alternatives, Temple City came to the following conclusion:

> The present contractual agreement with the Sheriff is least costly, attempts to provide acceptable levels of service for the most part, lacks any measure of local control, provides minimal level of supervision of patrol function, has poor communications with the public, lacks coordination between dispatcher and desk, furnishes adequate technical and supportive services.
> A consolidated law enforcement program with other cities conducted as a police district or by joint powers agreement provides many benefits resulting from centralized administration with joint use of technical services and facilities. Local control is improved by involving local legislative officials in determination of policy.
> The cooperative plan provides each participating agency with the direct opportunity to determine local needs and establish the patrol force re-

quired to accomplish the level of service desired. Technical services including communication, records, and identification and other supportive services are provided from a centrally located facility and related costs are apportioned to each participating agency.

The development of a totally functional city department provides the highest degree of local control, improved level of service, and of course is the most costly. [E11, p. 5.]

The importance of local control and the disadvantages of consolidation are noted in a report recommending the establishment of an independent police department in Bell Gardens.

I would recommend the organizing of the Bell Garden's police department for the following reasons. The city of Bell Gardens is basically a residential oriented community with the inherent police problems. The bulk of the law enforcement, called for services, consists of individual and family problems. This type of call can best be handled by a police department with a personal interest in the city and complete familiarity with the community as obtained by those employees, employed and paid by the local tax payers and by working with the local residents on a daily basis. Turnover, unlike that of the Sheriff's Department, would be held to a minimum.

Community needs would be more easily satisfied due to the direct contact of the city officials and citizens. These needs could be met immediately without being delayed as sometimes happens in the hierarchy of larger organizations. I think that the community interests, participation, and assistance would be stimulated to a new high as needed by any law enforcement agency. [E5, p. 1.]

The L.A. Sheriff's Department seeks to achieve the advantages of consolidation without its disadvantages by providing contract services on a decentralized basis. Therefore the LASD has fourteen stations, and each station can provide all the basic police services to the unincorporated areas and contract cities in its area. This includes the basic field patrol function, traffic control services, investigative support services, maintenance of records, communications, and administrative sustaining services. Each station is organized like a municipal police department and includes a captain, watch commanders, field supervision, field patrol, traffic units, investigative units, and support units. In addition to the station units, the countywide services described earlier are provided from LASD headquarters.

The expansion of the contract cities program brought about substantial changes in the policing operations of the LASD. By 1958 it became apparent that the stations servicing contract cities needed to be operated like municipal police departments. Detective and juvenile investigators were reassigned from the detective division to the stations under the direction of the station commanders.

Headquarters specialized investigative support became available to the stations and independent cities on the same basis. Stations, like those of the small- and medium-size independent cities, required back-up support for complex investigations, for emergencies, and for civil disturbances. This led to the creation of the Metropolitan Bureau in the Detective Division and the Special Enforcement Bureau in the Patrol Division, and to the development of information and records processing systems that can be countywide.

So it can be seen that not only has the L.A. Sheriff's Department, through its impact on contract law enforcement, determined how the contract services plan would operate, but also contracting has, to a large extent, determined how the LASD would operate. Whether this symbiotic relationship will continue is highly uncertain.

Chapter Four

Contracting of Municipal Services

THE EFFECT OF CONTRACTING ON CITY BUDGETS

Some proponents of contracting with Los Angeles County claim that it enables a city with a low tax base to obtain a full array of municipal services while holding down property taxes and limiting expenditures. This chapter seeks first to develop a statistical model based on this contention and then to test its validity. A system of multiple regression equations in which explanatory factors are introduced in a recursive fashion has been developed, and relationships among contracting, community characteristics, city revenue sources, and city expenditures have been examined by the model.

The model is recursive because it seeks first to explain why cities contract, then to show the effects of contracting on tax rates, which in turn affect the level and composition of expenditures. More formally, the model specifies three stages or steps:

Step I: Contracting = F_1 (community characteristics, tax bases)

Step II: Tax Rates   = F_2 (community characteristics, tax bases, contracting)

Step III: Expenditures = F_3 (community characteristics, tax bases, contracting, tax rates)

The analysis is of cities in Los Angeles County and is based on 1970 data. Although there were seventy-seven cities in Los Angeles County in 1970, only seventy-two are in the sample. Los Angeles and Long Beach are excluded because of their large size, while the industrial communities of Vernon, Irwindale, and Industry were also eliminated because their resident populations were below 1,000 persons, which provides them with a per capita budget expenditure substantially different from those of other cities. The seventy-two Los Angeles cities included in the analysis had 1970 populations ranging between about 5,000 and 135,000 persons; budget sizes between $50,000 and $20 million; and per capita budget expenditures ranging between $10 and $350.

On the average, all seventy-two cities contracted for about 15 percent of their city budget. However, forty-four of the seventy-two cities contracted for less than 10 percent of their respective budgets, while the other twenty-eight cities contracted for between 10 and 100 percent. On the basis of this distinction, all cities were separated into two groups. The forty-four cities contracting for less than 10 percent of their budgets have been called the *self-provision cities*. The twenty-eight contracting for more than 10 percent have been called *contracting cities*,[1] and on the average they contracted for about one-third of their budgets. The analysis which follows both pools two groups of cities and treats them separately in determining the causes and effects of contracting. The specific cities in each of these groupings are listed in Appendix Table A-10, which also shows selected data about each city.

Table A-11 lists the variables incorporated in the analysis and their data sources. As a first test of whether these variables are related to contracting we can examine whether the average values for the contracting cities are different from the averages of the self-provision cities.

Table 4-1 indicates that, as compared with contracting cities, self-provision cities not only have a significantly lower share of contracting in their budgets but also significantly higher budget property-tax rates, higher revenues from property taxes, higher budget expenditures per capita, higher commercial sales per capita, more city government employees per capita, and a higher median age of residents. Also, self-provision cities have a higher, but not significantly higher, property-tax base. Thus it appears that the extent of contracting does have some relationship to the city budget, which will become more explicit in the recursive model that is described below.

What Influences the Degree of Contracting?

The general mathematical form of the Step I contracting equation is:

$$LPER70 = F_1(CONSTANT, LOUTLET, LVALUE, EDUC, SPAN, AGE, DIST)$$

where variable names are discussed in Appendix Table A-11. Each of these variables has a specific analytic interpretation as described below.

---

1. Among the twenty-eight contracting cities, twenty-seven incorporated after 1954 and one before 1954. Two cities incorporated after 1954, but contract for less than 10 percent of their budgets. Among the forty-four self-provision cities, all but four contract for under 1 percent of their budgets. Contract cities, as identified in Chapter 2, are the cities which contract for the police service, which includes twenty-seven of the twenty-eight contracting cities, as defined here.

It is expected that a community with low incomes and few resources would be prone to contract because lower income communities are less likely than others to be able to afford the level of property taxes required to set up for self-provision. As a result, more contracting is expected to be found in the newer cities, which also tend to be located on the outskirts of the Los Angeles metropolitan region. By means of contracting, the residents in these communities believe they are able to obtain some of the benefits of living in a city without escalating their property tax rate, and they are apparently willing to give up some measure of local control for these benefits.

The extent of contracting relates to the portion of city expenditures made through county contracts. For our purposes it is measured by the logarithm of the share of contracting in the city budget (*LPER70*).

In the regression equation, median school years completed (*EDUC*) is interpreted as an approximation for an index of household incomes in the community. Miles from the city of Los Angeles (*DIST*) is the measure of outlying communities. Education is used as an income measure because it is a better approximation to the long-run earning capabilities of families than is the actual income obtained in any particular year.

Another factor expected to affect the extent of contracting is the degree to which citizens differ in what they want from public services. It is expected that contracting would be more likely when service needs of the citizens are similar. This is because when tastes are similar, there tends to be less dispute over what the service outputs are and what the community is receiving, so that contracts become easier to negotiate and monitor. Also, when there is a diversity of tastes, city departments are likely to be more flexible in responding to this diversity than is a contracting provider. In our analysis, the variable used to approximate similarity of service tastes is the proportion of the population that is Spanish surnamed (*SPAN*).

A commonly perceived benefit of incorporation is the achievement of a greater degree of local control than exists in unincorporated areas. To the extent that incorporation is dependent on contracting, the desire for local control would encourage contracting. However, once cities are incorporated, greater control over the delivery of services is achieved through self-provision. In this case a taste for local control discourages contracting. Studies of citizen evaluations of public services indicate that older citizens evaluate governments highly, believe that they can influence government decisions, and display a greater interest in local government activities. For these reasons, median age of the city's population (*AGE*) is used as an index of taste for local control in this study.[2]

The tax base of a community affects the kind and mix of public services that can be offered. To the extent that contracting is an inexpensive mode of service provision, then a low tax base would be associated with contracting. However, the tax base also reflects who bears the cost of services. If commercial sales are relatively high, there is a likelihood that some of the sales are made to noncity

---

2. Age of the population is, at best, only a crude approximation for local control.

Table 4-1. Mean Values for Selected Variables in Selected Los Angeles County Cities[a]

Variables	Units of measure	Selected cities in L.A. County	Selected contract cities in L.A. County	Self-provision cities less selected contract cities
Degree of contracting in budget	%	14.6	39.8	-39.5[b]
City budget property tax rate	%	.87	.17	1.10[b]
Special district property tax rate	%	1.48	2.20	-1.14[b]
Municipal services property tax rate	%	2.34	2.37	-.04
Property taxes per capita	$	25	5	32[b]
Intergovernmental transfers per capita	$	24	22	4[b]
City budget expenditures per capita	$	105	61	70[b]
Municipal service expenditures per capita	$	144	117	43[b]
Special district expenditures per capita	$	39	56	-27[b]
Sales tax base per capita	$	2,220	1,583	999
Property tax base per capita	$	2,912	2,623	453
City government employees per 1,000 persons	no.	4.9	1	6.1[b]
Median age	years	28.9	25.8	4.9[b]
Distance from central city	miles	14.5	16.7	-3.4[b]
Spanish surname share of population	%	17.9	20.4	-3.9
Median education	years	11.9	11.7	.3
Service expenditures per capita:				
Police	$	23	15	13[b]
Fire	$	12	0	19[b]
Streets	$	20	19	2[b]
Refuse	$	4	1	5[b]
Parks & recreation	$	11	7	6[b]
Library	$	3	0	4[b]

Table 4-1. contunued

Variables	Units of measure	Mean Values		
		Selected cities in L.A. County	Selected contract cities in L.A. County	Self-provision cities less selected contract cities
Service employees per 1000 persons:				
Police	no.	1.1	.0	1.7[b]
Fire	no.	.8	.0	1.2[b]
Streets	no.	.5	.1	.6[b]
Refuse	no.	.2	.0	.3[b]
Parks & recreation	no.	.6	.3	.5[b]
Library	no.	.2	.0	.3[b]

[a]In 1970 there were 77 cities in Los Angeles County. Only 72 have been included in the analysis. Los Angeles and Long Beach were excluded because of their extremely large size while Vernon and Irwindale and Industry were excluded because of their small size (less than 1,000 people).

These 72 cities, including 28 contracting cities and 44 self-provision cities, were used in the regression equations reported in Tables 4-2 to 4-10. However, for purposes of this table, which compares means of the self-provision and contracting cities, three additional contract cities have been excluded, leaving 69 cities, with 25 contracting cities and 44 self-provision cities. The cities of Commerce, Avalon, and Santa Fe Springs differ from the other contract cities in that they contract for less than 20 percent of their budget and have exceptionally high per capita expenditures, tax bases, or tax rates.

For comparison of means which do not exclude these three cities see Appendix Table A-12.

[b]Statistically significant difference in means at 5 percent probability level (two-tailed test, $p<0.05$).

residents. To the extent that commercial sales are an important source of revenue, a high sales base would lower the extent of contracting, for not all of the cost burden of public services would be falling on city residents. The per capita volume of sales by retail stores and other outlets, expressed in logarithmic form (*LOUTLET*), is taken as an index of the commercial sales base.

The property taxpayer prefers lower property tax rates but also would like a high level of municipal services, many of which are specifically for the purpose of protecting and enhancing property. Homeowners, we expect, would be more willing to support high levels of expenditures when their property values are high. Therefore, for residential communities a high property base would tend to lower the extent of contracting.

A community's property values may also be high because its business (commercial and industrial) base is relatively large. Different nonresidential land users often have similar requirements for municipal services, and do not require exceptional flexibility and responsiveness on the part of the provider. In addition, nonresidential land users are often attracted to communities that can assure them a low porperty tax rate. Therefore, in nonresidential communities a high property base would tend to increase its extent of contracting.

It would appear that the likelihood of a community increasing its extent of contracting is affected by how the cost burden of services is shared between residential and nonresidential land users. If the residential land user or homeowner dominates, we would expect high property values to lower the extent of contracting; if the industrial and commercial land users dominate, we would expect high property values would raise the extent of contracting. The assessed property value per capita, expressed in the logarithmic form (*LVALUE*), is taken as an index of the property base, which includes commercial, industrial, and residential property. We expect that as among contracting cities, increases in the property base reflect a growing importance of residential land users; therefore we would expect that among contracting cities a high property base will lower the extent of contracting. On the other hand, we expect that among self-provision cities a rising property tax base reflects a growing importance of industrial and commercial land use; therefore we would expect that among self-provision cities a high property base will increase the extent of contracting.

On the basis of the estimated contracting equations found in Table 4-2 we can draw the following conclusions. For all cities, the extent of contracting tends to increase significantly with increases in the property base per capita. This suggests that industrial and commercial preferences are of critical importance in deciding the extent of contracting in a community. The extent of contracting also tends to increase significantly as the result of a declining sales base per capita, lending support to the conjecture that the contracting alternative is less attractive in commercial communities. Among all cities, contracting increases are associated with declining family incomes, so the conjecture that low-income families prefer contracting is also supported, particularly as among the self-

Table 4-2. Estimated Regressions for City Budgets in Los Angeles County, by Group—Step I: Contracting Equations

Estimated coefficients

Dep. variable	CONSTANT	LOUTLET	LVALUE	EDUC	SPAN	AGE	DIST
All cities ($N = 72, DF = 6, 64$) $R^2 = 0.48, F = 9.68$	LPER70	15.68	-1.26^a	1.62^a	-1.02^a	0.01	-.27^a	0.04
Contracting cities ($N = 28, DF = 6, 20$) $R^2 = .37\ F = 1.93$	LPER70	5.73	-.02	-.20	.04	-.00	-.04^b	.02
Self-provision cities ($N = 44, DF = 6, 37$) $R^2 = 0.43\ F = 4.68$	LPER70	15.04	-.61	.17	-.92^a	-.02	-.10	.04

^{a}Significant at 5 percent level without direction predicted.
^{b}Significant at 10 percent level without direction predicted.

provision cities. Finally, contracting seems to decrease as the age of the population increases, supporting the conjecture that a desire for local control is a barrier to contracting.

Considering separately the equations for the contracting and self-provision cities shows, as expected, that an increasing taste for local control reduces the extent of contracting; while an increasing sales base also lowers the extent of contracting. For the contracting cities only, the extent of contracting is also lowered by an increased property base; while among self-provision cities it is raised. This suggests that among contracting cities the preferences of homeowners dominate, while among the self-provision cities business interests have an important effect on determining the extent of contracting.

In summary, a high nonresidential property base, a low residential property base, and a low sales base tend to raise the extent of contracting in both contracting and self-provision cities. An increasing taste for local control significantly lowers the extent of contracting among contracting cities, while also lowering contracting (though not significantly) for self-provision cities.

Does Contracting Affect Taxes?

The Step II equations are of the following general form:

Tax Rate (or Revenues) = F_2 (*CONSTANT, LOUTLET, LVALUE, EDUC, AGE, DIST, LPER70*)

The second stage of our recursive model tests the expectation that contracting results in lower city budget property tax rates and property tax revenues. For our purposes the city budget property tax rates are measured by the ratio of property tax payments made to city government divided by assessed property values (*TAXRATE*). City government property tax revenues are expressed as the log of per capita property taxes paid to the city government (*LPROPTX*).

It has sometimes been argued that contracting cities are much more dependent than noncontracting cities on intergovernmental transfers, particularly state-rebated sales and gas taxes. In our equation, intergovernmental transfers are expressed as the log of per capita transfers (*LREBATE*) and also as the ratio of transfers to total city government revenues (*PERREB*). These conjectures about the relation between contracting and revenues have been tested, and the results are reported in Table 4-3.

The results show that as the extent of contracting increases among cities, whether they are contracting or self-provision cities, the property tax rate tends to become smaller, and so do property tax revenues. Also, whether or not increased contracting raises the amount of intergovernmental transfers, it does tend to increase the share of transfer revenues in the city budget for both contracting and self-provision cities. Thus, the conjectures about the effects of contracting on revenues are essentially confirmed.

Of course there are factors other than contracting that also affect city government tax rates and revenues. As increasing taste for local control tends to increase the property tax rate, since higher rates would help in achieving local control. An increasing sales base lowers the property tax rate because alternatives to the property tax are available. An increasing industrial and commercial property base tends to lower the tax rate, because business tries to avoid high-tax places. Surprisingly an increasing residential property base tends to raise the property tax rate, apparently because wealthy homeowners seek to protect and enhance their property. Thus, the nonresident tax base and taste for local control have expected effects on the property tax rate for both contracting and self-provision cities.

It would also be expected that the tax bases and the taste for local control would affect the property tax revenues in the same way they affect tax rates. This, however, is not consistently the case. Among contracting cities, as expected, a decreasing commercial sales base and an increasing property base raise property tax revenues; however, an increasing taste for local control lowers, rather than raises, property revenues. Among self-provision cities an increasing taste for local control, as expected, rasies the property revenues; however, increases in the sales base and the property base raise property tax revenues even though they lower the property tax rate. It would seem that the extent of contracting and variables closely related to contracting have a more consistent and reasonable effect on the property tax rate than they have on property tax revenues.

In summary, for both contracting and self-provision cities, increases in the extent of contracting, in the commercial sales base, and in the nonresidential property base tend to *lower* the tax rate; increases in the taste for local control and in the residential property base will *raise* the property tax rate. Increases in the extent of contracting also lower property tax revenues in both contracting and self-provision cities; however, the effects of changes in the tax bases and taste for local control on property tax revenues seem to be different for contracting and for self-provision cities.

Does Contracting Affect Budget Expenditures?

It has been argued that contracting lowers budget expenditures, because contracting providers are more efficient and thereby lower costs, or because when the county provides the service then contracting cities tend to be financially subsidized, or because residents in contracting cities prefer to support a lower level of expenditures. Although this statistical study does not distinguish among these factors, it does test the more general statement that contracting tends to lower city budget expenditures. As our measure of budget expenditures, the log of city expenditures per capita (*LEXPTOT*) is used. In formal terms the city expenditure equation is:

$$LEXPTOT = F_3 \ (CONSTANT, LOUTLET, LVALUE, EDUC, SPAN, AGE, DIST, LPER70, TAXRATE)$$

Table 4-3. Estimated Regressions For City Budgets in Los Angeles County, by Group—Step II: Tax Rate and Revenue Equations

Step IIA: Tax Rate Equations

Estimated coefficients

Dep. variable	CONSTANT	LOUTLET	LVALUE	EDUC	SPAN	AGE	DIST	LPER70
All cities ($N = 72, DF = 7, 63$) $R^2 = 0.61\ F = 14.07$								
TAXRATE	0.61	-0.06	-0.11	0.01	0.01	0.02	0.04[a]	-0.18[a]
Contracting cities ($N = 28, DF = 7, 19$) $R^2 = 0.49\ F = 2.59$								
TAXRATE	-.63	-.04	.02	-.01	.01	.05[a]	.03[b]	-.22
Self-provision cities ($N = 44, DF = 7, 36$) $R^2 = 0.36\ F = 2.89$								
TAXRATE	.97	-.05	-.25	.11	.01	.02	.04[a]	-.08

Step IIB: Revenue equations

Dep. variable	CONSTANT	LOUTLET	LVALUE	EDUC	SPAN	AGE	DIST	LPER70
All cities ($N = 72, DF = 7, 63$) $R^2 = 0.52\ F = 9.72$ $R^2 = 0.55\ F = 11.21$ $R^2 = 0.71\ F = 22.19$								
LPROPTX	1.56	-1.00[a]	2.00[a]	-0.89[b]	-0.01	0.02	0.13[a]	-0.89[a]
LREBATE	1.96	.15[a]	.11	-.06	-.00	-.00	-.00	-.01
PEREB	137.65	-.80	-9.69[a]	-.97	-.11	-.32	-.36[a]	2.06[a]
Contracting cities ($N = 28, DF = 7, 19$) $R^2 = 0.35\ F = 1.48$ $R^2 = '0.81\ F = 11.67$ $R^2 = 0.70\ F = 6.34$								
LPROPTX	1.30	-1.15	2.30	-.66	.01	-.07	.25	-2.04
LREBATE	3.89	.16[a]	.13[a]	-.18[a]	-.01	.01	-.00	-.25[a]
PEREB	142.24	.41	-10.59[a]	-3.48	-.18	.13	.28	5.66

Table 4-3. continued

Step IIB: Revenue equations

Dep. variable	CONSTANT	LOUTLET	LVALUE	EDUC	SPAN	AGE	DIST	LPER70
LPROPTX	-7.01	.11	.71[a]	.22	.02[a]	.02	.03[a]	-.09
LREBATE	2.39	.05	.11	-.01	.00	-.01[b]	-.00	.01
PEREB	161.13	-6.35[a]	-3.99	-3.17[b]	-.10	-.45[b]	-.36[a]	.28

Self-provision cities
($N = 44$, $DF = 7, 36$)
$R^2 = 0.65$ $F = 9.59$
$R^2 = 0.17$ $F = 1.08$
$R^2 = 0.68$ $F = 11.07$

[a]Significant at 5 percent level without direction predicted.
[b]Significant at 10 percent level without direction predicted.

The results are shown in Table 4-4.

Increases in the property tax rate, the sales base and the property base would be expected to raise budget expenditures, and the regression equation indicates that this does indeed happen, for both contracting and self-provision cities. Our conjectures tell us that increases in the taste for local control would raise budget expenditures, and this again is confirmed by the results. We would also expect that increases in the extent of contracting would lower budget expenditures. This turns out to be the case only for contracting cities. Within the limited range of contracting which takes place in self-provision cities, changes in contracting seem to have no appreciable effect on the level of budget expenditures.

Two kinds of questions have so far been raised. The first question is, Why are some cities contracting cities (that is, contracting for over 10 percent of their budgets), while other cities are self-provision cities in the sense that they contract for less than 10 percent of their budgets? The recursive model has not been of much help in answering this question because it does not include variables that would describe the structural selection decision process.

The second question that has been raised is, What is the relationship between the degree of contracting and specific other variables, and are these relationships the same for contracting and self-provision cities? The recursive model, by separating the contracting cities from the self-provision cities, has been extremely helpful in answering this question. It turns out that the relationships are about the same (but not identical), for both contracting and self-provision cities.

As among the cities of either group, the extent of contracting is influenced by the desire to achieve local control of service delivery and by the sources of financial support for services. If local control is desired and can be afforded (because of high commercial sales or residential property base), then the extent of contracting will be low. If the extent of contracting is low, this leads to low property tax rates for both contracting and self-provision cities. Low property tax rates lead to low budget expenditures. And, at least among contracting cities, increases in the extent of contracting lead to lower budget expenditures, independent of the property tax rate.

THE EFFECT OF CONTRACTING ON MUNICIPAL EXPENDITURES

The city budget represents only a part of public expenditures on municipal-type services. Services that are funded through the city's budget include primarily those provided through city departments and city contracts. Often excluded from the budget are many services funded and provided through other structures.

We know that cities vary in the extent to which they use special districts and other structures, as well as in the types of services they choose to fund outside the city budget. Therefore, it is possible that the relationships shown in the last

Table 4-4. Estimated Regressions for City Budgets in Los Angeles County, by Group—Step III: City Expenditure Equations

Dep. variable		Constant	LOutlet	LValue	Educ	Span	Age	Dist	LPer70	TAXRATE
All cities ($N = 72$, $DF = 8, 62$) $R^2 = 0.88$ $F = 58.34$	LEXPTOT	-1.02	0.16^a	0.66^a	-0.12^a	-0.00	0.02^b	-0.00	-0.01	0.38^a
Contracting cities ($N = 28$, $DF = 8, 18$) $R^2 = 0.97$ $F = 66.67$	LEXPTOT	2.00	.12^a	.57^a	-.11^b	-.00	.01	-.01	-.57^a	.31^a
Self-provision cities ($N = 44$, $DF = 8, 35$) $R^2 = 0.89$ $F = 34.98$	LEXPTOT	-1.32	.26^a	.51^a	-.05	-.00	.01	.00	.01	.30^a

Estimated coefficients

[a] Significant at 5 percent probability level without direction predicted.
[b] Significant at 10 percent probability level without direction predicted.

section between contracting and budget expenditures or revenues are counterbalanced by the relationship between contracting and special districts. Specifically, the lower budget expenditures induced by contracting may be offset by higher special district expenditures, also induced by contracting. If this is the case, total municipal expenditures, which for our purposes are the sum of city budget and special district expenditures, may not be affected at all by contracting. Similarly, the overall tax rate for municipal services may also be independent of contracting. This suggests that the importance of contracting may be more in terms of its organizational consequences than in terms of the municipal services residents receive and the costs they bear for these services.

The following section analyzes these issues in two ways. First, it replaces the contracting variable in the regression system by a city bureaucracy variable. Second, it examines more directly the relationship between contracting, special districts, and overall municipal expenditures.

The Effects of City Bureaucracy

The size of the city bureaucracy is an index of the use of city departments for provision of municipal services. The number of city government employees per capita (*LTOTPC*) is the measure used to differentiate city department from all other structures for providing services. Thus it includes a somewhat broader perspective than that of the analysis in the preceding section, which focused on the role of contracting in city budgets.

Although the efficiency with which cities utilize labor is likely to vary, we conjecture that the major reason for large differences in per capita city employment is the variation in the extent to which city departments are used to provide municipal services. Our expectation, therefore, is that the effects of changes in the size of the city bureaucracy will be the opposite of the effects of the extent of contracting.

To test this conjecture, we again implemented the recursive system for contracting and self-provision cities in Los Angeles County, keeping all variables the same as in the earlier equations but replacing the degree of contracting in the city budget by the number of city government employees per capita. The results are reported in Table 4-5.

An increasing taste for local control increases the use of city departments, just as it reduces the extent of contracting; increased use of departments, just as decreased contracting, increases the property tax rate in both contracting and self-provision cities; increased use of city departments increases budget expenditures only among the self-provision cities, just as decreased contracting raises budget expenditures only among the contracting cities. In addition, when holding constant the effects of city employment, increases in the tax bases and tax rate tend to increase budget expenditures, which is comparable to the effect of these factors when the degree of contracting is held constant.

In summary, the city department analysis, in all but one important respect, is a mirror image of the contracting analysis. The exception is that among con-

Contracting of Municipal Services 131

Table 4-5. Estimated Regressions for All Cities in Los Angeles County: Self-Provision Equations

Estimated coefficients

Dep. variable	Constant	LOutlet	LValue	Educ	Span	Age	Dist	TOTPC	Tax-Rate
All cities (N = 72)									
Step I: Contracting equation									
$R^2 = 0.62$ $F = 17.15$ $DF = 6, 64$									
TOTPC	−26.96	1.34[a]	1.60[a]	−0.27	−0.01	0.43[a]	0.05		
Step II: Tax rate equation									
$R^2 = 0.62$ $F = 14.54$ $DF = 7, 63$									
TAXRATE	1.90	−.04	−.63[a]	.23[a]	.01[b]	.01	.02[b]	.15[a]	
Step III: City exp. equation									
$R^2 = 0.89$ $F = 62.63$ $DF = 8, 62$									
LEXPTOT	−.51	.14[a]	.57[a]	−.09[b]	−.00	.01	−.00	.03[a]	.31[a]
Contracting cities (N = 28)									
Step I: Contracting equation									
$R^2 = 0.63$ $F = 5.77$ $DF = 6, 20$									
TOTPC	14.90	.23	2.11[a]	−.57	.02	.25[a]	−.10		
Step II: Tax rate equation									
$R^2 = 0.95$ $F = 50.23$ $DF = 7, 19$									
TAXRATE	.84	−.08[a]	.33[a]	.08[b]	.00	.01[b]	.05[a]	.18[a]	
Step III: City exp. equation									
$R^2 = 0.90$ $F = 19.65$ $DF = 8, 18$									
LEXPTOT	−1.46	.18[a]	.83[a]	−.16	−.00	.02	−.05	−.09	.91
Self-provision cities (N = 44)									
Step I: Contracting equation									
$R^2 = 0.75$ $F = 18.04$ $DF = 6, 37$									
TOTPC	−35.39	.52	4.92[a]	−1.02[b]	.01	.31[a]	.16[a]		
Step II: Tax rate equation									
$R^2 = 0.52$ $F = 5.53$ $DF = 7, 36$									
TAXRATE	3.91	−.06	−.83[a]	.29[a]	.01[b]	−.01	.01	.12[a]	
Step III: City exp. equation									
$R^2 = 0.93$ $F = 55.69$ $DF = 8, 35$									
LEXPTOT	.72	.23[a]	.21[a]	.02	−.00	−.00	.00	.05[a]	.16[a]

[a] Significant at 5 percent level without direction predicted.
[b] Significant at 10 percent level without direction predicted.

tracting cities increased contracting lowers budget expenditures, while increased use of city departments does not raise expenditures. This suggests that although city departments are a substitute for contracting, there are also other structures for providing municipal services which will have an influence.

The Effects of Special Districts

As has been suggested, one such other structure could be the special district. And the relationship between contracting and special districts may be such that the observed relation between contracting and city budgets is different from the relation between contracting and all municipal services. To examine the effects of special district service delivery we have introduced into the analysis the special district tax rate ($SPDISTRT$), special district expenditure per capita ($SPDISTEXP$), the overall municipal property tax rate ($MUNIRATE$), and overall municipal service expenditure per capita in its logarithmic form ($LMUNIEXP$).

The municipal property tax rate is defined as the total property tax rate paid by all governments in a city minus the school district and county property taxes. The special district tax rate for a city is then calculated as the difference between the estimated municipal property tax rate and the city government property tax rate. Multiplying the estimated special district rate by the assessed value in the city provides an estimate of special district expenditure that, when added to the city government expenditure, shows the total of public expenditures for municipal services in the city. These municipal expenditures per capita are expressed in logarithmic form when used in the regression equations.

These estimates were made to provide a comparable coverage for expenditures and revenues among the cities in the sample. The estimates do provide approximate comparability; the major discrepancies relate to municipal services that are not publically financed in some cities but are in others.

As shown in Table 4-1, the special district tax revenues for all cities in L.A. County is estimated at about 1.5 percent of the property base on the average, while it is 2 percent in contracting cities. Thus the contracting cities, as a group, have a significantly higher special district tax rate than do the self-provision cities. These higher special district rates also seem to lower the property tax rates in contracting cities, which are calculated at 0.9 percent for all cities and 0.2 percent for only contracting cities, on the average. Thus the overall average municipal service tax rate of 2.3 percent is identical for contracting cities and self-provision cities.

The special district tax rate, when translated to expenditures, came to about $40 per capita for the average of all cities and $55 per capita for the average of contracting cities. These district expenditures are about one-third the size of the average budget expenditures for all cities in the county; however, for contracting cities only, district expenditures almost equal the average level of budget expenditures. Thus, high district expenditures in contracting cities do indeed offset their low budget expenditures; contracting does seem to be tied to special districts in some fashion. The end result is that self-provision cities have a 25 percent higher average level of per capita expenditures for the total of municipal services than do contract cities—about $145 as compared to $115.

Special district funding was introduced into the recursive model and its effects on city budgets and total municipal services were examined. The equations are reported in Table 4-6 and 4-7. The results indicate that, among contracting cities, increases in contracting tend to raise special district activities. However, among self-provision cities, increased contracting is associated with reductions in special district activities. It would appear that in cities which do a fair amount of contracting, special district and contracting expenditures together substitute for city departments; however, in cities which do not contract much, special district structures are a substitute for contract structures. Thus we would expect to find, and do find, that special districts have a more important effect on contracting than on self-provision cities.

It was earlier shown that increased contracting lowers the budget tax rate for contracting cities. An increasing special district rate also lowers the budget tax rate. However, when the special district rate is included in the budget tax rate equation, the lowering effects of contracting on the budget rate disappear. In addition, increases in residential property are shown to lower the budget tax rate when special districts are included, rather than raising the budget rate which occurs when special districts are not included. Thus, when special districts are considered, the residential property owners behave similarly to nonresidential property owners; that is, when the tax base increases they prefer that some of the increase go to tax reductions as well as to expenditure increases.

Increases in commercial sales, in the residential property base, and in the nonresidential property base tend to lower the overall municipal tax rate. This is because the greater tax base makes it easier to fund municipal service expenditures. Also, increases in the special district tax rate raise the overall municipal rate among both contracting and self-provision cities. However, while increased contracting tends to raise the overall municipal rate among contracting cities, the effect is reversed for self-provision cities.

Even though increased contracting tends to raise the budget and overall property tax rates among contracting cities, it tends to lower their budget and overall municipal service expenditures. It would seem that when cities use a combination of special district and contract structures in place of city department structures, overall expenditures are kept relatively low in order to prevent an increasing burden on property taxpayers. As among self-provision cities, alternatives to the department structure are not extensively used so that comparable results are not realized.

In summary, the effects of contracting are different for contracting and for self-provision cities. Among self-provision cities, increased contracting reduces the budget and municipal tax rates, but does not importantly affect their expenditures. Among contracting cities, increased contracting does not affect the

Table 4-6. Estimated Regressions for All Municipal Services in Los Angeles County: Step II: Tax Rate Equations

Estimated coefficients

Dep. variable	Constant	LOutlet	LValue	Educ	Span	Age	Dist	LPer70	Spdi-Strt
All cities ($N = 72$)									
$R^2 = 0.47$ $F = 7.85$ $DF = 7, 63$ SPDISTRT	5.68	-.18[b]	-0.14	-0.07	-0.01	-0.03	-0.00	0.11[a]	
$R^2 = 0.74$ $F = 22.47$ $DF = 8, 62$ TAXRATE	2.95	-.13[a]	-.16	-.02	.00	.01	.04[a]	-.13[a]	-0.41[a]
$R^2 = 0.73$ $F = 21.21$ $DF = 8, 62$ MUNIRATE	2.96	-.13[a]	-.16	-.01	.00	.01	.03[a]	-.13[a]	.59[a]
Contract cities ($N = 28$)									
$R^2 = 0.75$ $F = 8.23$ $DF = 7, 19$ SPDISTRT	3.93	-.06	-.24	.01	-.01	-.04[b]	.03[b]	.34[b]	
$R^2 = 0.80$ $F = 8.82$ $DF = 8, 18$ TAXRATE	2.64	-.09[b]	-.18	-.00	-.00	-.01	.05[a]	.06	-.83[a]
$R^2 = 0.75$ $F = 6.72$ $DF = 8, 18$ MUNIRATE	1.98	-.11	-.03	-.02	-.01	.01	.02	.07	.36
Self-provision cities ($N = 44$)									
$R^2 = 0.33$ $F = 2.56$ $DF = 7, 36$ SPDISTRT	11.76	-.75[a]	.20	-.55[a]	-.02[b]	.00	.01	-.13	
$R^2 = 0.57$ $F = 5.92$ $DF = 8, 35$ TAXRATE	5.38	-.33[a]	-.17	-.10	.00	.02	.04[a]	-.13[a]	-.37[a]
$R^2 = 0.81$ $F = 18.95$ $DF = 7, 36$ MUNIRATE	5.38	-.33[a]	-.17	-.10	.00	.02	.04[a]	-.13[a]	.63[a]

[a] Significant at 5 percent level without direction predicted.
[b] Significant at 10 percent level without direction predicted.

Table 4-7. Estimated Regressions for All Municipal Services in Los Angeles County: Step III: City Expenditure Equations

Estimated coefficients

Dep. variable	Constant	LOutlet	LValue	Educ	Span	Age	Dist	LPer70	Taxrate	Spdi-Strt
All cities (N = 72)										
$R^2 = 0.89$ $F = 54.88$										
DF = 9, 61										
LEXPTOT	-0.32	0.13[a]	0.63[a]	-0.13[a]	-0.00	0.01[b]	0.00	-0.01	0.28[a]	-0.11[a]
$R^2 = 0.94$ $F = 99.89$										
DF = 9, 61										
LMUNIEXP	-1.28	.08[a]	.75[a]	-.08[a]	-.00	.01[a]	.01	.00	.22[a]	.11[a]
Contracting cities (N = 28)										
$R^2 = 0.97$ $F = 58.10$										
DF = 9, 17										
LEXPTOT	1.54	.13[a]	.60[a]	-.11[b]	-.00	.01	-.02	-.59[a]	.41[a]	.13
$R^2 = 0.99$ $F = 165.52$										
DF = 9, 17										
LMUNIEXP	-.82	.07[a]	.78[a]	-.05	-.00	.00	-.01	-.25[a]	.29[a]	.23[a]
Self-provision cities (N = 44)										
$R^2 = 0.89$ $F = 30.43$										
DF = 9, 34										
LEXPTOT	-1.03	.25[b]	.51[a]	-.06	-.00	.01	.01	.01	.28[a]	-.02
$R^2 = 0.91$ $F = 31.86$										
DF = 9, 34										
LMUNIEXP	-1.68	.20[a]	.61[a]	-.03	-.00	.01	.01	.01	.24[a]	.16[a]

[a]Significant at 5 percent level without direction prediction.
[b]Significant at 10 percent level without direction prediction.

budget and municipal tax rates, but does reduce their expenditures. Part of the reason for these differences is that special districts are much more important in contracting than in self-provision cities.

CONTRACTING, CITY BUDGETS, AND MUNICIPAL SERVICES FOR CITIES IN L.A. COUNTY

What can be inferred about contracting if we interrelate the variety of equations adopted for the recursive model? In general, the conclusions emerging from such an integration are consistent with the interview results in Chapter 2 and with the conjecture that contracting results from balancing the desire for local control of service delivery against the cost burdens associated with the service, while the consequence of contracting is to affect the quantity and mix of different types of municipal expenditures and revenues.

What Affects Contracting?

Cities generally consider it desirable to maintain local control over service delivery, to keep service expenditures low, and to minimize the burden on the property taxpayer. The extent of contracting adopted by a city is determined by the trade-offs between these three objectives. Cities differ in the kinds of trade-offs they make because they differ in their preferences or taste for local control; in the amount of their commercial sales, which affects the tax base and therefore the affordable extent of local control; and in their assessed property values, which affect the tax burden imposed on the homeowner and nonresidential landowner.

There are some cities in L.A. County that prefer to engage in a fair amount of contracting—above 10 or 20 percent of their budgets. In addition to these contracting cities, there are self-provision cities that prefer to engage in very little contracting—less than 1 percent of their budgets. The contracting cities tend to have a smaller tax base than self-provision cities, and also tend to spend less on municipal services in general. Contracting cities generally have smaller budget expenditures than self-provision cities, and these lower budget expenditures are offset partially, but not completely, by higher special district activities.

The extent of contracting in cities seems to increase when the value attached to local control goes down. But whatever the taste for local control, declining commercial sales appear to induce cities to increase their contracting because they cannot afford the added expenditure associated with achieving local control through the use of city departments.

No matter what level of city revenues is provided by commercial sales, nonresidential property owners prefer to avoid bearing the added costs associated with local control. Therefore, a high nonresidential property tax base leads to an increase in the extent of contracting. However, residential propertyowners appear less averse to bearing the extra tax burden associated with obtaining an added degree of control over the level and mix of service expenditures. Therefore a high residential property base leads to a decrease in the extent of contracting as greater reliance is placed on the use of city department structures.

According to our statistical analysis, these relationships between contracting on the one hand and the tax bases and taste for local control on the other hand apply to both contracting cities and self-provision cities. However, while the statistical analysis has been able to explain how some factors influence the degree of contracting among contracting cities and among self-provision cities, it has not been able to explain why some cities become contracting cities and others do not.

We believe that a low taste for local control, a low commercial sales base, a low residential property base, and a high nonresidential property base each encourage cities to pass that threshold which moves them from a self-provision to a contracting city status, but there also are additional factors involved in causing cities to become contracting cities. It is likely that these factors, which have not been incorporated in the recursive model, relate to the availability of law enforcement contracting. Almost all of the contracting cities received police services from the L.A. County Sheriff's Department prior to incorporation. Only a few of the cities that became incorporated after the police contracting option became available refused to exercise the option. Almost none of the cities that had their own police departments prior to the availability of the police contracting decided to become contracting cities. So even though we have not been able to include it in our statistical analysis, we believe that the extent of satisfaction with the city's police department and the extent of satisfaction with county service delivery—particularly the police service—will affect a city's decision to become a contracting city.

How Does Contracting Affect Revenues and Taxes?

Since contracting is associated with budget expenditures, we would expect contracting to affect city tax rates and revenues. And, in fact, contracting cities have lower city property tax rates and lower city property taxes per capita than do self-provision cities. Furthermore, so long as special district activities are not explicitly considered, increasing the extent of contracting results in a declining property tax rate as well as declining property tax revenues. When special district alternatives to city departments are made explicit, a different conclusion emerges, for, as among contracting cities, it is not increased contracting but increased special district activities that lower the budget tax rate. However, the use of special districts does not lower budget financing by as much as it increases special district financing, so increasing the extent of contracting among contracting cities does not lower the overall municipal property tax rate.

Below the contracting threshold, increases in both special district and contracting activities lower the budget and the overall municipal property tax rates.

However, among self-provision cities there is not much use of contracting or special district structures, so their impact in terms of lowering the budget rates is not large. It is partly for this reason that the overall municipal tax rate is not higher, but about the same, on average, in contracting cities as in self-provision cities.

How Does Contracting Affect Expenditures?

Increased contracting tends to lower city budget expenditures. As among contracting cities, for example, a 1 percent increase in the extent of contracting lowers budget expenditures by 0.5 percent. Increased contracting also leads to increased special district expenditures. But this increase is not enough to counterbalance the reduction in city budget expenditures due to contracting. So on balance, the overall effect of increasing the extent of contracting is to lower municipal government expenditures, particularly among contracting cities.

But we have already seen that once beyond the contract threshold, further increases in contracting do not lower the overall municipal tax rate, even though it lowers municipal expenditures. This is in part because increased contracting results in a smaller amount of intergovernmental transfers, which could account for the lowering of budget and overall municipal expenditures without affecting the property tax rates. It also appears possible, although it has not been tested, that not only do lower residential property values result in increasing the extent of contracting, but increased contracting, in turn, leads to lowering residential property values. This also could account for increased contracting having the effect of lowering expenditures but not the property tax rate.

Clearly, the effect of contracting on city government (that is, on city budget expenditures) is related to its effect on different revenue sources and on expenditures for municipal services that are not carried in the city budget. Cities that decide to increase contracting at the same time seem to decide to increase the expenditures made through special districts. This means that expenditures through city departments are lower not only because there is contracting but also because there is a relatively high level of district expenditure. Cities that contract are not only contracting cities; they are, more generally, non-city-department cities.

And to a large extent they are non-city-department cities because they choose to avoid adding to the financial burdens of property taxpayers. Thus, we find that contracting cities have relatively low per capita municipal expenditures and a relatively low tax base but about the same municipal property tax rate as the self-provision cities. It appears that in contract cities the property taxpayer is not willing to be taxed at the higher rate needed to raise municipal expenditures to the level achieved by the wealthier self-provision cities.

What Affects Structural Competition?

The comparison of contract cities with self-provision cities makes it clear that city departments are in competition with alternative providers—particularly contract and special district providers. Departments are rejected when the taste for local control is low. Departments are rejected when they cannot be afforded because of a low commercial sales value. Departments are rejected even when the nonresidential property base is high, because the higher base is not used to generate more taxes but to achieve the lower budget tax rates associated with contracting. All of this is consistent with the city manager interviews, which also indicated that structural competition exists in varying degrees among different cities.

The city manager interviews suggested that there is a two-level sequential type of structural competition in cities. First, the decision is made either to provide or not to provide most services through city departments. Then, if the decision has been made not to deliver all municipal services through city departments, the preferred provider of specific services or service components is selected among available alternatives, including (but not limited to) contract, district, and even city department providers. The multiple regression results relating to the extent of contracting illuminate these views and indicate that the competition among contract, district, and city department providers is affected differently by the share of contracting in the budget, by the city's taste for local control, and by the size and composition of the economic base in the community.

The results are summarized in Table 4-8, which shows how contracting, local control, and the economic base affect contract, city departments, and special district expenditures for all cities in L.A. County. If the impacts on providers are in the same direction, we can assume that the indicated variable does not place the providers in a competitive relationship with each other. By a competitive relation we mean that a change in the municipal expenditures results in an expenditure increase for one type of provider, accompanied by an expenditure decline for some other types of provider; by a complementary relationship we mean that a change in municipal expenditures causes two providers to share in the municipal expenditure increase or decline, although not necessarily to share equally. According to these definitions, we can conclude that there tends to be competition between contract and department providers or between district and department providers, but there is complementarity between contract and district providers. How does this come about?

As the percentage of contracting in the city budget increases, budget expenditures are reduced while the level of contracting expenditures is increased. Since contracting and departments are the components of budget expenditures, and since total budget expenditures do not grow as a result of increased contracting, we can conclude that increased extent of contracting is accompanied by decreased self-provision—that is, there is competition between contract and department providers.

From the evidence in the manager surveys and the police study to be presented in Chapter 5, it appears that levels of expenditure are lower when services are provided through contract than when these same services are provided through city departments. These "savings" could result in increased expenditures

Table 4-8. Summary of Structural Competition

As Share of Contracting in Budget Increases	This Results in	decrease in municipal expenditures increase in district expenditures decrease in city government expenditures increase in contracting expenditures decrease in department expenditures	Therefore	competition occurs between contract and department and also district and department	complementarity occurs between contract and district
As Taste for Local Control Increases	This Results in	increase in municipal expenditures no change in district expenditures increase in city government expenditures decrease in contracting expenditures increase in department expenditures	Therefore	competition occurs between contract and department	complementarity occurs between contract and district
As Commercial Base Increases	This Results in	increase in municipal expenditures decrease in district expenditures increase in city government expenditures decrease in contracting expenditures increase in department expenditures	Therefore	competition occurs between contract and department and also district and department	complementarity occurs between contract and district
As Property Base Increases	This Results in	increase in municipal expenditures increase in district expenditures increase in city government expenditures increase in contracting expenditures increase in department expenditures	Therefore		complementarity occurs between contract and district and department

or in decreased city budgets. It appears that they actually result in a combination of reduced city budgets and increased district expenditures. As a result there is competition between district and department providers while there is a complementary relation between contract and district providers.

Competition or complementarity among departments, districts, and contractors may result not only from increased contracting but also from other factors. We find this is true when we look more closely at the consequences of changes among contracting cities in their taste for local control and in their commercial sales and property tax bases.

As the taste for local control goes up, the size of the city budget increases while city government employment, and therefore city department expenditures, also increase. However, even though the share of contracting in the budget goes down, the amount of contracting might increase because of the rising city budget. We judge this to be unlikely since the effect of a taste for local control on budget expenditures is quite small as compared to its effect on the share of contracting in the budget. As a result we conclude that the taste for local control generates competition between contract and department providers.

As the commercial sales increase the share of contracting goes down while the city budget goes up. However, the effects on the share of contracting are much more substantial than the effects on the city budget, so we would expect the amount of contracting to decrease. This indicates that there is competition between contract and department providers. At the same time increasing commercial sales lower district expenditures, which means that the size of the commercial sales generates competition between district and departmental providers and complementarity between contract and district providers.

The regression equations indicate that increases in the property base result in increasing the budget expenditures and therefore increasing the amount as well as the share of contracting. Since municipal expenditures will increase even more than budget expenditures as a result of the rising property base, the district expenditures will also increase. This indicates a complementary relation between contract and district providers. Since city employment and therefore city department expenditures also increase as a result of a rising property base, this indicates a complementary relation between contract, district, and department providers.

In summary, we can say that changes in the degree of contracting, in the taste for local control, and in the commercial sales all contribute to competition between contract and city department providers; changes in the degree of contracting and the commercial sales contribute to competition between city departments and special districts; changes in the degree of contracting and the commercial sales establish a complementary relationship between contract and district providers; and changes in the property tax base establish complementarity among contract, district, and department providers.

THE EFFECT OF CONTRACTING ON SPECIFIC SERVICES

It is sometimes suggested that contracting cities have a different set of service priorities and service costs than do noncontracting cities. This is because they are thought to have fewer resources and smaller budgets, which compels them to concentrate their funds on provision of a few traditional municipal services, while relatively small amounts are spent on the newer, amenity-type services. Furthermore, it is suggested that because contracting cities are seeking to avoid internal bureaucracies, they will not only contract for police, street, recreation, and refuse collection services, but also they will tend to provide those traditional services for which they are not contracting, such as fire protection and library services, through special districts. Thus we would expect that an increasing extent of overall service contracting in the budget will tend to lower the level of per capita expenditures for the traditional services that are also contracted, but will raise their share of the budget. Also we would expect that as the extent of overall service contracting increases, this will lower the per capita expenditures of traditional services which are provided through special districts, and will also lower their share of total municipal expenditures.

We can test whether the extent of budget contracting has an effect on specific service expenditures by extending the three-equation recursive system to include a fourth step for specific service equations, as follows:

Step IV-A: Specific Service
Budget Expenditures = F_4 (community characteristics, contracting, tax rates, total expenditures)

In addition, we can test the related question of whether the extent of use of city departments affects budget expenditures for the same selected services. We do this by deleting from the service-specific regression equations the percent of contracting as an independent variable and adding the total city government employment and the service-specific city government employment per capita. The results of extending the recursive system to include the specific services are shown in Tables 4-9 and 4-10. Six traditional services are examined: police, fire protection, street repair and maintenance, refuse and garbage collection, parks and recreation, and library services.

Police ($LEXPOL$)

Contracting cities, as shown in Chapter 5 and confirmed in Table 4-1, generally spend less per capita on police services than do self-provision cities. Is this directly attributable to the extent of contracting in the city or is it associated with other factors related to increased contracting? The regression analysis indicates that increasing the extent of contracting tends to raise, not to lower, per capita police expenditures. What lowers police expenditures are factors associated with increased contracting—namely the property tax rate, the residential property tax base, and the total budget expenditure.

Low tax rates are a significant factor in reducing per capita police expenditures. Since contracting results in lowering the budget property tax rate we can infer that increased contracting indirectly lowers police expenditures even if it does not do so directly.

Increases in residential property base tend to raise per capita police expenditures. This is in part because more police are required to provide the needed protection, and in part because the added resource base makes it easier to raise the revenues required to support the added expenditures. We can therefore infer that the declining residential property base associated with increased contracting tends to lower police expenditures. However, the increasing nonresidential property base, which is also associated with increased contracting, tends to raise police expenditures.

For cities in L.A. County an increase in total budget expenditures is related to an increase in police expenditures; roughly a 1 percent increase in the budget is associated with a 0.2 percent increase in police expenditures for contracting cities, and a 0.5 percent increase for self-provision cities. Thus, lowering the budget tends to raise the share of police in total budget expenditures. To the extent that increased contracting is associated with lowering budget expenditures, it appears that is is also associated with raising the share of police expenditures in the budget.

These results are about the same for all cities in L.A. County when police and total city employment are introduced into the equation. Increases in the economic base, the tax rate, and total expenditures continue to raise police expenditures among all cities in L.A. County, while the extent of city government employment does not raise police expenditures. Increasing police employment does tend to raise police expenditures, although it adds surprisingly little to the explanatory power of the regression equation.

In summary, it appears that while the extent of contracting does not have an important direct effect on police expenditures, some factors closely associated with increased contracting, as expected, lower per capita expenditures and raise the police share of budget expenditures. Put differently, the "savings" associated with lower police expenditures in contracting cities do not go to expand other municipal services, but rather are reflected in lower tax rates—a conclusion that we have also drawn in earlier analyses.

Fire Protection (*LEXFIRE*)

In L.A. County the structural options for fire protection services are city fire departments or county fire districts. The contracting cities report very low budgeted expenditures for the fire service, indicating that most of them are in the fire district. Indeed, many of the contracting cities describe their participation in

Table 4-9. Estimated Regressions for Specific Service Expenditures in Los Angeles County: Step IVA: Excluding Employment Effects

Estimated coefficients

Dep. variable	Constant	LOutlet	LValue	Educ	Span	Age	Dist	LPer70	Taxrate	LexPtot
All cities ($N = 72, DF = 9, 61$)										
LEXPOL $R^2 = 0.81$ $F = 28.53$	-1.45	0.10^a	0.27^a	0.02	-0.00	-0.00	-0.01	0.01	0.27^a	0.30^a
LEXFIRE $R^2 = 0.82$ $F = 30.12$	-5.24	.11	.44	-.06	.01	-.01	-.03	$-.17^a$	$.69^a$	$.77^a$
LEXHIGH $R^2 = 0.63$ $F = 11.40$	2.27	.07	$-.91^a$	-.03	-.01	.00	.02	.02	$-.57^a$	1.71^a
LEXGARB $R^2 = 0.33$ $F = 3.28$	1.64	-.05	-.29	-.22	-.02	-.03	.01	-.03	.25	1.15^a
LEXPARK $R^2 = 0.58$ $F = 9.38$	-4.63	.28	.29	.07	.01	-.00	.00	-.03	.12	.32
LEXLIB $R^2 = 0.31$ $F = 3.01$	-2.31	-.06	.55	-.26	-.01	.01	-.04	-.03	-.02	.60
Contracting cities ($N = 28, DF = 9, 17$)										
LEXPOL $R^2 = 0.89$ $F = 15.76$	4.78	$.16^a$	.28	$.20^a$	.01	.01	$-.03^a$	.25	$.50^a$	.18
LEXFIRE $R^2 = 0.79$ $F = 7.08$	-4.94	-.08	$.64^b$	-.24	.01	-.03	$-.07^b$	.43	1.32^a	.84
LEXHIGH $R^2 = 0.79$ $F = 6.98$	4.93	.12	-1.16^b	-.28	-.02	.05	.05	-.17	-1.16^b	2.05^a
LEXGARB $R^2 = 0.43$ $F = 1.41$	-.57	-.19	-.35	-.00	-.00	-.02	.01	.19	$.76^b$	1.17
LEXPARK $R^2 = 0.60$ $F = 2.84$	-5.78	$.11^b$	-.36	-.02	.00	$-.03^a$	.02	.96	-.23	1.63
LEXLIB $R^2 = 0.81$ $F = 7.95$	-1.69	$-.19^b$	.43	-.12	-.00	$-.06^a$	-.02	.05	-.35	.75
Self-provision cities ($N = 44, DF = 9, 34$)										
LEXPOL $R^2 = 0.78$ $F = 13.38$	-.52	-.01	$.26^b$	-.03	.00	-.01	-.00	$.03^b$	$.02^a$	$.51^a$
LEXFIRE $R^2 = 0.86$ $F = 22.55$	-13.71	1.18^a	$.49^b$	$.49^a$	.01	.00	-.02	.07	$.60^a$	-.59
LEXHIGH $R^2 = 0.61$ $F = 5.97$	2.66	$-.25^b$	-.36	-.09	.00	-.02	.01	-.05	$-.36^a$	1.44^a
LEXGARB $R^2 = 0.39$ $F = 2.44$	-2.94	-.40	-.14	-.31	-.01	-.01	-.00	.23	.51	2.57^b
LEXPARK $R^2 = 0.66$ $F = 7.50$	-3.08	-.24	.22	.01	-.01	.01	-.00	-.03	.03	1.02^a
LEXLIB $R^2 = 0.35$ $F = 2.02$	-.44	-.61	.09	-.53	-.03	.06	-.05	.05	.27	2.24

[a] Significant at 5 percent level without direction prediction.
[b] Significant at 10 percent level without direction prediction.

Table 4-10. Estimated Regressions for Specific Service Expenditures in Los Angeles County Step IVB: Including Employment Effects

Estimated coefficients

Dep. Variable	CONSTANT	LOUTLET	LVALUE	EDUC	SPAN	AGE	DIST	TOTPC	TAXRATE	LEXPTOT	SERV. PC[a]
All cities ($N = 72$, $DF = 10, 60$)											
$R^2 = 0.83$ $F = 28.31$ LEXPOL	-1.52	0.07[c]	0.31[b]	0.01	0.00	-0.00	-0.01	-0.02	0.19[b]	0.32[b]	0.14[b]
$R^2 = 0.84$ $F = 31.10$ LEXFIRE	-3.57	0.10	0.08	0.06	0.00	-0.02	-0.04[b]	0.03	0.77[b]	0.65[c]	0.60[b]
$R^2 = 0.67$ $F = 12.43$ LEXHIGH	0.79	0.10	-0.71[b]	-0.11	-0.01	0.02	0.02	-0.11[b]	-0.42[b]	1.87[b]	0.20
$R^2 = 0.38$ $F = 3.68$ LEXGARB	3.95	-0.11	-0.47	-0.10	-0.01	-0.06	0.01	0.13	0.01	0.83	0.26[b]
$R^2 = 0.67$ $F = 12.15$ LEXPARK	-2.27	0.31[b]	-0.06	0.13	0.00	-0.01	0.01	0.02	0.07	0.15	0.43[b]
$R^2 = 0.53$ $F = 6.89$ LEXLIB	1.99	-0.01	-0.04	-0.26	-0.02	0.03	-0.01	-0.02	-0.22	0.36	2.44[b]
Contracting cities ($N = 28$, $DF = 10, 16$)											
$R^2 = 0.97$ $F = 53.48$ LEXFIRE	3.75	-0.56[b]	-1.40[b]	0.25[c]	0.03[b]	0.02	0.20[b]	1.09[b]	-4.39[b]	0.79[b]	0.20[c]
$R^2 = 0.81$ $F = 6.77$ LEXHIGH	3.88	0.09	-0.69[b]	-0.45	-0.03	0.04	0.02[b]	-0.19[b]	-0.85[b]	2.03[b]	0.78
$R^2 = 0.78$ $F = 5.55$ LEXPARK	4.00	-0.22[b]	-1.81[b]	0.37	0.02	0.01	0.26[b]	0.99[b]	-5.02[b]	0.89	-0.01
$R^2 = 0.71$ $F = 3.97$ LEXLIB	-6.50	0.95[b]	1.41[b]	-0.14	-0.04[b]	-0.04	-0.31[b]	-1.48[b]	7.69[b]	-0.46[b]	5.55[b]
Self-provision cities ($N = 44$, $DF = 10, 33$)											
$R^2 = 0.88$ $F = 25.09$ LEXPOL	1.19	-0.05	0.04	-0.04	-0.00	-0.00	-0.00	-0.02	-0.06	0.53[b]	0.30[b]
$R^2 = 0.87$ $F = 22.12$ LEXFIRE	-8.70	0.82[b]	0.28	0.33[b]	0.00	0.00	-0.01	-0.04	0.54[b]	-0.36	0.49[b]
$R^2 = 0.66$ $F = 6.38$ LEXHIGH	-0.59	-0.31[b]	-0.13	-0.16	0.00	0.00	0.01	-0.09[b]	-0.25[c]	1.97[b]	0.04
$R^2 = 0.40$ $F = 2.17$ LEXGARB	0.38	-0.79	0.42	-0.53	-0.01	-0.05	-0.00	-0.10	0.38	2.41[b]	1.24
$R^2 = 0.73$ $F = 9.12$ LEXPARK	-3.15	0.03	-0.08	0.11	0.01	-0.00	-0.01	-0.03	0.02	0.95[b]	0.45[b]
$R^2 = 0.66$ $F = 6.33$ LEXLIB	-7.30	-0.72	0.56	-0.83[b]	-0.00	0.09	0.00	-0.41[b]	-0.48	3.96[b]	3.83[b]

[a]Indicates city government employment per capita for each indicated service.
[b]Significant at 5 percent level without direction prediction.
[c]Significant at 10 percent level without direction prediction.

the fire district as a county contract. Since contracting cities, as a group, have substantially lower budgeted fire expenditures than self-provision cities, it is clear that they also use the fire district structure more extensively.

Furthermore, we find in the regression equations that an increasing budget tax rate leads to higher budget fire expenditures, for both contracting and self-provision cities. It would seem that at least part of the reason for the relatively low budget tax rate in contracting cities is because of their greater reliance on fire districts. Also, increases in the extent of contracting for all services seem to be associated with increases in budgeted fire expenditures. This suggests that participation in fire districts is not encouraged by more extensive contracting of other services, either for self-provision cities or for contracting cities.

It is generally believed that expenditures for fire protection services in cities using fire districts are lower than in cities with their own fire departments. Since contracting cities tend to use fire districts more than self-provision cities, and if it is the case that their per capita fire protection expenditures are also lower, we can conclude that contracting cities spend proportionately less of total municipal expenditures on fire protection services, potentially releasing "savings" for use in increasing expenditures for other municipal services.

In summary, the important structural competition for the fire protection service is between fire departments that tend to be used by self-provision cities and fire districts that tend to be used by contracting cities.

Street Maintenance, Cleaning, and Lighting (*LEXHIGH*)

A declining property tax rate increases per capita budget expenditures on street services. Since increased contracting is accompanied by lower budget property tax rates, it appears that increased contracting indirectly, even if not directly, raises street expenditures. However, a high nonresidential property tax base and low levels of total budget expenditures, which we have seen are also associated with increased contracting, are significant in reducing budgeted street expenditures. Since the per capita budget expenditures on street services in contracting cities is about the same as in self-provision cities, it would appear that the decreasing effects of the property tax base on streets expenditures just about balance the increasing effects of the property tax rate. This is not consistent with our expectation that factors associated with increased contracting would tend to lower the street service budget expenditures. Furthermore, the regressions indicate that a 1 percent increase in total budget expenditures results in almost twice that percentage increase in street service expenditures. This indicates that, contrary to expectation, factors closely associated with increased contracting tend to reduce the share of street service expenditures in the budget.

Why does the street service behave contrary to expectation? In part the answer may be that some street service expenditures are postponed when a city's total budget is high. This is suggested by the regression equation showing that street service expenditures tend to decline as the total of city government employment increases.

Another part of the reason for street services behaving contrary to expectation is that a large portion of street expenditures per capita are funded through state rebates of the gasoline tax. The level of such rebates seems unrelated to contracting factors, suggesting that street expenditures would also be unrelated to contracting. Thus we find that the similarity of per capita expenditures for street services between contracting and self-provision cities is consistent with the approximate equality of per capita intergovernmental transfers between both groups of cities.

Other Services (*LEXGARB, LEXPARK, LEXLIB*)

The regression equations used to explain parks and recreation, library, and refuse collection services did not perform well. Not only was the explanatory power low for each of the three equations, but almost none of the independent variables in the equations was significant.

Neither the extent of contracting in the city budget nor the number of city government employees has an independent effect on the budget expenditures for these services. However, employment increases in the specific services do tend to be associated with budget expenditure increases for the service. Thus by adding service-specific city government employment to the regression equations, we are able to improve our ability to explain budget expenditures for the refuse, recreation, and library services.

The reason for the poor explanatory power of these equations is that substantial portions of the expenditures for these services are not made through city budgets. In many cities the refuse service is not budgeted because it is handled through private franchise, while parks and library services are provided through districts. Since contracting cities, as a group, have lower expenditures than self-provision cities for the refuse, library, and probably the recreation services as well, it seems that they rely more heavily on these alternative providers. But any useful attempt to understand these services must go beyond the contracting and city department structures incorporated in the city budget to include consideration of expenditures made through other governments and private franchise.

On an overall basis it appears that the extent of contracting in a city does not importantly affect the budget expenditures for specific traditional services provided by the city. However, factors associated with increased contracting do affect the police and fire protection services—tending to lower their per capita expenditures while also affecting their importance relative to other services, just as expected. On the other hand, for streets, libraries, parks, and refuse services, which in many cities are provided neither through contract nor city departments, the factors associated with contracting seem to have little effect.

Other Counties in California

Although contracting is not widespread among cities outside L.A. County, the city department structure is only one among a number of alternatives. Therefore, through use of the employment regression equations we can assess the factors related to use of city departments in the state of California and determine whether there are differences betweeen L.A. County and other counties in the state. This, in turn, will test the generality of the recursive model, which has so far been applied only to L.A. County.

The California sample includes 72 cities in L.A. County and 42 cities in five other California counties, including 9 cities in Alameda County, 7 in Contra Costa County, 12 in Orange County, 8 in Santa Clara County, and 6 in Ventura County. Each of these 42 cities had a 1970 population of at least 10,000 persons.

Table 4-11 indicates that the budgets of cities in L.A. County are very like the budgets of cities in other counties. In spite of significant differences between the two groups of cities in the various community characteristics (age, education, distance from central city, and Spanish-surname population), there are only two budget variables that are significantly different: the city budget property tax rate and property tax revenues per capita are significantly lower in L.A. County cities than in other cities.

As shown in Table 4-12, Step I, the recursive model does not explain the extent of use of city departments in cities outside L.A. County as well as it explains their use in cities within the county. In L.A. County cities and in other cities the extent of use of city departments increases significantly as a result of increases in the taste for local control. Thus it would seem that cities outside L.A. County will also use nondepartment structures when their taste for local control is low, even if contract structures are not readily available. However, unlike cities in L.A. County, the size of the commercial sales and property tax base in other cities does not seem to affect the extent of use of city departments.

Among both L.A. County cities and other cities, increases in the use of city departments raise the property tax rate. However, in L.A. County cities a declining property tax base tends to raise the tax rate, while in other cities it is a declining commercial sales base which has this result. It appears that in L.A. County the emphasis on contracting as an alternative to city departments is related to a desire for lowering the property tax rate; however, outside L.A. County the emphasis on other alternatives is related to a desire to reduce the government charges imposed on commercial sales.

Both in L.A. County and in other counties, budget expenditures increase significantly as a result of increases in the property base, the commercial sales base, the property tax rate, and the extent of reliance on city departments. Thus it appears that the more extensive contracting in L.A. County does not result in the L.A. County cities having different levels of expenditures than other California cities. It would seem to be the case that adherence to the city department

Table 4-11. Mean Values for Selected Variables in California and Cities Outside L.A. County

		Mean values		
Selected Variables	Units of measure	114 Cities in Calif.	42 Cities Outside Los Angeles	L.A. County Cities less Non-L.A. County Cities
City budget property tax rate	%	1.02	1.27	-0.40[a]
City budget expenditures per capita	$	121	124	-4
Commercial sales per capita	$	2,704	2,267	692
Property tax base per capita	$	3,238	2,992	389
City government employees	per 1,000 people	5.2	5.4	-.3
Property rates per capita	$	30	36	-10
Median age	years	28.3	27.3	1.6[b]
Distance from central city	miles	12.6	9.7	4.7[a]
Spanish surname share of population	%	16.8	12.9	6.1[a]
Median education	years	12.2	12.7	-0.9[a]
Service expenditures per capita:				
Police	$	24	23	2
Fire	$	15	15	0
Streets	$	22	21	1
Garbage	$	4	3	1
Parks & recreation	$	14	14	0
Libraries	$	3	3	0
Service employees per 1000 persons:				
Police	no.	1.2	1.3	-.2[b]
Fire	no.	.8	.9	-.1
Streets	no.	.5	.5	.0
Garbage	no.	.2	.2	.0
Parks & recreation	no.	.7	.6	.1
Libraries	no.	.2	.2	.0

[a] Statistically significant at 5 percent probability level.
[b] Statistically significant at 10 percent probability level.

structure raises expenditures; that contracting is one way to escape the city department and thereby reduce expenditures, but that there are other structures which will do the same, particularly for cities outside L.A. County.

As shown in Table 4-13, for both L.A. County cities and other cities increases of total budget expenditures and in service-specific employment tend to increase budget expenditures for the service. However, only in L.A. County does the size of the property tax rate affect the specific service expenditures. This again seems to reflect the efforts of L.A. County propertyowners to reduce their budgeted property tax rates, even if it means spending less for important services.

Table 4-12. Estimated Regressions for City Budgets in California and Cities Outside L.A. County

Estimated coefficients

	Depend. variable	CONSTANT	LOUTLET	LVALUE	EDUC	SPAN	AGE	DIST	TOT-PC	TAX-RATE
California cities (N = 114)										
Step I: Contracting $R^2 = 0.55$ $F = 21.46$ $DF = 6, 106$	TOTPC	−25.87	1.27[a]	1.55[a]	0.01	−0.01	0.34[a]	−0.02		
Step II: Revenues $R^2 = 0.55$ $F = 18.19$ $DF = 7, 105$	TAXRATE	3.82	−0.10	−0.69[a]	0.24	0.01	−0.02	−0.00	0.18	
Step III: Expenditures $R^2 = 0.88$ $F = 95.60$ $DF = 10, 102$	LEXPTOT	−0.54	0.15[a]	0.48[a]	−0.02	0.00	0.00	−0.00	0.05[a]	0.26[a]
Cities outside L.A. (N = 42)										
Step I: Contracting $R^2 = 0.34$ $F = 3.00$ $DF = 6, 35$	TOTPC	−20.92	1.06	0.71	0.52	0.06	0.21[a]	−0.06		
Step II: Revenues $R^2 = 0.65$ $F = 8.92$ $DF = 7, 34$	TAXRATE	10.35	−0.46[a]	−0.55	−0.23	−0.00	0.02	−0.00	0.23[a]	
Step III: Expenditures $R^2 = 0.91$ $F = 40.56$ $DF = 8, 33$	LEXPTOT	0.77	0.14[a]	0.24[a]	0.03	0.00	−0.00	0.00	0.11	0.14[a]

[a]Statistically significant at 5 percent level without direction predicted.

Table 4-13. Estimated Regressions for Specific Service Expenditures in California and Cities Outside L.A. County Including employment effects

Estimated coefficients

Dep. Variable	CONSTANT	LOUTLET	LVALUE	EDUC	SPAN	AGE	DIST	TOTPC	TAXRATE	LEXPTOT	SERV. PC
California cities ($N = 114$, $DF = 102$)											
$R^2 = 0.77$ $F = 33.85$ LEXPOL	−0.59	0.05	0.21[a]	−0.05	0.00	0.01	0.00	0.01	0.10[b]	0.37[a]	0.16[a]
$R^2 = 0.80$ $F = 41.39$ LEXFIRE	−4.13	0.15	−0.03	0.09	0.01	−0.01	−0.01	0.03	0.48[a]	0.68[a]	0.73[a]
$R^2 = 0.58$ $F = 13.93$ LEXHIGH	−0.07	0.09	−0.52[a]	−0.06	−0.01	0.02[b]	−0.01	−0.12[a]	−0.24[a]	1.62[a]	0.26
$R^2 = 0.33$ $F = 5.08$ LEXGARB	2.36	−0.18	−0.55	−0.01	0.00	−0.05[b]	0.02	0.12[b]	−0.41[b]	1.07[a]	0.84[a]
$R^2 = 0.59$ $F = 14.80$ LEXPARK	−1.17	0.17[b]	−0.18	0.14	0.00	−0.01	−0.01	0.02	0.05	0.41	0.53[a]
$R^2 = 0.49$ $F = 9.70$ LEXLIB	4.03	−0.16	−0.28	−0.17	−0.02[b]	−0.04	−0.02	0.03	−0.50[a]	0.72	2.92[a]
Cities outside L.A. ($N = 42$, $DF = 31$)											
$R^2 = 0.77$ $F = 10.58$ LEXPOL	1.31	0.09	−0.25	0.02	−0.01	−0.00	0.00	−0.02	−0.01	0.55[a]	0.36[a]
$R^2 = 0.80$ $F = 12.35$ LEXFIRE	−4.68	−0.02	0.12	−0.07	0.03	−0.02	−0.01	−0.17	−0.13	1.48[b]	1.71[a]
$R^2 = 0.29$ $F = 1.26$ LEXHIGH	1.12	0.03	−0.20	0.05	0.00	0.02	0.01	−0.04	0.03	0.43	0.21
$R^2 = 0.53$ $F = 3.52$ LEXGARB	−5.01	−0.48	0.46	−0.22	0.02	−0.08	0.01[b]	−0.02	−0.89[a]	2.39[b]	2.05[a]
$R^2 = 0.65$ $F = 5.81$ LEXPARK	−0.82	−0.34	−0.14	−0.01	0.01	−0.02	−0.02[b]	−0.09	−0.15	1.60[b]	1.02[a]
$R^2 = 0.69$ $F = 6.82$ LEXLIB	1.43	−0.54	0.27	−0.04	0.00	−0.19[a]	0.02	−0.08	−0.64	1.53	5.28

[a] Statistically significant at 5 percent level without direction prediction.
[b] Statistically significant at 10 percent level without direction prediction.

In general, then, it seems that the recursive model explains reasonably well the budgeted property tax rate, the total budget expenditures, and the budgeted police and fire expenditures both for cities in L.A. County and for other cities in the state. In addition, if we are seeking to explain the extent to which cities use structures other than city departments, the model performs reasonably well for cities like those in L.A. County, which tend to use the contracting alternative.

❋ Chapter Five

The Case of Police: Chief or Sheriff

POLICE CONTRACTING: ISSUES AND TRENDS

Many of the perceptions about service contracting in Los Angeles County are based on the issues and trends that have evolved for police contracting. In Chapter 3, for example, it was shown that new incorporations were encouraged by availability of police contracting; that contract pricing and subsidy controversies were essentially a debate over the proper charge for police patrol units; that the decentralization of service delivery as adopted by the L.A. County Sheriff's Department has been duplicated by other county departments; that the countywide law enforcement responsibilities of the sheriff are an important component of the efforts to consolidate service delivery on a countywide basis. Similarly, in Chapter 4, it was shown how a low tax base favors contracting, including police contracting, and that total budget as well as police expenditures per capita were lower in contract cities. In Chapter 2 it was indicated that city managers did not expect a significant trend toward either policy contracting or contracting in general; that in spite of the potential for economies of scale, police contracting and contracting in general were thought to be less efficient than city departments; and that both police contracting and contracting in general ranked low in terms of quality of service, sensitivity to community needs, and the confidence of citizens.

It seems clear that attitudes held about contracting as a structure for service delivery in general are largely influenced by the specifics of contracting as a structure for delivering the police service. This is not surprising in view of the large role of law enforcement in most city budgets, and the dominating role of police contracting in contract services offered by Los Angeles County.

For these reasons we have selected law enforcement to more precisely assess the validity of the claims made for and against contracting. Is contracting less efficient than city department? Does it lead to lower levels of expenditures? Does it result in greater similarity of service delivery? These are some of the questions for which reliable, quantitative responses are essential, and which we seek to answer with this case study of police contracting.

Police contracting in L.A. County has arrived at an important juncture. The number of cities contracting has remained fairly stable, and the rate of turnover has been low in the last decade. Two contracting cities recently formed their own departments, while a third elected to contract for police services from a neighboring city.

Despite the stability in the number of participants, contract cities have shown signs of increasing restlessness with the L.A. County Sheriffs' Department (LASD). One of the major concerns in the past has been contract prices. Although agreed-upon pricing formulas have now reduced this source of contention for the future, the price controversy has had the effect of stimulating contract cities to inquire seriously about the desirability of the county as a supplier of police services and about alternative arrangements available for providing law enforcement.

It has been argued that one beneficial effect of the contract structure has been to increase the LASD internal evaluation of its own performance. It is suggested that, since contract cities demand such evaluations, the LASD is encouraged to generate and provide such information in order to retain its present customers and attract new ones.

The LASD collects considerable data and undertakes numerous statistical analyses. Since 1973 the department's Regional Allocation of Police Services Program (RAPS) has regularly made available to contract cities information dealing with crimes committed, response time, calls for service, preventive patrol, arrests, and cases handled. In addition, other data, such as successful prosecutions and cases filed, are made available upon request. These data have considerably improved the capability of contract city managers to evaluate how well their cities are being policed.

Although participation in the contract services plan has remained relatively stable over the last decade, contract city managers do consider adopting alternative ways to deliver law-enforcement services. This continuous threat of withdrawal, combined with the growing concern for cost and effectiveness, has induced the LASD to revise delivery policies in certain station areas, revisions that could strengthen its attractiveness to both present and potential customers.

The principal innovation is regional policing, which currently involves three district stations (Lakewood, Norwalk, and Temple) and encompasses 14 of the 30 contract cities. Each of these three stations serves a total of 200,000 to 300,000 population, thus representing a sizeable urban area. In regional policing, the entire station area is treated as a single patrol district, and patrol units are deployed according to crime and service-call patterns rather than according to city or unincorporated district boundaries. Regional deployment has also been accompanied by increased specialization in the patrol function. The cost of the service is shared by each city on the basis of its ranking in terms of the seven major crimes, its calls for services, its assessed property valuation, its geographic area, and its population. The cost-sharing formula is agreed upon by the cities involved and is slightly different for each station.

Although decentralization of LASD activities would probably have occurred in any event, contracting hastened the process and shaped the particular form of regionalization that it has taken. In recent years, the LASD has advocated the consolidation of small city departments into a regional police services district with a separate taxing authority and with control in the hands of the sheriff. Police chiefs and city managers of independent cities, according to the interviews in Chapter 2, hesitate to give the sheriff such control. The LASD, on the other hand, sees the current experiment in regional law enforcement as an important stride in the direction of full-scale county consolidation.

A second development with potentially important ramifications for contracting is exemplified by the newly incorporated city of Rancho Palos Verdes, which has entered into a kind of performance contract with the LASD. Rather than merely purchasing a given quantity of inputs, the city has stipulated certain desired objectives, such as reduced crime and traffic accident rates, which the LASD has agreed to attempt to meet, even though it cannot be legally bound to meet them. The terms of the agreement were negotiated bilaterally, and both parties agreed that the terms were reasonable and attainable given the manpower level purchased by the city.

The potential for this type of agreement to affect the relationship between the LASD and contract cities could be quite extensive. For example, a city manager could become involved with arrest policies, response time, the handling of juveniles and drunks, and patrol deployment policies within the city. In essence, performance contracting permits service standards to be set by both the city and the LASD rather than unilaterally by the LASD; in addition, the contract city is provided with better information to evaluate daily performance of the provider.

Thus the LASD is experimenting and probing in new and fundamentally diverse directions. Regional policing seeks to move away from contracting toward the consolidated regional police service district envisioned by the LASD. Performance contracting seeks to tie contracting expenditures to the quantity and quality of law enforcement service received. The current regional policing plan tends to dilute the direct control of the individual contract cities, and the proposed police services district might eliminate it entirely. The performance contract experiment would tend to strengthen local control over the LASD's policing activities, in part because more adequate evaluative criteria could be established.

Improved evaluations of service delivery depend on developing indicators of output produced by the police agency and relating such indicators to the objectives of law enforcement and the resources needed to produce the outputs. A listing of indicators of service performance distinguishing among final output, intermediate output, workload, and service quality indicators for each of the four major police services is presented in Table 5-1. The footnotes to Table 5-1 indicate the current and likely future availability of data to implement each indicator.

SOME STATISTICAL COMPARISONS OF POLICE SERVICE IN CONTRACT AND INDEPENDENT CITIES

Having identified some indicators for evaluating police service delivery, we can now examine whether contract and independent cities have different levels for these indicators. The variables used in these comparisons are listed and defined in Table 5-2. The data for fiscal year 1968/69 are shown in Table 5-3. The specific indicators are grouped according to whether they are output, input, expenditure, or productivity indicators. For each indicator the mean values for the contract cities and the independent cities are shown, and whether or not the difference between these two groups of cities is statistically significant is indicated.

Table 5-3 indicates that in 1968/69 the extent of property crime and arrests for property offenses was essentially the same for contract cities, on the average, as for independent cities, on the average. However, violent crimes were significantly higher in contract cities, and the probability of arrest for such crimes was significantly lower. Most violent crimes and arrests relate to aggregated assaults for which there is no Penal Code definition. As a result, the difference in violent crimes between the contract and independent cities may be mostly attributable to differential reporting practices. Since there is some indication that the LASD tends to report felony aggravated assaults in some cases where the independent cities would report misdemeanors,[1] we have been particularly cautious in interpreting the statistical results as they relate to violent crimes.

Even if the violent crime differences are real and not caused by a reporting artifact, when per capita property and violent crimes or arrests are combined, there is no significant difference between contract and independent cities in these overall measures of police output. Yet the independent cities had, on the average, a significantly higher per capita expenditure for police services than contract cities. As a result, independent cities spent significantly more than contract cities relative to the crimes committed and arrests made—twice as much for each property crime or arrest and three times as much for each violent crime and arrest.

Independent cities not only spent more per capita than contract cities in 1968/69 but also had significantly more sworn officers on their force. Both

---

1. See the section entitled "A Note on Crime and Arrest Data" later in this chapter.

Table 5-1. Indicators Important for Assessing Police Performance

Police service	Final output	Intermediate outputs	Workload indicators	Quality measures
Crime repression (patrol, answer calls for service [CFS])	Crimes deterred[c] Social loss saving[c] Victimizations prevented[c]	Crime rates[a] Victimization rates[b] Average response time[b] On-scene arrests[d]	Calls for service answered, by type[b] Street miles patrolled[b] Suspicious persons/vehicles checked[e] On-view criminal cases detected Court appearances	Percentage of callers satisfied[b] Patrol frequency[d] Fear of crime[b] Crime seriousness index[b]
Crime investigation and apprehension	Crimes deterred[c]	Arrest rates[a] Clearance rates[b] Filing rate[a,b] Conviction rate[a,b]	Crime cases handled[d] Arrests or citations[b] Bookings[d] Warrants served Follow-up investigation[d] Court appearances[d]	Property recovered[b] Length of investigation
Traffic safety and control (traffic patrol; accident investigation)	Traffic accidents (TA's) prevented[c] Safety level[e] Congestion[e]	TA accident rate[a]	Citations issued[b] TAs investigated Street miles patrolled[b] Arrests[b] Accident reports written	Traffic accident investigation policy[b] TA reporting policy[b]
Community services; community relations	Community cooperation with police[b] Percentage of crimes unreported[d]	Response time to noncrime CFS[b]	Incidents handled[b]	Citizen satisfaction with police[b]

[a] Data available.
[b] Data collected or being collected by survey or interview.
[c] Data can be generated by statistical estimation.
[d] Data to be collected in future.
[e] Data unavailable and unlikely to be generated.

Table 5-2. Description of Variables

Source	Variable designation	Definition
a	VOLT	Total number of reported violent offenses (homicide, assault, rape).
a	PRPTY	Total number of reported property offenses (robbery, burglary, larceny, auto theft).
a,e	VIOL	Violent offenses per 1,000 population (homicide, assault, rape); violent crime rate.
a,e	PROP	Property offenses per 1,000 population (robbery, burglary, larceny, auto theft); property crime rate.
a	VARST	Ratio arrests for violent offenses to reported violent offenses; violent crime arrest probability.
a	PARST	Ratio arrests for property offenses to reported property offenses; property crime arrest probability.
a	VIOL-ARST	Total arrests for violent offenses.
a,e	ARSTVPC	Arrests for violent offenses per capita, violent crime arrest.
a	PROP-ARST	Total arrests for property offenses.
a,e	ARSTPPC	Arrests for property offenses per capita; property crime arrest rate.
c,d	ACDNTS	Fatal and injury traffic accident rate per street mile.
b	EXPEND	Total police expenditures.
b,e	EXPD	Police expenditures per capita.
f,g	PATROL	Total street patrol officers (including traffic enforcement officers).
f,g,e	PATROLPC	Street patrol officers (including traffic enforcement officers) per capita.
f,g,c	PTDEN	Street patrol officers (including traffic enforcement officers) per street mile.
f,g,e	NONPT	Nonpatrol sworn police officers per 1,000 population.
f,g	SWORN	Total sworn police officers.
f,g	ONEMAN	One-man patrol units as percentage of total patrol units deployed.

Sources:
a. State of California, Bureau of Criminal Statistics, *Law Enforcement Extended Data 1968.*
b. State of California, Office of State Controller, *Annual Report of Financial Transactions Concerning Cities of California, 1968-1969.*
c. State of California, Division of Highways, *California County Roads and Streets, 1965.*
d. State of California, California Highway Patrol, *Fatal and Injury Motor Vehicle Traffic Accidents 1968.*
e. U.S. Bureau of the Census, *Census of Population: 1970 General Social and Economic Characteristics, California.*
f. Los Angeles County Department of the Sheriff, *Contract Patrol Services, 1968-69* (mimeo).
g. UCLA Special Survey of Independent Cities.

Table 5-3. Significance Test of Differences Between Means of Police Service Variables for Independent and Contract Cities, Fiscal Year 1968/1969

	Mean		Standard Deviation		
Variables	Independent cities (N = 46)	Contract cities (N = 26)	Independent cities	Contract cities	T-test[a]
Output					
VARST	0.736	0.379	0.354	0.20	4.84[a]
PARST	0.159	0.193	0.116	0.09	1.33[a]
VIOL-ARST	64.59	37.82	58.03	36.19	2.16[a]
ARSTVPC	0.973	2.45	0.63	5.19	1.95
PROP-ARST	222.74	139.46	165.2	127.75	1.11
ARSTPPC	3.61	10.94	2.55	30.22	1.68
ACDNTS	3.17	2.68	1.39	1.76	1.30
PROP	23.37	28.13	10.58	14.88	1.61
VIOL	1.556	3.679	1.53	2.46	2.26[a]
Expenditure					
EXPD	$ 25.62	$ 18.15	6.85	16.54	2.70[a]
EXPEND/SWORN (000's)	$ 19.33	$ 31.70	2.42	22.96	3.48[a]
EXPEND/VIOL-ARST (000's)	$ 33.65	$ 12.37	15.53	13.55	5.80[a]
EXPEND/PROP-ARST (000's)	$ 9.18	$ 4.02	4.31	4.35	4.90[a]
EXPEND/VOLT (000's)	$ 25.21	$ 6.50	19.93	9.28	4.50[a]
EXPEND/PRPTY (000's)	$ 1.26	$ 0.687	0.63	0.54	3.30[a]
Input					
PATROLPC	0.746	0.366	0.22	0.35	5.85[a]
PTDEN	0.324	0.124	0.105	0.08	8.58[a]
NONPT	0.584	0.218	0.17	0.14	10.46[a]
ONEMAN	80.43	51.0	30.94	16.32	4.46[a]
Productivity					
VIOL-ARST/PATROL	1.34	4.95	0.80	3.92	10.58[a]
PROP-ARST/PATROL	4.73	17.05	2.32	9.01	10.80[a]
VOLT/PATROL	2.15	11.57	1.83	6.97	19.56[a]
PRPTY/PATROL	32.74	87.52	14.67	26.86	11.00[a]

[a]Indicates statistically significant difference between independent and contracting cities at 0.05 percent level.

[b]The NONPT variable is not strictly comparable between the two classes of cities, since in independent cities it includes sworn officers who perform non-detective duties, whereas in contract cities it includes only detectives.

street patrol officers and nonpatrol sworn officers per capita and per street mile were higher in the independent cities. In part this is because independent cities utilize one-man patrol units to a significantly greater extent than contract cities.

Since independent city per capita expenditures were 40 percent higher than in contract cities and the number of sworn officers per capita was over twice as high, the expenditures per sworn officer were significantly higher in contract than in independent cities. This may be attributable to higher wages in the LASD or that some independent cities do not include retirement costs in the police budget. It may also be the case that the LASD has a larger support staff or that some of the support activities recorded by the LASD were performed by sworn officers in the independent cities, which would account for some of their relatively high sworn officer and patrol inputs.

In 1968/69 there were significantly more crimes and arrests per patrol officer in contract cities than in independent cities. So even though contract cities were getting a greater return per dollar, in the sense that their expenditure per crime and per arrest was lower, contract cities also seemed to be getting a smaller return in terms of crime deterrence, since their crime-per-patrol-officer ratio was significantly higher than for the independent cities. This lower ratio of crime per officer may signify a lower efficiency in LASD because less crime is being deterred; alternatively it can be perceived as higher efficiency because more cases are being "handled" by the average LASD deputy than by the average independent city police officer.

These simple comparisons between the groups of contract cities and independent cities raise several important questions. Does contracting for police services result in lower costs? If so, is the saving achieved at the expense of potentially lower crime rates? Does contracting affect crime and arrest rates, perhaps differently for property and violent crimes? Does contracting affect police productivity? For answers to such questions, a simple comparison of group means is not sufficient. Rather, we must turn to a more elaborate analysis of police performance.

MODELS OF POLICE PERFORMANCE

Chapter 4 showed that, on average, contract cities tend to be smaller and to have lower expenditure and tax levels than do independent cities. This suggests that contract cities might be characterized as having residents with relatively homogeneous tastes for public services—they prefer the mix of lower expenditures and fewer services even though this might mean lower levels and quality of service output. In Chapter 3 it was indicated that proponents of contract law enforcement, and of police service consolidation in general, argue that such arrangements benefit the entire metropolitan area by providing a minimum service level in all areas served and by increasing the similarity of police services provided to all areas. In addition, these proponents argue that such structures reduce the interjurisdictional spillovers within a metropolitan area, thereby improving resource allocation and effectiveness of service delivery for the metropolitan area as a whole. For these reasons it has been argued that contracting results in lower police expenditures and greater efficiency than would be obtained if each independent jurisdiction maintained its own police department.

The Los Angeles County Sheriff's Department currently sells police services to contract cities on the condition that the contract city purchase at least a minimum service level, which is defined to be "at the same level as provided to unincorporated areas plus additional patrol service for general law enforcement and/or traffic law enforcement at the level desired by the contract city" [cited in E12, p. 2-2]. Thus the level of service provided to unincorporated areas represents an acceptable minimum. However, the LASD does not specify what constitutes police service when determining the minimum level, what level is provided to unincorporated areas, or how a comparison between contract cities and unincorporated areas can be made. Therefore, the procedure for determining minimum service levels has been for each station captain to analyze the policing needs of the contract city and come to some judgment, usually in consultation with city officials. Currently the LASD is attempting to systematically introduce more information into this process by implementing the "Field Unit Requirement" formula devised by Booz, Allen, and Hamilton to determine patrol needs [E2]. This procedure uses historical and current data on the factors determining workloads in the community, which are then used to determine patrol requirements.

Any empirical test of the existence and importance of the minimum service level depends on how this level is defined and measured. If it is defined as output (crime prevention, for example), then two contract cities with widely divergent socioeconomic and physical characteristics may require a considerably different number of patrol units to achieve an equal amount of crime prevention. Conversely, if it is defined as input (such as patrol units), and each city purchases the minimum, then the amount of crime prevention in each could differ considerably.

It is important to note that there is fairly widespread agreement among police officials that policing standards (minimum or otherwise) can be objectively determined. Booz, Allen, and Hamilton presented a fairly comprehensive set of standards, such as maximum response time, minimum time available for officer-initiated activities, minimum number of crime stops, minimum patrol unit visibility, and 24-hour traffic investigation capability [E2]. Despite this agreement, however, such standards are not widespread in most medium-size police departments [E2, Appendix C], and often not present in very large cities [F3]. Input- and output-level differences are still likely to be great.

The notion of a minimum level of police services is very closely related to the concern with an equitable distribution of the police service benefits. This is true even though recent studies, partly in response to court cases challenging the distribution of police and other municipal services, have analyzed the distribution of officers and other inputs rather than the distribution of benefits. Even if benefit or output data were available, however, difficult questions would still be encountered in determining an equity rule. For example, if in distributing police protection the sheriff chooses an equity rule that seeks to equalize the (marginal) amounts of crime reduction in each city or area, this probably would result in a higher crime rate than if he tried to minimize the average crime rate throughout the country. Clearly the choice of an equity rule can conflict with the choice of a minimum service rule.

Insofar as the data permit, we have incorporated both input and output measures to determine how the minimum service level is defined, and then sought to determine whether service levels are more similar among the areas policed by the LASD than among independent cities. We have also attempted to determine whether the service level provided in the LASD area exceeds the average service level provided in independent cities; whether the actual level of service provided to contract cities exceeds the levels that would be provided if they were to behave like independent cities with their own police departments; and whether the service provided to contract cities exceeds that provided in unincorporated areas.

To summarize, there are four hypotheses tested in the following sections:

1. Contracting is expected to result in greater similarity of police service output and expenditures than results from self-provision through independent cities. (This is found not to be the case.)
2. Such factors as community wealth, crime rates, population density, and traffic accidents are expected to influence the number of patrol officers in a city. But, independent of these factors, contracting is expected to lower the amount of patrol personnel provided. (This is shown to occur.)
3. Contracting is expected to result in lower police expenditures per capita even after taking account of the effects on expenditure of those same factors which influence amounts of patrol personnel. (The data confirm this expectation.)
4. Contracting is not expected to significantly affect crime rates. (The results are mixed. Holding constant other factors affecting crime rates, contracting does not significantly affect property crimes and raises violent crimes. However, when coupled with lower manpower, contracting raises both property and violent crimes.)

An Analysis of Similarity of Service Delivery

One way to examine whether the LASD promotes similarity in the delivery of service is to test whether the variation among independent cities is different from the variation among contract cities. If it is not, then the degree of similarity in delivery would be no greater among areas served by the LASD than among other areas.

Table 5-4 reports the comparison for selected variables. The variables whose variance among contract cities is significantly different from that among independent cities are essentially the same variables whose means are significantly different, as reported in Table 5-3. For three of the output variables—violent crimes, arrests for violent crimes, and arrests for property crimes—the variation is greater in contract cities. For two other output variables—the ratio of violent arrests to crimes, and arrests for violent offenses—variation is greater in independent cities. It cannot be concluded from these data that contracting has the effect of standardizing police output among the areas serviced by the LASD.

The standardizing effect is made even more questionable by the finding that expenditure per capita is more variable among contract cities than among independent cities. The greater variability in per capita expenditures suggests that preferences for police services are less homogeneous among contract cities than independent cities. This evidence does not support the assumption that production of police services by a single supplier will increase the similarity of service levels among cities. Contract cities appear to have greater flexibility in their expenditure levels than independent cities. Independent cities, perhaps because most police departments have considerable influence over the budget process, come to more similar expenditure decisions than do contract cities, even though

Table 5-4. Significance Test of Difference in Variance of Police Service Variables for Contract and Independent Cities, Fiscal Year 1968/69

Variables	Independent cities ($N_1 = 46$)	Contract cities ($N_2 = 26$)	F-Value[a]
VARST	0.125	0.040	3.19*
PARST	0.014	0.008	1.72
VIOL-ARST	3,367	1,310	2.53*
ARSTVPC	0.404	26.915	0.015*
PROP-ARST	27,290	16,320	1.64
ARSTPPC	6.50	913.01	0.007*
PROP	111.98	221.43	0.50
VIOL	2.35	6.06	0.38*
ACDNTS	1.92	3.09	0.61
EXPD	$ 46.89	$273.70	0.171*
EXPEND/SWORN	$245.85	$527.26	0.011*
EXPEND/VIOL-ARST	$241.30	$183.60	1.29
EXPEND/PROP-ARST	$ 18.58	$ 18.90	0.96
EXPEND/VOLT	$397.35	$ 96.20	4.53*
EXPEND/PRPTY	$ 0.39	$ 0.29	1.33
PATROLPC	0.049	0.122	0.39*
PTDEN	0.011	0.007	1.57
NONPT	0.031	0.021	1.48
ONEMAN	957.23	266.40	3.59*

[a]The asterisk denotes F-values that do not fall within the range to accept the null hypothesis, which is from 2.29 to 0.44.

the LASD is a common provider for contracted police services. Also, the difference in variance for expenditures per sworn officer is significantly greater among contract cities than independent cities. This result is somewhat puzzling, since we would expect comparable expenditures per officer in the area served by the LASD. One explanation may be that station overhead charges vary considerably among the various stations of the LASD.

To further examine whether comparable levels of service are provided by the LASD, we compared police outputs of unincorporated areas and contract cities. Data for four output variables in unincorporated areas are available, and the differences in means and variances for these variables are shown in Table 5-5.

Unincorporated areas show a significantly higher average property crime arrest probability and a larger variance in violent crime arrest probability than do contract cities. But the means and the variance of violent and property crimes are similar among contract cities and the unincorporated places. It seems to be the case that although there is considerable variability in output among contract cities and also among unincorporated areas, the LASD provides similarity in services between the contract cities taken as a group and the unincorporated areas taken as a group. Thus we conclude that, although contracting does not result in greater similarity among cities than does self-provision, it does result in services provided to the less urbanized areas becoming more similar to the services provided in contract cities. Since, as has been earlier noted, the service provided in unincorporated areas is perceived as an acceptable minimal standard, then either contract cities tend to move down toward the minimum or the standard adopted for unincorporated areas tends to be raised to the contract city levels.

Even if richer data were available, the simple tests performed above can provide only limited evidence about the differences in police output between contracting and self-provision. The relationships between police inputs and crime prevention, accident prevention, accident investigation, crime investigation, and

Table 5-5. Significance Test of Differences in Means and Variances of Variables for Unincorporated Areas and Contract Cities, Fiscal Year 1968/69

	Mean		Variance			
	Unincorporated areas ($N = 14$)	Contract cities ($N = 26$)	Unincorporated areas	Contract cities	t-value	F-value
VARST	0.448	0.379	0.002	0.040	1.25	0.049[b]
PARST	0.253	0.193	0.005	0.008	2.21[a]	0.61
VIOL	4.63	3.679	7.74	6.06	1.13	1.25
PROP	27.785	28.13	210.19	221.43	0.07	0.93

[a] Statistically significant at the 0.01 level.
[b] Statistically significant at the 0.05 level.

other police services are complicated and relatively unknown. Clearly more empirical testing is called for.

For example, we reported in Table 5-3 that the violent crime rate is significantly higher in contract than in independent cities, but that the property crime rate is not. This conclusion was based on a statistical test of the difference between the means of these variables for the two groups of cities. But suppose we asked whether crimes are distributed between contract and independent cities in the same way as population is distributed. On the basis of the chi-square test, Table 5-6 indicates that the distribution between contract and independent cities of property crimes and of violent crimes is significantly different from the population distribution. Furthermore, independent cities, on the basis of this calculation, have a significantly lower share of both violent and property crimes than they have of population not only for violent crimes, as earlier reported, but also for property crimes.

Although there is not much reason to expect crime to be distributed according to population levels, the chi-square test does indicate that a simple test of means should be supplemented by other tests seeking to account for differences in population characteristics and physical makeup of the two groups of cities that might explain observed differences in output, input, and effectiveness.

An Analysis of Patrol Personnel Levels

Patrol personnel is the most important input to the police service. In an effort to determine what factors might affect personnel levels, we computed simple correlation coefficients for 29 contract cities; the results are shown in Table 5-7.

Table 5-7 shows that total man-hours are positively correlated with total felony violations and with total felony arrests. However, there is no significant correlation between man-hours input and crime or arrest rates. Since it is difficult to believe that more patrol man-hours generate more crime (unless crime-reporting is positively related to patrol man-hours), it seems safe to conclude that the LASD determines city needs for personnel input more on the basis of

Table 5-6. Chi-Square Test of Crime Rate Differences, Fiscal/Year 1968/69

	Independent cities		Contract cities		Totals of actuals	Contract city percent of actuals
	Actual	Expected	Actual	Expected		
Property crimes *(PRPTY)*[a]	1,568	1,822	682	427	2,250	30.3%
Violent crimes *(VOLT)*[b]	104	158	91	37	195	46.7%
Population (000)[c]	3,049		700		3,749	18.7%

[a] For property crimes: Chi² = 187.
[b] For violent crimes: Chi² = 96.
[c] Both values exceed Chi² · 99 = 6.63.

Table 5-7. Simple Correlation Coefficients Between Inputs and Outputs in Contract Cities, Fiscal Year 1968/69

	(1) General and traffic patrol man-hours (annual)	(2) Ratio one-man to total patrol units per shift
Population	0.89	0.25
Total seven major felonies	0.92	0.33
Violent crimes (*VOLT*)	0.82	0.26
Property crimes (*PRPTY*)	0.93	0.33
Total felony arrests (*VIOL-ARST* & *PROP-ARST*)	0.87	0.32
Felony arrest rate (*ARSTVPC* & *ARSTPPC*)	0.17	0.09
Felony crime rate	−0.16	0.30
Violent crime rate (*VIOL*)	−0.18	0.28
Property crime rate (*PROP*)	−0.16	0.30

the total number of crimes and arrests, rather than the perhaps more meaningful rates of crimes and arrests per capita.

The relative use of one-officer patrol units seems unrelated to both total number of crimes or arrests and to rates of crime or arrests. These data clearly reflect the former LASD policy of assigning one-officer cars on day shifts and two-officer cars on evening and night shifts. A relatively high use of two-officer patrol cars appears to have been the source of a considerable proportion of the total cost to contract cities. For example, a Booz, Allen, and Hamilton study found that, merely through the use of one-officer patrol units, service goals could be achieved and costs reduced by almost 20 percent in contract cities [E2, p. 149].

It has earlier been shown that the average level of patrol officers per capita in contract cities is only half that in independent cities, whereas the variance in patrol officers per capita is three times greater in contract cities. These differences are statistically significant and suggest equally large variations in the factors influencing the demand for patrol and traffic officers. These factors include community income levels, physical aspects of the community, and factors affecting the demand for crime prevention and traffic safety. Therefore these factors have been incorporated in a model formulated to explain the variation in patrol officers per capita across cities.

The demand for patrol personnel can be viewed from the perspective of a conventional labor demand function, which indicates that the number of patrol officers employed depends on wage rates, community income or wealth, price of close substitutes and complements, demands for the police services, and variables reflecting workload normally handled by patrol or traffic officers. Data are available for both contract and independent cities on per capita assessed property valuation representing community wealth (*WEALTH*), property and violent crime rates (*PROP* and *VIOL*), fatal and injury traffic accidents per street mile (*ACDNTS*), and population density of the city (*DENSITY*).

The expected relationship between each of these variables and patrol officers per capita (*PATROLPC*) can be examined with some *a priori* reasoning. There are two kinds of effects associated with community wealth, and they would be expected to move in opposite directions. If we assume that publicly provided police services are a normal good, and that wealthier communities would tend to purchase more of all normal goods, then because of the income effect, *WEALTH* and *PATROLPC* should be positively related. However, privately provided protection is also likely to be a normal good and, if private efforts are viewed as more effective than public activities, wealthier communities may substitute private for public protection. This substitution effect would lead to a negative relation between *WEALTH* and *PATROLPC*. Although the relative strength of these two effects is unknown, it is believed that the income effect is more important than the substitution effect, so that the net effect of *WEALTH* on the demand for patrol officers is expected to be positive.

A variable used to represent the effect of the city's physical aspects on the demand for patrol officers is population density. As *DENSITY* increases, a fixed amount of police input can provide the greater population with the same (or a higher) level of some police services. For example, certain aspects of patrol, such as routine visible patrolling and answering calls for service, benefit an entire neighborhood no matter how many people live there. Thus, economies of density may exist and may be reflected in a negative association between *DENSITY* and *PATROLPC*. On the other hand, greater density also may stimulate higher crime rates, which would require more, rather than fewer, police officers. The net impact of *DENSITY* will depend on the strength of these two opposing effects. We expect the economies of density to dominate so that the relation between density and patrol officers is likely to be negative.

We would expect a positive relationship between workload and number of patrol officers. Three variables are used to represent the effect of workload on the demand for patrol officers—property and violent crime rates, each lagged one year, and fatal and injury traffic accidents per street mile. If it is assumed that crime rates and calls for service and arrests are highly correlated, then property and violent crime rates can be used as measures for the crime-related workload of the police. Offense rates are lagged one year because previous workload indicators are usually used to determine current manpower budget allocations. The injury traffic accident rate reflects traffic workload, since all such accidents customarily are reported and investigated by the police. Property damage accidents are not always investigated, although they are usually reported.

Lack of data for both contract and independent cities precluded testing the effect of other potentially important factors. One of the most important of these is the wage rate of patrol officers. (For other important variables, see F2 and F4). A negative relationship is expected between wage rates and number of patrol officers hired. Indeed, it has been suggested that one reason contract cities as a group hire fewer patrol officers may be traced to the relatively higher wages paid to sheriff's deputies as compared with patrol officers in small city departments. Since wage rates are invariant across contract cities, they cannot easily be used in a regression analysis seeking to compare contracting and other cities. However, we can compare the wage of the LASD with the wages of other law-enforcement agencies to assess which is higher. Comparative 1970 wages are shown in Table 5-8. It appears that the LASD pays lower starting salaries than the L.A. City Police Department. However, when compared with salaries in other cities the LASD pays somewhat more at the top of each rank but seem to be at the upper end of the range across cities for both the entry level and the top of each rank.

The basic model was estimated in linear form by ordinary least-squares as follows:

$$PATROLPC = \alpha + \beta_1(WEALTH) + \beta_2(PROP_{t-1}) + \beta_3(VIOL_{t-1}) + \beta_4(ACDNTS) + \beta_5(DENSITY) + \mu$$

It is anticipated that $\beta_1, \beta_2, \beta_3, \beta_4$, are positively, and β_5 is negatively related to the patrol officers per capita.

Table 5-8. Comparison of County and City Police Salaries

	Monthly salaries ($)			
			Range of other cities	
Rank	LASD	LAPD	High	Low
Chief				
Entry level	—	—	1,649	1,203
Top	3,297		2,000	1,463
Captain				
Entry level	1,170	1,306	1,292	941
Top	1,458	1,458	1,571	1,137
Lieutenant				
Entry level	992	1,007	1,063	856
Top	1,236	1,107	1,292	1,034
Sergeant				
Entry level	842	940	940	780
Top	1,048	1,048	1,063	941
Police officer				
Entry level	755	755	756	698
Top	889	839	918	844

[a]Other cities included: Inglewood, Monterey Park, Gardena, Whittier, Downey, Alhambra, Lynwood, Montebello, Compton, Vernon, South Gate, Hawthorne, and Bell.

Source: Holston, Billie. Proposed police department for city of Bell Gardens, 1970 (mimeo) p. 6.

The results obtained from testing this model are presented in Table 5-9, which shows four estimating equations: one for the sample of 42 independent cities; another for 26 contract cities; a third for independent and contract cities together; and a fourth that includes contracting as a dummy independent variable. The separate independent and contract city estimates in Table 5-9 tend to confirm *a priori* expectations; most of the signs are as predicted and the coefficients are statistically significant. Moreover, the high R^2s indicate that the model explains a sizeable proportion of the variation in patrol officers per capita (*PATROLPC*), although the strength of this conclusion is diminished somewhat by the likely effects of multi-colinearity in the estimated equations. As expected, the wealth, violent crime rate, and traffic accidents are all positively related to number of patrol officers. One result that runs contrary to expectations is the coefficient of the property crime rate, which is negative rather than positive as expected. It may be either that property offenses are not correlated with calls for service and other workload indicators, as assumed, or that the colinearity between property crime rate and the violent crime rate has created unstable parameter estimates.

Although the indicated variables significantly affect the number of per capita patrol officers in both contract and independent cities, the question remains as to whether the magnitude of their effects is similar. It turns out (as indicated by the statistical Chow test, which identifies whether there are differences between two sample populations such as independent and contract cities) that the effects are not similar. The influence of the same set of explanatory variables appears to differ between the contracting and independent cities. It is possible that the governmental structure accounts for some of the variation in patrol personnel levels.

We can examine the independent effect of contracting by pooling both sets of cities and reestimating the model with a dummy variable to represent whether a city contracts with the LASD for law enforcement. When this is done, as shown in Table 5-9, the contract structure is highly significant; the procedure indicates that, other things held constant, contract cities on average hire 0.48 fewer patrol officers per capita than do independent cities, a difference of over 60 percent. Thus, virtually all of the difference in the average patrol-officer-per-capita level between contract and independent cities that was shown in Table 5-3 is explained by whether a city does or does not contract, and not by the other factors influencing the demand for patrol officers.

It appears that either independent cities are employing more than the optimum number of patrol officers or contract cities are employing less than the optimal number. Or it may be that independent cities undertake a wider range of functions than the LASD provides to contract cities and, in that sense, is providing a higher quality of services.

Since patrol personnel inputs may be influenced by geographic factors, the patrol input variable was reformulated as patrol officer per street mile (*PTDEN*),

Table 5-9. Demand for Patrolmen Per Capita (PATROLPC), 1968/69 (t-ratios in parentheses)[a]

Equation/ sample	Dep. variable	CONSTANT	WEALTH	$PROP_{t-1}$	$VIOL_{t-1}$	ACDNTS	DENSITY	Contract structure	Correlation
46 independent cities	PATROLPC	0.407 (5.66)	0.00015 (9.35)	−0.00067 (.16)	0.027 (.95)	0.027 (1.77)	−0.000016 (1.49)		$R^2 = 0.72$ $SSR = 0.61657$ $N = 46$
26 contract	PATROLPC	0.370 (4.41)	0.00006 (5.30)	−0.016 (3.52)	0.036 (1.51)	0.096 (3.70)	−0.00003 (2.96)		$R^2 = 0.84$ $SSR = 0.433885$ $N = 25$
72 independent and contract cities	PATROLPC	0.530 (6.07)	0.000047 (4.79)	−0.0039 (.84)	−0.057 (2.09)	0.079 (3.27)	−0.000013 (1.16)		$R^2 = 0.93$ $SSR = 4.221$ $N = 71$
72 cities including structure variable	PATROLPC	0.736 (11.85)	0.00005 (7.52)	−0.0016 (3.79)	0.0405 (1.94)	0.056 (3.40)	0.000013 (1.63)	−.482 (8.94)	$R^2 = 0.93$ $SSR = 1.896$ $N = 71$

[a]Chow test: $F = \dfrac{0.6342}{0.0172} = 36.87$

and the model reestimated, with results shown in Table 5-10. The results are nearly identical to those for patrol officer per capita. Except for $VIOL_{t-1}$ in independent cities, and $PROP_{t-1}$ in contract cities, the signs are as anticipated and usually are statistically significant. Again, the Chow test indicates that the two samples are not drawn from the same population and, again, most of the difference (approximately 85 percent) in the mean *PTDEN* level between the two groups of cities is explained by the contract status of the community.

In summary, we find that if community wealth, crime rates, traffic accidents, and density are held constant in the two groups of cities, contract cities hire significantly fewer patrol personnel. Either LASD patrol officers are more productive than their independent city counterparts, or patrol officers perform fewer tasks in contract cities. Clearly, we need both more extensive information on the tasks performed by the two groups of officers and fuller output data, such as for calls for service, response time, clearances, and filing, to determine which of these is the case.

An Analysis of Expenditure Levels

Since the number of patrol officers deployed in contract cities is relatively low compared to that in independent cities, we would expect expenditures per capita also to be low. We have found that, in contract cities, expenditures per capita are about 30 percent less than in independent cities. Since labor costs constitute about 90 percent of police expenditures, we would expect that if the factors affecting the number of patrol officers in a city were held constant, the difference in per capita expenditures between contract and independent cities would be even greater than 30 percent. This expectation is fulfilled by Table 5-11, when expenditures per capita are regressed on the same set of explanatory variables that were used in the personnel equations.

For contracting cities, increases in wealth, violent crime rates, and traffic accident rates tend to raise police expenditures per capita, while increasing density and property crime rates tend to lower expenditures—just as they affected the number of patrol officers. For independent cities, increasing wealth and crime rates tend to raise expenditures per capita, while increases in traffic accidents and density tend to lower expenditures—which is a somewhat different effect than occurred for patrol officers. Thus there seem to be some differences between independent cities and contract cities, which is confirmed by the Chow test that shows that the independent cities are significantly different from the contract cities with respect to the factors affecting expenditures per capita.

When we seek to determine whether the contract structure can explain this difference, we find that it does. When the dummy variable *CONTRACT* is introduced, it is negative and highly significant. The regression coefficient indicates that expenditures per capita are, on the average, $13 less in contract cities, and

172 How Cities Provide Services

Table 5-10. Demand for Patrolmen Per Street Mile (*PTDEN*), 1968/69 (t-ratios in parentheses)[a]

Equation/ sample	Depend. variable	CONSTANT	WEALTH	$PROP_{t-1}$	$VIOL_{t-1}$	ACDNTS	DENSITY	Contract structure	Correlation
(10-A) 46 independent cities	PTDEN	0.024 (.62)	0.00004 (4.86)	0.001 (.45)	−0.0007 (.05)	0.031 (3.95)	0.0001 (2.29)		$R^2 = 0.64$ $SSR = 0.178$ $N = 46$
(10-B) 28 contract cities	PTDEN	0.070 (4.29)	0.00001 (4.99)	−0.005 (5.57)	0.010 (1.85)	0.034 (5.82)	0.000003 (1.26)		$R^2 = 0.83$ $SSR = 0.0213$ $N = 25$
(10-C) 72 independent and contract cities	PTDEN	0.107 (3.23)	0.000004 (1.00)	0.002 (1.22)	−0.041 (4.08)	0.045 (4.65)	0.000006 (1.35)		$R^2 = 0.43$ $SSR = 0.6641$ $N = 71$
(10-D) 72 cities including a structure variable	PTDEN	0.189 (7.00)	0.000005 (1.93)	−0.002 (1.34)	−0.0013 (.14)	0.037 (5.10)	0.000007 (2.00)	−0.174 (7.40)	$R^2 = 0.70$ $SSR = 0.3577$ $N = 71$

[a]Chow test: $F = \dfrac{0.09296}{0.00327} = 28.45$.

Table 5-11. Determinants of Police Expenditures Per Capita (*EXPD*), 1968/69 (t-ratios in parentheses)[a]

Equation/ sample	Depend. variable	CONSTANT	WEALTH	$PROP_{t-1}$	$VIOL_{t-1}$	ACDNTS	DENSITY	Contract structure	Correlation
(11-A) 46 independent cities	EXPD	14.99 (7.98)	0.005 (11.73)	0.122 (1.15)	1.145 (1.53)	-0.113 (0.30)	-.00064 (2.28)		$R^2 = 0.80$ SSR = 420.218 N = 46
26 contract cities	EXPD	16.605 (6.11)	0.0025 (7.41)	-0.900 (6.32)	2.11 (2.32)	4.50 (4.60)	-.0012 (3.24)		$R^2 = 0.97$ SSR = 610.91 N = 25
(11-C) 72 independent and contract cities	EXPD	21.438 (7.34)	0.0013 (4.05)	-0.164 (1.13)	-0.944 (1.08)	2.45 (2.89)	-0.0007 (1.69)		$R^2 = 0.77$ SSR = 5112.6 N = 71
(11-D) 72 cities including a structure variable	EXPD	27.62 (10.59)	0.0014 (5.41)	-0.452 (3.53)	2.04 (2.33)	1.83 (2.63)	-0.00065 (1.94)	-13.18 (5.82)	$R^2 = 0.85$ SSR = 3345.12 N = 71

[a]Chow test: $F = \dfrac{816.3}{16.9} = 48.3$

that the difference is due to the contract structure.[2] Since contract cities, on the average, spend about $18 per capita on police services, while independent cities spent about $25.50, almost as much is "saved" in contract cities as is spent. Further, since the actual differences between contract and independent cities is about $7.50, while the difference attributable to contracting is $13, there must be a number of other factors present that tend to raise expenditures in contract cities while lowering them in independent cities.

Analysis of Difference in Output Levels

What of the differences in output levels for police services in contract and independent cities? Do lower input levels in part lead to higher crime rates, lower arrest rates, or other indicators of poor quality of service? Or are independent cities simply "overpoliced," in the sense that their greater expenditures do not result in important gains in output?

When variables meant to represent output levels were analyzed above, the simple tests of difference in means indicated that only rates of violent crime are significantly higher in contract cities. However, the significant difference in patrol personnel and expenditure levels in the two groups of cities and the failure of workload and other factors to fully explain these differences suggest that lower output quality might be the end result in contract cities. Thus, an attempt was made to determine whether the factors affecting property and violent crime rates are significantly different in the two groups of cities and, if so, whether such differences are due to variations in factors related or unrelated to a city's contract status.

We have sought to explain the variation in property crimes per capita and violent crimes per capita across the two groups of cities by using assorted police inputs and service condition variables in regression equations, as follows:

$$PROP = \alpha + \beta_{11} (PATROLPC) + \beta_{12} (ONEMAN) + \beta_{13} (POOR) + \beta_{14} (NW) + \beta_{15} (SALESPC) + \beta_{16} (CONTRACT) + \mu$$

$$VIOL = \alpha + \beta_{21} (PATROLPC) + \beta_{22} (ONEMAN) + \beta_{23} (POOR) + \beta_{24} (NW) + \beta_{25} (STABLE) + \beta_{26} (CONTRACT) + \mu$$

where

PATROLPC = patrol officers per capita
POOR = percentage of community below poverty line
NW = percentage of community population which is nonwhite
SALESPC = retail sales (annual dollar value) per capita

2. Chapter 4 presents some data suggesting that once the contract structure is adopted, further increases in the extent of contracting (that is, share of contracting in total budget expenditures) do not further reduce police expenditures.

STABLE = percentage of community males who are married
ONEMAN = one-man patrol units as percentage of total patrol units deployed

The two police input variables, patrol officers per capita and the share of one-man patrol units, represent mainly patrol inputs, which is the essential activity in both contract and independent cities. *ONEMAN* is included to measure the independent effect on crime rates of differential deployment policy between the two groups of cities. It is assumed that potential offenders assess the relative costs and gains of contemplated offenses, and that visible police patrolling, answering calls for service, and the like can affect this assessment. So we would expect a positive deterrent effect from higher police input levels and from a greater use of one-man patrol units; in both cases the visibility of patrol and the risk of capture and conviction are greater, so that the expected costs to potential offenders are higher. Thus it is anticipated that $\beta_{11}, \beta_{12}, \beta_{21}, \beta_{22}$ are positive.

Similarly, service conditions are factors that affect the gains and losses for potential offenders and thus the deterrent affect of a given level of police inputs. Poverty families would incur relatively less loss of legal earnings from participation in crime and would gain a higher reward from crime participation relative to legal employment. So we would expect poverty conditions to increase crime. Nonwhites are disproportionately poor. But even apart from this we would expect that discrimination would reduce their legal earnings and further encourage crime. Thus, we expect the coefficients $\beta_{12}, \beta_{14}, \beta_{23}, \beta_{24}$ will be positive.

In the property crime equation, the retail sales variable is added to reflect the opportunities for crime across communities. Cities with relatively high retail sales include more retail establishments and therefore elicit more opportunities for property crime. Thus, the individual offender's gross return from property crimes in such cities tends to be higher, if other factors are equal, and we would expect β_{15} to be positive. In the violent crime equation, the percent-of-males variable is added to capture differences in family stability. To a large extent crime is committed by single males, and we expect communities with more married males and thus more stable families to experience less crime—that is, β_{25} would be negative.

The estimated property crime equations are presented in Table 5-12. All anticipations are confirmed for the independent cities sample, and all of the estimated coefficients are statistically significant. Both the number of patrol officers and share of one-man units have significant deterrent effects on property crime rates. Increasing income and sales variables encourage property crimes. For contract cities, however, the comparable results do not occur. Although, except for number of patrol officers, all of the signs are as expected, the coefficients are not significant.

When the two sets of cities are pooled and a dummy variable is introduced to represent contracting, the contract structure, as well as increasing the number of

Table 5-12. Determinants of Property Offense Rates *(PROP)*, 1968/69 (t-ratios in parentheses)[a]

Equation/ sample	Depend. variable	CONSTANT	PATROLPC	ONEMAN	POOR	NW	SALESPC	Contract structure	Correlation
(12-A) 46 independent cities	PROP	21.167	−12.619 (2.43)	−0.108 (3.45)	1.323 (3.54)	0.387 (4.18)	0.0039 (3.63)		$R^2 = 0.75$ $SSR = 1279.85$ $N = 46$
(12-B) 26 contract cities	PROP	7.36	24.385 (1.04)	−0.047 (0.52)	0.903 (2.49)	0.361 (1.08)	0.0005 (0.54)		$R^2 = 0.84$ $SSR = 898.49$ $N = 26$
(12-C) 72 independent and contract cities	PROP	20.31	−3.87 (1.23)	−0.081 (2.84)	0.909 (3.61)	0.432 (4.91)	0.002 (9.12)		$R^2 = 0.77$ $SSR = 2588$ $N = 72$
(12-D) 72 cities including a structure variable	PROP	21.29	−4.77 (1.00)	−0.985 (2.64)	0.907 (3.58)	0.428 (4.75)	0.0017 (7.02)	−0.716 (0.25)	$R^2 = 0.77$ $SSR = 2585.58$ $N = 72$
(12-E) 72 cities excluding police input variables	PROP	10.07			1.05 (4.06)	0.502 (5.73)	0.0014 (10.25)	3.84 (2.31)	$R^2 = 0.74$ $SSR = 2878.84$ $N = 72$

[a]Chow test: $F = \dfrac{81.94}{35.13} = 2.34$

patrol officers and one-man units, all independently act to lower crimes even though their coefficients are not significant. However, since contracting lowers patrol officer and one-man units, the effect of contracting on crimes is not independent of the effects of these inputs. When the equation is reestimated with patrol officer and one-man units not included, as is also shown in Table 5-12, the results indicate that the contract structure is associated with significantly higher property crime rates, and the three remaining service condition variables are highly significant. So long as contracting is associated with a lower patrol personnel level and lower relative use of one-man patrol units, then contracting will tend to raise property crime rates. When the violent crime equations are estimated, as reported in Table 5-13, contracting is shown to result in higher violent crime rates whether the patrol inputs are included in the equation or not.

AN INTEGRATED ANALYSIS

The analyses both in Chapter 4 and in this chapter indicate that contracting cities, as a group, have lower law-enforcement expenditures per capita than do independent cities; probably the greater the extent of contracting, the lower are the expenditures. The explanation for this is not that contract cities are also relatively high users of a third structure, such as districts or joint powers, to provide police services. For relatively few police services are provided through means other than departments or contracting.

What does seem to account for the lower police expenditures is that certain community characteristics that influence expenditures are not the same in contract and independent cities, and that some of the means for providing police services differ between the L.A. County Sheriff's Department and independent city police departments.

City government revenues are lower in contract cities. This is partly because the sales tax bases in contract cities tend to be relatively low and partly because the property tax rates in contract cities are low. The lower revenues in contract cities tend to lower expenditures on law enforcement, which is the major user of city government revenues.

Another factor affecting police expenditures is the preference for local control of services. A city that prefers local control tends to select a city department rather than contract structure. Such cities seem willing to bear the added costs in exchange for the perceived benefits of local control. The willingness to forego some local control, then, by itself contributes to the lower expenditures in contract cities, and the greater the amount of local control foregone the lower are police expenditures.

Contract cities have fewer patrol officers than independent cities. This is consistent with their lower expenditures and would certainly be expected, since labor costs are the major component of police expenditures. However, it is not appropriate to say that there are fewer patrol officers in contract cities because

Table 5-13. Determinants of Violent Offense Rates (VIOL), 1968/69 (t-ratios in parentheses)[a]

Equation/ sample	Depend. variable	CONSTANT	PATROLPC	ONEMAN	POOR	NW	STABLE	Contract structure	Correlation
46 independent cities	VIOL	2.268 (1.27)	-0.217 (0.58)	-0.0036 (1.16)	0.284 (7.88)	0.065 (7.13)	0.037 (1.41)		$R^2 = 0.89$ $SSR = 11.868$ $N = 46$
26 contract cities	VIOL	3.08 (0.28)	4.007 (4.98)	0.022 (0.79)	0.227 (1.43)	0.256 (0.36)	-0.428 (0.38)		$R^2 = 0.74$ $SSR = 26.5284$ $N = 20$
72 independent and contract cities	VIOL	-3.36 (5.18)	2.052 (3.79)	-0.006 (0.98)	0.371 (6.49)	0.055 (3.02)	0.133 (5.88)		$R^2 = 0.68$ $SSR = 93.9971$ $N = 66$
72 cities including a structure variable	VIOL	-3.36	2.415 (5.01)	0.00273 (0.48)	0.343 (7.73)	0.0601 (3.79)	0.0046 (0.76)	3.073 (8.17)	$R^2 = 0.76$ $SSR = 80.3414$ $N = 66$
72 cities excluding police input variables	VIOL	2.69 (0.83)			0.283 (4.62)	0.061 (3.54)	-0.050 (1.10)	3.095 (3.61)	$R^2 = 0.67$ $SSR = 97.0496$ $N = 66$

[a]Chow test: $F = \frac{11}{7} = 15.7$

of their lower expenditures; rather what should be said is that fewer patrol officers and lower expenditures occur together in contract cities.

Lower expenditures and fewer patrol officers are the result of lower tax bases and less willingness to be taxed in contract cities. Additionally, the unwillingness of contract cities to fund more patrol officers does not seem to be the result of lower crime rates in contract cities. Rather, the smaller number of patrol officers in contract cities is an important factor in raising the crime rates above what they would otherwise be. Thus, contract cities are paying for fewer police inputs than independent cities and they are receiving fewer inputs. Because it is associated with fewer inputs, contracting has the effect of lowering the quality of service.

Although police expenditures are somewhat lower in contract than in independent cities, the number of patrol officers is much lower. As a result, unit labor costs—expenditures per patrol officer—are over one and a half times as high in the contract cities. Does this indicate that the LASD is relatively inefficient? Not necessarily, for a part of the differential is probably attributable to the fact that sheriff's deputies command higher wages than are generally paid to independent city police officers (other than those in the city of Los Angeles). In addition, the higher unit labor costs of the LASD are to some extent offset by cost-saving deployment policies. Thus, for example, when the contract price for a patrol unit increased substantially, the LASD adopted the selective use of one-man patrol units and regional contracting, both of which appear to have kept costs down by more than they reduced output. Furthermore, the LASD may be selective in the way it responds to calls for service, for it may provide a relatively rapid response to calls leading to arrests, while providing a relatively slow response to calls that might prevent crimes or are unrelated to criminal acts. Such a deployment policy would be consistent with the observation that arrests for patrol officer and crimes per patrol officers are higher in contract than independent cities. Whether such deployment practices are considered effective depends on whether city residents believe it is more important for police to make arrests than to prevent crimes or to engage in noncrime-related activities.

Thus, on an overall basis, there is some evidence that contracting is a "bargain" in the sense that contract cities are getting more for their money than independent cities. However, contracting is not a bargain in the sense that it provides a higher quality of service. It appears that the great advantage of contracting, so far as contract cities are concerned, is that it offers an opportunity to choose a lower input of law enforcement than would be possible if the service were being provided directly through a city police department.

A NOTE ON CRIME AND ARREST DATA

The Los Angeles County Sheriff's Department made available the crime and arrest data shown in Table 5-14. The LASD was particularly interested in determining whether the relationship between contract and independent cities that

180 How Cities Provide Services

Table 5-14. Crimes and Arrests in Contract and Independent Cities

(per 1,000 persons)

	Crimes 1968	Crimes 1973	Crimes 1974	Arrests 1968	Arrests 1973	Arrests 1974
Property plus violent						
Contract cities	27.0	34.4	36.7	5.9	9.8	8.3
Independent cities[e]	27.1	35.5	39.7	4.1	12.4	10.6
Selected independent cities[f]	28.2	36.8	41.2	3.8	12.3	10.6
Property[a]						
Contract cities	23.1	28.3	29.4	4.2	6.2	5.1
Independent cities[e]	23.7	29.8	33.4	3.5	8.5	7.2
Selected independent cities[f]	24.5	30.7	34.4	3.3	8.4	7.1
Violent[b]						
Contract cities	38.9	61.7	72.4	1.7	3.5	3.2
Independent cities[e]	33.8	57.4	63.4	.5	3.8	3.4
Selected independent cities[f]	36.9	60.6	67.5	.5	3.9	3.5
Violent, excluding aggravated assault						
Contract cities	16.1	22.2	23.8	.7	1.2	1.1
Independent cities[e]	19.2	33.9	35.5	.3	2.0	1.8
Selected independent cities[f]	21.7	37.3	39.5	.3	2.1	1.9
Violent, excluding robbery[c]						
Contract cities	26.6	40.2	52.5	1.2	2.6	2.3
Independent cities[e]	17.2	27.8	33.0	.3	2.3	2.0
Selected independent cities[f]	18.2	27.9	33.4	.3	2.3	2.0
Property plus robbery[d]						
Contract cities	24.3	30.4	31.4	4.8	7.2	6.0
Independent cities[e]	25.4	32.7	36.7	3.8	10.1	8.6
Selected independent cities[f]	26.4	34.0	38.0	3.6	9.9	8.6
Willful homicide						
Contract cities	.4	.7	.6	.02	.06	.07
Independent cities[e]	.5	.7	.9	.01	.15	.12
Selected independent cities[f]	.6	.8	.9	.01	.15	.13
Forcible rape						
Contract cities	.3	.3	.3	.10	.21	.14
Independent cities[e]	.2	.3	.4	.02	.30	.25
Selected independent cities[f]	.2	.4	.4	.02	.32	.29
Robbery						
Contract cities	1.2	1.8	2.0	.54	.91	.89
Independent cities[e]	1.7	3.0	3.0	.28	1.56	1.43
Selected independent cities[f]	1.9	3.3	3.4	.29	1.59	1.49
Aggravated assault						
Contract cities	2.3	3.9	4.9	1.05	2.31	2.11
Independent cities[e]	1.5	2.4	2.6	.24	1.85	1.56
Selected independent cities[f]	1.5	2.3	2.7	.23	1.86	1.54

[a] Property includes burglary, grand theft, and grand theft auto.
[b] Violent includes homicide, robbery, rape and aggravated assault.
[c] Analagous to violent crimes (*VIOL*) and violent arrests (*APSTVPC*) as reported in Ch. 5.

The Case of Police: Chief or Sheriff 181

existed in 1968 has persisted in more recent years. Although precise tests have not been made, it does not appear to us that the conclusions of Chapter 5 would be markedly changed by the more recent data.

The LASD was also interested in determining why violent crimes appear to be higher in contract cities than in independent cities. Their conclusion is that the violent crime and arrest data are distorted because of differential reporting practices for aggravated assaults, as indicated by the following LASD comment.

> As can be seen by a perusal of the statistical data, the contract cities have lower crime rates overall when property and violent crimes are combined. Contract cities also have lower property crime rates. Contract cities have a higher overall violent crime rate. Further investigation of this factor indicates that contract cities are lower in the violent crimes of willful homicide, forcible rape, and robbery. Only in the category of aggravated assaults are contract city crime rates higher than the independent cities. The question that arises is why is there such a large disparity in this single category? Can a homicide or rape or robbery be reported as anything else but a homicide, rape, or robbery? The answer is no. What about assaults? Who determines what is aggravated and what is not aggravated? It is possible that the Los Angeles County Sheriff's Department, as policy, reports some assaults as aggravated that independent police departments do not report as aggravated? There is a lot of room for conjecture in this category because of the nature of the crime. An assault can be a felony or a misdemeanor. As a rule, the L.A.S.D. when taking an assault report wherein a gun, a knife, or some other offensive weapon is used or *displayed* will classify the report as a felony or aggravated assault. The Penal Code does not use the term *aggravated* assault. The L.A.S.D. also reports wife beating and child beating as aggravated assaults.
>
> Under the L.A.S.D. Uniform Reporting Number (URN) system, the code 051 (Aggravated Assault—Gun used) could be used to classify a misdemeanor crime, 417 P.C. (displaying a firearm or deadly weapon in a rude or threatening manner).
>
> The point being made is that because of the variety in the nature of the crime and because there is no Penal Code definition for *aggravated* assault, the classifications and policies for qualifying this particular crime category can be widely divergent. This is not the case in homicides, rapes, and robberies, which are all felonies. [Private correspondence]

---

[d] Analagous to property crimes (*PROP*) and property arrests (*ARSTPPC*) as reported in Ch. 5.
[e] Includes all independent cities except Los Angeles.
[f] Includes all independent cities except Los Angeles, Long Beach and Pasadena.

APPENDIX

Selected Methodological Issues

SELECTED METHODOLOGICAL ISSUES

Local government performance and decision processes can be analyzed from a variety of perspectives, employing alternative analytic methodologies and requiring multiple sources of data. According to James Coleman, building such variety into analysis is among the principles that should govern policy research:

> For policy research, the criteria of parsimony and elegance that apply in discipline research are not important; the correctness of the predictions or results is important, and redundancy is valuable. [G12, p. 4.]

When the alternative analyses converge toward the same conclusions, then the general results become more reliable and the detailed results more useful to policy. In this way the inadequacies of any specific methodology or data set become less serious if a variety of analyses are pursued.

In this study eight alternative methodologies have been employed leading to noncontradictory and usually similar conclusions:

- An historical analysis of municipal service contracting trends in Los Angeles County.
- An econometric analysis of factors affecting and affected by contracting for municipal service delivery.
- A structural analysis of the modes for delivering services in California.
- A cost analysis of police services provided to contracting and independent cities in Los Angeles County.

- A literature review of citizen orientations toward local governments.
- A regression analysis of the effects of contracting and other factors on citizen evaluations of municipal services provided in the Los Angeles region.
- An attitudinal analysis of elite (city managers, police chiefs, and county officials) interviews dealing with the performance characteristics of municipal service structures.
- An attitudinal analysis of citizen surveys concerned with citizen evaluations and preferences for municipal services.

This technical appendix is concerned primarily with the data input for the attitudinal analyses. It first reviews some methods of incorporating attitudinal data in analyses of local government performance; it then considers some specific measurement and interpretation aspects of the data developed in the citizen surveys and elite interviews of this study. It then describes procedures for developing the structural typology, and, finally it discusses some specific methodological issues relating to the empirical analysis of contracting.

MULTIPLE DATA SOURCES AND RESEARCH STRATEGIES

Eugene Webb and his colleagues argued a decade ago that social scientists, by relying too heavily on single data collection methods, were in danger of neglecting issues that focused on measurement questions in general and on validity more particularly [G51]. They suggested that researchers must consider the use of multiple data collection techniques. More recently, economists, political scientists, and sociologists have been urging the use of multiple data sources for policy analyses. We shall illustrate with examples from each of these disciplines.

Economists at the Urban Institute have been advocating and developing municipal service models that have conceptualized productivity measurement in terms of several types of input measurements. Harry Hatry suggests their reasoning:

> Unfortunately, the state of the art of productivity measurement for local government services is disappointing. The temptation is and will be great to stick with the more readily available and traditional workload type of measurements. But used alone these measurements can lead to perversities and misallocations of effort. The collecting and at least arraying of various quality considerations should also be undertaken and used in interpreting workload productivity calculations. Single, readily available, physical measurements, tempting as they may be, should be viewed with a jaundiced eye. Inevitably, for a government to obtain a reasonable perspective of its productivity for any service, it will need multiple measurements. [C3, p. 783.]

Hatry's concern is that if such a complex phenomenon as public service output is measured by a single dimension, its use for policy decisions will be misleading. A complex phenomenon is multi-dimensional and its measurement should be specific for each of the relevant dimensions.[1]

One of the most ambitious efforts using multiple indicators in measuring the output of local government agencies is being undertaken by a team of political scientists headed by Eleanor Ostrom. The focus of her project is the conceptualization and operational development of multiple modes of measurement of three municipal services: street lighting, street repair, and the provision of parks and recreation facilities. Ostrum also is concerned with physical, cost, and attitudinal dimensions of service output.

By examining more than one service Ostrum will be able to make interservice comparisons about the quality of the data used for output measures and the relationships among output dimensions. For example they will

> ascertain what kinds of relationships exist between the physical measures of service output and citizen perceptions and evaluations of that output. In regard to street lighting, for example, we will examine the relationship between light-meter readings and citizens' perceptions of street lighting on their block. In a relative sense do citizens perceive differences in output as measured with a light meter? We will also explicitly analyze environmental factors affecting citizen preferences for street lighting which could affect evaluations of lighting service independent of the level of light provided. [G32, p. 89.]

Sociologist Terry Clark proposes the use of multiple indicators in formulating community decision-making models [H27]. Clark argues that policy outputs are a function of five variables: citizen values, community characteristics, resources, community leadership, community power and decision-making structures. Clark's model specifies the use of aggregate data, structural data, and survey data.[2]

Hatry, Ostrom and Clark [G1] advocate the use of multiple indicators because the phenomenon they are interested in measuring are multi-dimensional. Psychometric theory suggests the use of multiple measures because a single

---

1. For example, in the area of solid-waste collection Hatry suggests that there are four dimensions: tons of solid waste collected, dollar costs of collection, average street cleanliness rating, and citizen satisfaction with the collection. The first two dimensions are objective physical dimensions, which can be measured by using reported agency data. The third dimension relates to elite evaluations, which can be obtained from the reported observations of "judges" who calculate the streets' cleanliness. The fourth dimension relates to citizen attitudes, which could be obtained from citizen survey responses.

2. Up to now much of Clark's work involves correlation analysis. He has, however, given considerable attention to the theoretical and operational questions dealing with measurement, and concludes that two types of survey data are needed—citizen values and community power or decision-making structures, the mass and elite attitudes.

measure of any concept will contain design, operational, and random measurement errors. Psychometric theory addresses the issue of to what extent the measured value closely reflects the true value, or to what extent it contains substantial error.

As Webb [G51] and Blalock [G4] have argued, reliance on a single measure decreases reliability while it also creates data analysis problems. Random error attentuates bivariate correlation and regression coefficients and also produces attenuating biases in multivariate estimates where there is random error in the independent variables. Scott [A8] demonstrated that when a number of indicators (each of which has a random error component) are combined into a single index, a more reliable and therefore stronger relationship exists.

Our review of methodology suggests that there are six research strategies that tend to be adopted and discussed.[3] The most prevalent type of research design includes only a single measure or indicator obtained from a single method of data collection. Leege and Francis argue that even when validation problems are recognized, the use of single indicators as outside criteria in the criterion-validation process is undesirable for dealing with systematic error. They further argue, "Not only the measure of the concept itself, but also the criterion for validation should be based on multiple indicators" [G25, p. 139].

An improvement on the single-indicator/single-method strategy is the single-indicator/multiple-method strategy. In this approach a single concept, such as quality of solid-waste collection, is measured by different sources of data. Hatry's research on productivity is an example of an attempt to obtain two measures of "quality." For decision-making purposes this is an appealing strategy because models are kept simple [G12, p. 5], and multiple data sources are more manageable. Such a strategy, however, can potentially suffer most of the problems articulated by Leege and Francis.

A third strategy is the use of homogeneous multiple measures with a single data collection method. Leege and Francis call this "multiple indicators of the same kind," which have played a major role in attitude and personality measurement. The key to this strategy is the use of homogeneous indicators [G1, p. 2] in combination. For example, an underlying trait is hypothesized and a battery of items utilizing the same stimulus is administered. All indicators—of the same kind—are then combined to create a new scale score. The problem with this strategy is that despite the fact that the test may be relatively homogeneous *in toto*, the individual indicators may have been subject to biases in either the measurement technique or the data collection method.

---

3. By methodology we mean an elaboration of an entire research strategy: design, sampling, measurement, and so on. A method is a general rationale employed to specify and structure empirical observations. For example, we would speak of a data collection method. Following Leege and Francis [G25], a technique "is a specific instrument for the generation and analysis of data." Thus, for example, a self-anchoring scale is a measurement technique, while key cluster analysis is a data analysis technique.

A fourth strategy is to employ multiple but homogeneous indicators with more than one data collection method. This will provide an external control for distinguishing error that is peculiar to a data collection method. This is a variation of the Leege and Francis strategy of "multiple indicators each based on different operations."

> ... If we argue that "people with a high rate of self-doubting run for political office," we might administer to a sample of candidates and non-candidates a series of tests where multiple items were designed to measure self-confidence, paranoid tendencies, and need inviolacy. But we might also ask for clinical observations on the sample, or we might design a set of experimental games to measure the same traits. Results of the latter measurement methods [e.g., data collection methods] would help us to estimate to what extent scores on the initial test were a function of the measurement method employed. [G25, p. 140.]

A fifth strategy is to use multiple heterogeneous measurement techniques within a single data collection method, such as, for example, a citizen survey. Newhouse [A6] indicates the lack of rigorous methodological investigation of surveys dealing with citizen perceptions, evaluations, and preferences of the outputs of urban governance; Scott [A8], however, noted that Milbrath, Ostrom, and their associates are notable exceptions.

This strategy is, of course, subject to method effect, as are all surveys. If measurement techniques and their items are operationalized well, then problems of method effect can be tackled. When measures are poorly operationalized or the execution of a measurement technique is not thoroughly considered, then we obviously obtain no reading on method effect.

The sixth, and most complete strategy, is the use of multiple heterogeneous measurement techniques and multiple data collection methods. Such a strategy has been termed "multiple operationalism." Leege and Francis argue:

> The strategy we espouse for conceptual-operation coordination, then, is one where the concept is carefully explicated and differentiated to derive its location in a theoretical network of concepts. Measures of the concept in all its aspects are developed, as well as measures of other concepts in the theoretical network; the measures are refined through empirical operations using multiple indicators of the *same* kind and multiple operations of *different* kinds. Then, the entire predictive network surrounding the concept is subjected to empirical examination. Through such procedures ... theory becomes cumulative and measurement error is less of a mystery. [G25, p. 141.]

In this study both the fifth and sixth strategies have been used. As earlier indicated, the sixth strategy has been adopted through the use of eight alternative methodologies for empirical and theoretical analyses of structures for delivering municipal services. The fifth strategy has been followed in the design of the elite interviews and citizen surveys. The citizen surveys included systematic experimentation with alternative measurement techniques, such as card sorts, self-anchoring scales, and budget pies; the elite interviews included systematic experimentation with feedback process in group and single respondent interviews.

THE CITIZEN SURVEY
The Los Angeles Metropolitan Area Survey (LAMAS VII) was utilized for a modest experiment with alternative evaluation and preference measurement techniques. LAMAS is an omnibus survey conducted biannually, obtaining around 1,100 respondents. As the primary sample frame is Los Angeles County (with a "stand-alone" subsample for Los Angeles City), LAMAS is not ideally suited for analyses comparing alternative structures of service provision. Only about 10 percent of the respondents come from cities which contract for law enforcement services, for example, with no assurance that these respondents are a valid sample of the universe of citizens receiving contract police service.[4]

As a vehicle for experimentation with alternative questionnaire construction techniques, however, LAMAS was acceptable. Moreover, many of the interviewers used had previous experience with LAMAS, and the quality control available on the survey encourages confidence in the fairly novel and complex question formats used. Three question format issues were of critical importance: the relation of scaling techniques to the measurement of attitudes; the relation of saliency to the measurement of attitudes; and the relation between evaluations and preferences in the measurement of attitudes.

Scaling and Measurement of Attitudes
Recent literature on attitude measurement generally accepts the proposition that much of the research is essentially predicated upon item analysis. This is true of work with attitude measurement instruments based upon scales composed by several items or single-item measures tapping generalized cognitive predispositions. By far the greatest concern with item analysis relates to what William A. Scott calls minimizing extraneous determinants [G38, p. 238]; that is, minimizing what contaminates scale scores. In studying such problems most of the research has centered on response sets, response styles, the lack of correlation of an item with other scale items, or with the scale itself.

Ordinal scale measures appear to be the most popular because they are easy to administer, whether by interview or self-administered questionnaire, and are simple to score. Our research used two ordinal techniques for rating specific local government services and a third was employed only for the police service.

---

4. Despite these limitations, a substantive analysis of these data was made with highly suggestive results [A10].

The use of multiple measurement techniques serves a dual and interlocking purpose in comparing the techniques and examining validity and reliability questions.

This effort is partially patterned after research undertaken in the Buffalo Metropolitan Area by Everett Cataldo and his associates [G8]. They were particularly interested in the advantages of a card-sorting technique in comparison with the more traditional closed-ended measures. The advantages they sought were in terms of the quality of data obtained and the ease of administration (interview-respondent interaction for example).[5] Cataldo reported that the card-sorting technique was easier to administer, and our study comes to the same conclusion. Cataldo also reported that the card-sorting technique provided a higher quality of data. However, our study could find no clear differences in the data quality produced by the two techniques.[6]

Scott reports the empirical results of the two types of data analysis he used to test for data quality: the multi-trait, multi-method matrix, and cluster analysis [A7]. The underlying assumption of the matrix analysis is that, when two techniques are compared, correlations of the same measures will be substantially larger than correlations among different measures. Thus, in interpreting such a matrix, a validity diagonal is established by the correlations obtained on similar measures between the two techniques. Where a panel study has been used [G8], or items have been apportioned on an instrument in a split-half manner, then a reliability diagonal can be designed by correlations of similar measures within the same technique.

Given that neither condition was possible with the LAMAS survey, a second data analytic strategy—the use of cluster analysis—was also adopted. By using a cluster analytic solution with the loading, similarity, and reliability coefficients, substantive findings can be linked to methodological considerations (such as validity, reliability, and technique comparison).[7]

---

5. The differences between the Cataldo research and the present project should be noted, so as not to leave the impression that a replication was undertaken. The Buffalo research was a part of a two-wave panel study, whereas LAMAS VII was a single cross-section of the Los Angeles County population. To examine "method effect," Cataldo employed the card sort and ordinal rating scales, using two different data collection methods. On the one hand, the card-sorting was done during the personal interview, while, on the other hand, the ordinal ratings were obtained by having the respondent complete a self-administered questionnaire after the interviews. In contrast, while our study employed equivalent measurement techniques, only one data collection method, the interview, was used.

6. This might be because the number of measures used on the interview and questionnaire in the Cataldo study was substantially greater than those used in the LAMAS survey, and the Cataldo outtake scale was composed of many more heterogeneous items than the service items on LAMAS.

7. A cluster analytic solution on its face appears to be analogous to factor analytic solutions because both consist of a number of dimensions or clusters defined by subsets of observed variables. The desired objective is to make each dimension as generally mutually exclusive of the others as possible. Both types of solutions are specified by loadings of an observed variable on dimensions as well as intercorrelations among the dimensions. It is at this point that the two types of solution employ dissimilar methodological criteria for

The loading, similarity, and reliability coefficients were developed for scales created from 17 service evaluation items [A7]. From the items, eleven scales were constructed, of which six were defined only by card sort and ordinal items. In each of the six scales both technique items had identical loading and matrix coefficients. In no case was there another item in the scale that exhibited a higher value. In all but one scale—police services—the loading matrix entries were substantially greater than all other entries, thus quantitatively defining the dimension. When coupled with identical similarity matrix entries within service scales, a strong content validity case is established for individual service scales.

In the case of the police scale, the card sort and ordinal items exhibit the same pattern as in the other scales, but the inclusion of a self-anchoring scale item rating police services shows a similar pattern. Therefore, when we specifically define a scale with all three measurement technique items, we find that both loading and similarity matrix entries are nearly identical for all three items and that they indeed define a better (that is, more error-free) police services cluster.

The relevance of a cluster analytic solution for validity and reliability concerns is demonstrated by the differences in the police service scales. The card-sort/ordinal scale has a reliability coefficient of 0.77, but when the self-anchoring scale item was introduced, a 0.82 reliability coefficient was obtained. However, when two adidtional police service evaluation questions, dealing with judgments comparing police services in different cities are included in a police services scale, the reliability coefficient obtained is reduced to 0.77. Upon inspection of the five items, we find the spread of the similarity coefficients is from 0.78 to 0.90, which is not great, but the corresponding range for the loading matrix coefficients is 0.41 to 0.81. When taken together, the coefficients suggest that the content validity of city comparisons is not as strong as other items.

---

establishing dimensions. In factor analysis it is sufficient for an observed variable to be highly correlated with other variables in the dimension. A cluster analytic solution imposes a more exacting criterion before admitting a variable to a cluster or dimension: it must have a similar pattern of relationships with all the variables in the predefined cluster. Thus, accompanying a matrix of loadings of the observed variables on the cluster is a second matrix of similarities that exhibits the extent to which a variable has a pattern of correlations that is similar to those of the items which are preselected to define the cluster. The similarity coefficient ranges from zero to one, indicating a total lack of similarity (0.0) to a perfect fit with the cluster items (1.0). As Hensler notes, "a cluster is a subset of variables which are strongly intercorrelated and are related to other variables in the same way . . . . While the loading matrix tells us the extent to which each variable is correlated with those defining each cluster, the similarity matrix gives us a measure of the extent to which each variable is similar to the definers of each cluster [and] in the way they are related to all the other variables in the analysis" [G21, pp. 69, 74]. A third coefficient, Cronback's Alpha, is employed because it measures the reliability of the scale formed by its defining variables. A reliability coefficient indicates how much of the total variance of a measured variable is "true" variance. Thus a high reliability coefficient means that the measure is relatively free of error variance and contains only uncorrelated measurement error.

While it is of major concern to examine the items within the individual scales, it is also interesting to examine the relationship between scales. A scale intercorrelation matrix demonstrates how mutually exclusive one scale is from the other [A7]. For example, the police city comparison scale is correlated (0.46 and 0.48) with the police ordinal measurement scales; they are obviously tapping different aspects of a law enforcement domain. The relationship between street cleaning and garbage collection is 0.40, which signifies a large refuse domain. Street cleaning is also mildly correlated (0.36) with street repair, suggesting a street maintenance domain.

On balance, then, we conclude that the card-sort and ordinal methods are both measuring service-specific areas and provide valid data. However, there is not sufficient evidence to conclude that the card-sort technique is superior.[8]

Salience and the Measurement of Attitudes

Although there are competing definitions of the concept of attitude, the social psychologists [G35; G36; G16; G38] and political scientists [G30; G21] distinguish three component characteristics: cognitive, evaluative, and conative. In such survey research an implicit assumption is made that a survey respondent has the appropriate level of cognitive skills and motivation necessary for valid responses. This may not always be the case. In this study we were particularly interested in whether respondents were aware of whether the city in which they lived contracted for its services.

Operationalizing the term "contracting" for conceptual purposes throughout this project has not been an easy task. It was readily assumed that one could not simply ask a citizen what contracting arrangements existed without specifying the concept more fully. We found in the survey pretest phase that the citizens who lived in contract cities did substantially recognize the idea of contracting in terms of service delivery; however, we also found that citizens in Los Angeles City, Long Beach, and independent cities believed that they also received ser-

---

8. There are however, some hints that further investigation may more fully support Cataldo's finding that the card-sort technique provides more reliable data. In the multi-trait/multi-method matrix, when comparing the within-method intercorrelations (e.g., the heterotrait or heteroitem-nonmethod submatrixes), all coefficients within the ordinal technique are larger than in the card-sort technique, except one (Construction Control). Optimally such correlations-within techniques should be low, otherwise one might suspect some type of method effects (e.g., yes-nay saying; position effect, etc.) In the cluster analysis, similarity coefficients can be examined within and then across the two techniques. Each technique across all eleven scales includes 66 similarity coefficients. When compared, 54 coefficients of the ordinal techniques are larger than their card-sort equivalents. The larger the similarity coefficient, the closer it comes to the largest scale-defining items. Thus, like the multi-trait/multi-method matrix, there tends to be a higher, more positive set of interitem correlations in the ordinal technique than in the card-sort technique. Because there are only six equivalent items in each technique, it would be hasty to conclude that a method effect has been uncovered. If a larger number of items had been included, such as reported by Cataldo, it may very well have led to an equivalent finding for response bias in ordinal scales.

vices from contract providers. Thus the need for a cognitive filter question was apparent.[9]

The responses showed that almost half the contract city residents and only one-quarter of the independent city residents indicated that their city contracted for services. However, the number of "don't know" responses was very high—about half of the respondent in each city.

In reviewing the literature measuring attitudes toward local government outputs we either do not find "no opinion" categories, or, if they were utilized, apparently they have gone unreported. When viewed against the standard works on attitude measurement, such findings are not unexpected, since the topic is seldom treated with much concern.[10]

In a great deal of the psychometric literature, efforts are undertaken to obtain what amounts to a 100 percent response rate for attribute categories. Irrespective of the number of response categories, the exclusion of a no-opinion category means that the question is of a forced-choice nature. Such an orientation allows the researcher to avoid dealing with problems of missing data. The question raised here is the extent to which this is considered a realistic state of affairs. The investigator interested in public opinion and public policy research must confront findings that suggest large sections of the American public are neither attentive nor informed in political matters [G20].

The need for no-opinion categories is directly related to the issue of the utility of cognitive filter questions. It is argued that, in the best of all measurement situations, before asking citizens to evaluate stimuli it is necessary to ascertain whether they have "thought about," "have knowledge of," or "have a opinion about" some particular matter. Those who answer negatively are not asked to provide evaluations, because at minimum the responses are difficult to interpret.

Preceding each item in a large battery of items with a cognitive filter question poses some strategic problems, such as substantially lengthening a questionnarie.

---

9. The question ultimately used for the citizen survey was worded as follows: "Do you happen to know whether some of the local government services you receive are provided by another government or private business under contract? That is, does (respondent's city name/Los Angeles County) pay some other government or private business to provide services for (repeat city name/Los Angeles County)?"

10. There appear to be several strategies toward the exclusion or inclusion of categories allowing the respondent no opinion. The first is the strict forced-choice format, which simply does not permit the respondent under any circumstances to opt out of the investigator's response categories. Missing data are simply not a part of that world. A second perspective is the one which, while not providing don't-know categories, does allow the respondent to spontaneously admit no answer. A third option is to include a don't-know category as a valid response read to the respondent in a manner that conveys its appropriateness. A fourth orientation is to include such a category because the response scale itself may have a central point (for example, establishing positive or negative direction) that the investigator does not want used as a surrogate for don't know. A fifth perspective builds on the fourth, but is concerned with not only a central-point/don't-know distinction, but also a differentiation among possible types of no opinion.

The cost of specific cognitive filter questions was too high for our study's resources. Therefore a compromise procedure was adopted that explicitly called attention to the possibility that the respondent might not have an opinion.[11]

One set of our questions directly addressed the no-opinion category. Citizens were presented with a set of ordinal categories that described how good a job their city was doing providing services. The categories were labeled on pockets on a card placed in front of the respondent, who then placed cards representing services in the pockets according to his or her evaluations. To see whether the inclusion of a no-opinion category made a difference in the evaluation of services, a random half-sample was given the sort categories without a no-opinion category, while the other half-sample included a no-opinion category.

The results indicate that respondents tended to report that the city was doing a better job when the no-opinion option was included than when it was not. When the simple marginal distributions of the two half-samples are compared, the response categories of the sample without the no-opinion option tend to be larger than the other sample, with the largest difference being in the positive categories. Furthermore, as services become more salient, the no-opinion responses tend to become fewer and the positivistic bias becomes smaller.

The Relationship Between Evaluations and Preferences in the Measurement of Attitudes

Ordinal measurement techniques are criticized as preference and evaluation measures because they have a tendency to lead to preferences for more of each service. For this reason Clark advocates use of techniques in which "intensity of preference is expressed under conditions of budget constraint" [H25, p. 1] —a factor only too obviously operating in the real world of local government decision-making. Hoinville and Clark both suggest that preferences must be examined in clusters so that citizens' responses are in the form of trade-offs [A1, p. 22]. The process is one of identifying relative priorities from a range of competing alternatives.

There are relatively few devices for obtaining opinions and preferences within a constrained decision-making context.[12] In this study we have adopted an

---

11. The lack of a no-opinion category should be classified with what Leege and Francis called distributional errors [G25, p. 209]. They suggest that the question format may lead respondents to select a specific alternative response. The temptation to force a choice in order to eliminate (ideally) as much missing data as possible by omitting a no-opinion category might force respondents to commit distributional errors. In cases where the question referent is very salient or of interest to the respondent (for example, maximum cognitive skills and motivation are present), such distributional errors may be slight. However, where the referent is ambiguous or the concept is poorly operationalized, it is not a wise course to accept the probability that all such respondents will admit to no opinion. Given what we know about response sets, it is not unreasonable to assume that the distributional errors may be positively biased.

12. In 1962, Robert Wilson developed a game-board technique for determining resource allocation choices of respondents [G53]. In 1970 Hoinville devised a pictoral system for

approach in which respondents were shown a budget pie depicting current service allocations and were asked to draw in new lines showing their service allocation preferences of the current total budget. Two-thirds of the respondents changed the budget allocation in some way, while one-third prefered the status quo; there were very few refusals or don't-know responses.[13]

The respondents were also given a second blank budget pie and told that each household in their city could distribute $100 of new money to the five service areas or could take all or some of that money in a tax reduction. Whereas 3.2 percent either refused or had no opinion on the reallocation budget pie, a slight increase to 3.9 percent was recorded for the $100 increment.

The incremental budget pie was employed to gauge the extent to which evaluation and preference measures relate to each other. Do citizens who evaluate a service highly also prefer to spend more money on that service? Or does a positive evaluation mean that there is a preference for augmenting other (not so highly evaluated) services? These questions were examined in the context of the multi-trait/multi-method matrix and cluster solutions. The preliminary finding from using the card-sort, ordinal scale, and self-anchoring scale (in the case of police services only) is that high service evaluations are not related to preferences for spending more money on high-performance services.

ELITE INTERVIEWS AND QUESTIONNAIRES

Three questionnaires and five sets of interviews were used to determine the attitudes and perceptions of city and county government officials who could be instrumental in selecting structures for service provision. Table A-1 indicates the cities which were sampled and responded to each of these instruments. Table A-2 summarizes the response rates by county.

Over 125 city managers responded to either an initial exploratory questionnaire or a structural incidence questionnaire. Ten city managers from Los Angeles County, all of whom responded to the questionnaires, were individually interviewed in their offices. Twenty-six city managers were interviewed in a group setting; all but one of these responded to the questionnaire and only one was individually interviewed as well. Twenty-five police chiefs responded to a police service questionnaire; fifteen police chiefs, eight of whom had responded to the police questionnaire, were interviewed in a group setting. Twelve Los Angeles County Sheriff's Department officials were interviewed; four as individuals and eight in a group setting. The exploratory questionnaire sample of cities

---

determining allocation decisions [G22]. In 1974, Beardsley used a device for manipulating chips (money) for allocating public budgets [G2].

13. The status quo responses might include those with no judgments. In the Beardsley study only one-tenth of the responses were status quo, indicating that moving chips between policy categories poses less difficulty for respondents than drawing lines on a budget pie, which requires addition and subtraction skills as decisions are made and recorded.

Appendix 195

Table A-1. Interview and Questionnaire Sample and Respondent Cities

| | | Questionnaires | | | Interviews | | | |
| | | | | | City Manager | | Police chief | County departments | |
City	City code no.	Exploratory (1)	Structural incidence (2)	Police (3)	Individual (4)	Group (5)	Group (6)	Group (7)	Individual (8)
Los Angeles County									
Alhambra	001	R	R	N					
Arcadia	002	R	R	R					
Artesia (C)	003	R	N						
Avalon (C)	004	R	R						
Azusa	005	R	R	N		R	R		
Baldwin Park	006	R	N						
Bell	007	R	R	N					
Bellflower (C)	008	R	R						
Bell Gardens	009	R	R	N					
Beverly Hills	010	R	N	N		R	R		
Bradbury (C)	011	N	N						
Burbank	012	R	R	R					
Carson (C)	013	R	R		R				
Cerritos (C)	014	R	R						
Claremont	015	N	N	N					
Commerce (C)	016	R	R		R				
Compton	017	R	N	N					
Covina	018	N	R	N		R	R		
Cudahy (C)	019	R	R		R	R	R		
Culver City	020	R	N	N					
Downey	021	R	R	N		R	R		
Duarte (C)	022	N	R						
El Monte	023	R	R	N					
El Segundo	024	R	N	R	R		R		
Gardena	025	N	N	R					

Table A-1. continued

		Questionnaires			Interviews			
						City Manager		Police chief	County departments
	City code no.	Exploratory	Structural incidence	Police	Individual	Group	Group	Group	Individual
		(1)	(2)	(3)	(4)	(5)	(6)	(7)	(8)
Glendale	026	N	R	R		R	R		
Glendora	027	R	R	N					
Hawaiian Gardens (C)	028	R	R						
Hawthorne	029	R	R	N		R			
Hermosa Beach	030	R	N	N					
Hidden Hills (C)	031	R	R						
Huntington Park	032	R	R	R			R		
Industry (C)	033	R	R						
Inglewood	034	R	R	N					
Irwindale	035	N	N	R					
Lakewood (C)	036	R	R		R				
La Mirada (C)	037	R	R		R	R			
La Puente (C)	038	R	R						
La Verne	039	R	N	N					
Lawndale (C)	040	R	R			R			
Lomita (C)	041	R	R						
Long Beach	042								
Los Angeles	043								
Lynwood	044	R	R	N	R				
Manhattan Beach	045	N	R	N					
Maywood	046	R	N	N					
Monrovia	047	N	N	N					
Montebello	048	R	N	N					
Monterey Park	049	R	R	N					
Norwalk (C)	050	R	N		R				
Palmdale (C)	051	N	N						

Table A-1. continued

		Questionnaires			Interviews			
		Exploratory	Structural incidence	Police	City Manager		Police chief	County departments	
	City code no.				Individual	Group	Group	Group	Individual
		(1)	(2)	(3)	(4)	(5)	(6)	(7)	(8)
Palos Verdes Est.	052	R	N	N					
Paramont (C)	053	R	R						
Pasadena	054	R	R	R	R		R		
Pico Rivera (C)	055	N	N			R			
Pomona	056	R	R	N					
Redondo Beach	057	R	R	N	R		R		
Rolling Hills (C)	058	N	N						
Rolling Hills Est. (C)	059	R	R						
Rosemead (C)	060	R	R						
San Dimas (C)	061	R	R						
San Fernando	062	R	R	N					
San Gabriel	063	R	R	N					
San Marino	064	N	N	N					
Sante Fe Springs (C)	065	R	R	R		R			
Santa Monica	066	R	R	N					
Sierra Madre	067	R	R	N					
Signal Hill	068	R	R						
South El Monte (C)	069	R	R			R			
South Gate	070	R	N	N					
South Pasadena	071	R	R	R					
Temple City (C)	072	R	R			R			
Torrance	073	R	R	N		R			
Vernon	074	N	N	N					
Walnut (C)	075	R	R						
West Covina	076	R	R	R			R		
Whittier	077	R	R	N					

Table A-1. continued

	City code no.	Questionnaires			City Manager Interviews		Police chief		County departments	
		Exploratory	Structural incidence	Police	Individual	Group	Group	Group	Individual
		(1)	(2)	(3)	(4)	(5)	(6)	(7)	(8)

Orange County

Anaheim	301	R	R	N					
Brea	302	N	R	R					
Buena Park	303	R	R	N					
Costa Mesa	304	R	R	R					
Cyprus	305	R	N	N					
Fountain Valley	306	R	R	R			R		
Fullerton	307	R	N	N					
Garden Grove	308	R	R	N					
Huntington Beach	309	R	R	N					
Irvine	310	N	N	N					
Laguna Beach	311	R	R	R					
La Habra	312	R	N	R					
La Palma	313	R	R	N					
Los Alamitos	314	N	R	N					
Newport Beach	315	R	R	R					
Orange	316	N	R	R					
Placentia	317	N	N	N					
San Clemente	318	R	R	R					
San Juan Capistrano	319	R	R	R					
Santa Ana	320	R	R	N			R		
Seal Beach	321	N	N	N					
Stanton	322	N	R	R			R		
Tustin	323	N	N	N					
Villa Park									

Table A-1. continued

		Questionnaires			Interviews			
	City code no.	Exploratory	Structural incidence	Police	City Manager		Police chief	County departments	
					Individual	Group	Group	Group	Individual
		(1)	(2)	(3)	(4)	(5)	(6)	(7)	(8)
Westminister	324	R	R	N					
Yorba Linda	325	R	N						
Alameda County									
Alameda	101	R	N	N					
Albany	102	R	N	N			R		
Berkeley	103	R	N	R					
Emeryville	104	N	N	R					
Fremont	105	R	R	N					
Hayward	106	R	N	N					
Livermore	107	R	R	N			R		
Oakland	108	R	R						
Piedmont	109	R	R	N					
Pleasanton	110	R	R	N					
San Leandro	111	R	R	N					
Union City	112	R	R	N					
Newark	113	R	R	N			R		
Contra Costa County									
Antioch	201	N	R	N					
Brentwood	202	N	N	N					
Clayton	203	R	R	N					
Concord	204	R	R	R					
El Cerrito	205	R	R	R					
Hercules	206	R	R	N					
La Fayette	207	R	R						

200 *How Cities Provide Services*

Table A-1. continued

		Questionnaires			Interviews			
				City Manager		Police chief	County departments	
	City code no.	Exploratory	Structural incidence	Police	Individual	Group	Group	Group	Individual
		(1)	(2)	(3)	(4)	(5)	(6)	(7)	(8)
Martinez	208	R	R	R					
Pinule	209	R	R	N					
Pittsburg	210	R	N	N					
Pleasant Hill	211	R	R	N			R		
Richmond	212	R	N	R					
San Pablo	213	R	R	N					
Walnut Creek	214	N	R	N			R		
Ventura County									
Camarillo	501	R	N						
Fillmore	502	N		N					
Ojai	503	R	N	N					
Oxnard	504	R	R	N					
Port Hueneme	505	R	R	R					
San Buenaventura	506	R	R				R		
Santa Paula	507	N	N	N					
Simi Valley	508	N	R	N					
Thousand Oaks	509	R	R						
Santa Clara County									
Campbell	401	R	R	N		R			
Cupertino	402	R	R			R			
Gilroy	403	R	R	N					
Los Altos	404	N	N	N					
Los Altos Hills	405	R	R			R			
Los Gatos	406	R	R	N		R			

Table A-1. continued

		Questionnaires			Interviews			
					City Manager		Police chief	County departments
	City code no.	Exploratory	Structural incidence	Police	Individual	Group	Group	Group	Individual
		(1)	(2)	(3)	(4)	(5)	(6)	(7)	(8)
Milpitas	407	R	R	R					
Monte Sereno	408	N	R			R			
Morgan Hill	409	R	R	N					
Mountain View	410	R	N	R					
Palo Alto	411	R	R	N					
San Jose	412	N	R						
Santa Clara	413	N		N		R			
Saratoga	414	N	N			R			
Sunnyvale	415	N	R	R					
Los Angeles County Departments									
Fire								R	
Library								R	
CAO								R	
Personnel								R	
Engineering								R	R
Roads								R	R
Sheriff								R	
Regional Planning								R	
Health									R

(C) = Contract City.
N = Sample City which did not respond.
R = Respondent City.

Table A-2. Interview and Questionnaire Response Rates

| | Questionnaires ||| Interviews ||||
| | | | | City Managers || Police Chief || County departments ||
	Exploratory	Structure incidence	Police	Individual	Group	Individual	Group	Individual	Group
All counties									
Responses	117	101	25	10	26		15	4	8
Sample	152	149	105						
Response rate	.77	.68	.24						
Los Angeles County									
Responses	61	59	11	10	14		11	4	3
Sample	75	75	45						
Response rate	.81	.79	.24						
All other counties									
Responses	56	52	14		12		4		
Sample	77	74	60						
Response rate	.73	.70	.24						
Orange County									
Responses	18	18	5				3		
Sample	26	26	24						
Response rate	.69	.69	.24						
Alameda County									
Responses	12	8	2		2				
Sample	13	13	11						
Response rate	.92	.62	.18						
Contra Costa County									
Responses	11	10	3		3				
Sample	14	13	12						
Response rate	.79	.77	.25						

Table A-2. continued

	Questionnaires			Interviews			
	Explor-atory	Structure incidence	Police	City Managers		Police Chief	County departments	
				Individual	Group	Group	Individual	Group
Ventura County								
Responses	6	5	1			1		
Sample	9	8	6					
Response rate	.67	.63	.17					
Santa Clara County								
Responses	9	11	3		7			
Sample	15	14	10					
Response rate	.60	.79	.30					

included 76 cities in Los Angeles County (excluding Los Angeles City and Long Beach) and 76 cities randomly selected from five urban counties in California. The structural incidence questionnaire sample was approximately the same. The police chief questionnaire sample excluded contract cities and therefore includes a fewer number of cities. The interviewed city managers were randomly selected, as were the police chief interviewees. County officials were specifically selected because of their interest and knowledge in Los Angeles County contracting.

Exploratory Questionnaire

This was the first of the questionnaires sent to city managers or city administrators. Its "exploratory" aspect was to assess whether city managers would respond to questions about the sources of finances, organizational structure, and decision processes for providing municipal services. The high response rate (77 percent) indicated both the capacity of city managers to respond as well as their interest in issues of governmental structures.[14]

The questionnaire was concerned with four specific services—police, refuse collection, parks and recreation, and streets. Subservices within each of these services were also identified.[15]

Respondents were asked to check, from a specified list, the source of financing and the type of government or private sector providing the subservice. Respondents were also asked to indicate, for those services not provided through city departments, how the provider was selected (through bids or otherwise), and what the terms of payment were (e.g., cost reimbursable or price per unit of work completed, for example). Respondents were finally asked to indicate how and when tasks or operating procedures were defined and workload assigned, who specifies the terms of performance, and who monitors the service performance. A summary of the results indicates the following:

Police: Municipal police services are generally provided by a public agency— either a city police department or under contract to a county department. Most police contracting occurs in Los Angeles County, where only about half the respondents provide the basic police services (patrol, traffic control, detectives, juvenile delinquency control, and community relations) through their own departments, and even fewer provide their own support services (jails and detention facilities, training, and laboratory work and record-keeping). This can be compared with much higher percentages of self-provision (50-85 percent) for respondents outside of Los Angeles County.

14. Respondents were asked if they wanted to receive a report of the findings, and most answered that they did want such a report.
15. Police included community relations, general law enforcement, detectives, jails, delinquency control, traffic control, training, crime labs, and records; refuse collection included residential and business; parks and recreation included parks, athletic facilities, cultural and social facilities, athletic programs, cultural and social programs; streets included sweeping, resurfacing and patching.

Of the cities which do contract for some police services, about one-third contract for only one of the services, usually a support service, and another third contract for all eight basic and support services. Thus relatively few cities seem to combine the contracting of several specific services with their own police department providing other services. If any one of the basic services is contracted for, then the other basic services also will usually be contracted; if the basic services are contracted, then the support services tend to be contracted; however, if a city contracts for the support services, this does not necessarily imply that it will also contract for the basic services.

Refuse Collection: In about 90 percent of the cases in both Los Angeles and other counties, municipal refuse collection is provided by a private firm. However, of these, less than half the respondents indicated that the city contracted with the private firm. In other cities the private firm usually, but not always, has a franchise from the city to charge the consumer directly for the service.

In those cases where cities contract with a private producer, they tend to contract for both residential and business collection (although not necessarily with the same firm). In those cases where the city does not contract, the residential collection tends to be franchised while the business collection is not. However, there is substantially more franchising of business refuse collection by cities outside of Los Angeles County than by cities within the county.

Street Maintenance: Municipal street services tend to be provided either by city departments or through contract. However, in the case of street services, unlike police, the contract is more likely to be with a private than a government provider. Also, there is substantially more contracting among Los Angeles County cities than among the cities in other counties.

The street resurfacing service is relatively more dependent on contracting than the street sweeping and patching services, both within and outside Los Angeles County. Cities which contract for the sweeping and patching services also tend to contract for the resurfacing service; however, the reverse does not necessarily occur.

Public Recreation: Most public recreation in both the Los Angeles County and other county respondent cities is provided by the city recreation departments. This is the case for the specific recreation services (parks, cultural and social activities, and athletic activities) as well as the aggregate of recreation services.

Financing: Police, recreation, and street services are usually paid for out of the General Fund in the city budget, although there is some special district financing for recreation and street services.

For police, the contract charges are based on patrol or other input units.

There is rarely more than one potential provider offering to contract police services. For refuse collection, contract charges are based on fees per household, while for streets the contract charges are essentially cost reimbursement for work done. For both refuse and street services there is usually more than one potential provider; most cities use a formal contract bidding process; and cities fairly often switch from one provider to another.

Decision-Making: For police and refuse collection services that are contracted, the terms of performance tend to be specified either by the city or by the city and the provider jointly, and monitoring of service delivery also tends to be done by the city alone, or jointly with the provider. For recreation and street services, however, specification of performance terms and monitoring of delivery is usually done only by the city.

These substantive results are essentially consistent with later surveys. From a methodological perspective the exploratory questionnaire indicated that we should separate our efforts to determine the structures currently being used to provide services from our efforts to determine the decision processes involved in service provision. The former is reasonably objective information that could be obtained from simple questionnaires; the later is complex information where simple questions are ambiguous questions, and there is a need for interview rather than questionnaire instruments.

The Structural Incidence Questionnaire

This questionnaire was designed to determine the structure used to provide 26 municipal services. It was deicded that rather than ask respondents to specify particular service structures in their cities, we would determine which structures are used by asking respondents to identify what actor performs which activity for each service. The exploratory survey confirmed our expectation that financing, producing, planning, and monitoring are the important activities that could be used as a basis for defining structures.

Each of the four questions in the survey was designed in a matrix format with specific rows and specific actor columns. Respondents were asked to check the appropriate cells in each matrix question. This approach proved to be very effective with a high response rate (68 percent) and all questions virtually always answered.

When more than one actor was involved with a specific activity for a specific service, respondents were asked to indicate their relative importance. Some respondents simply checked the multiple actors when this occurred. Also, there are indications that some respondents did not indicate multiple actors but checked only the dominant actor. Improved questionnaires should seek to correct for such underreporting.

The Police Services Questionnaire

Much of the data needed to estimate the costs and outputs of police agencies are not available. We sought to fill this data gap with a questionnaire to independent city police departments in California. One set of questions dealt with output or performance indicators.[16] We asked respondents to provide recent year data on these indicators and to specify whether they were used to evaluate performance of individual officers or the department.

Other questions dealt with inputs required to provide the police service, including data on patrol officers' time allocation, employment and expenditures for various police functions, wages and residence of police officers, and dispatch and investigatory policies. A final question dealt with who provides 17 specific police subservices to the city.[17]

The response rate to this survey was quite low (24 percent). Also, the questions requiring hard data were not completed as often as were the questions involving attitudes and judgments.

Individual City Manager Interviews

Ten city managers in Los Angeles County were interviewed in their offices. The city managers were asked to put aside a two- to three-hour block of time for the interview. The sample was drawn from the respondents to the exploratory questionnaire. Although the respondent's sample was selected randomly, the interviews were set up, as far as possible, through the use of personal contacts.[18]

Two interviewers were at each interview session. One took the lead in asking questions, while the second interceded, when necessary, for clarification or amplification. Both interviewers took complete notes, partly to make certain that all information was taken down and partly for post-interview comparisons.

The first set of questions dealt with the budgetary process. Included were questions about who was involved with budgeting, what they did, whom they interacted with, the sequence and timing of steps in the process, budget priorities, and the response to unexpected budget developments.

The second set of questions was concerned with costs and revenues, including identifying revenue sources, recent changes in such sources, and what the city is likely to do if service costs continue rising.

A third set of questions focused on four specific services—police, residential refuse, street sweeping, and building and safety inspection. The interview covered such questions as what standards were used in evaluating service performance; what were the sources of information about service performance; how

---

16. The pre-specified performance indicators included calls for service, average response time, traffic accidents, traffic accidents investigated, traffic enforcement index, investigations conducted, felony complaints filed, convictions obtained, citizen complaints, seven major felonies committed, clearances for major felonies, juvenile arrests, and narcotic arrests.

17. The pre-specified actors included city departments, county government, other cities, private firms, joint-powers agreements, and state government. Except for city departments a distinction was also made between contracting and noncontracting provision.

18. Two of the senior investigators, Ries and Kirlin, have extensive contacts among city managers, knowing most of them personally.

did services rank in terms of saliency; what changes in structure had recently been adopted and which were likely in the future; and who opposed or supported such changes.

A fourth set of questions was concerned with the duties of the city manager and staff, and whether this time allocation would be different under alternative structures.

In spite of pre-tests of the interview schedule, these interviews were unsuccessful in the field. Even though the city manager had the time set aside it was difficult to obtain an uninterrupted interview. Open-ended questions tended to result in long difficult-to-interpret answers; more structured questions were difficult to understand and were resisted. It was impossible to insure that respondents received similar interviews. Respondents tended to concentrate on specific areas in the interview. The pre-designed questions were excessively detailed, complex, and lengthy. The interviewers often disagreed on their interpretation of responses. The interview process was extremely costly, since usually only one a day could be scheduled.[19]

After ten interviews it became apparent that they were not being productive. The staff then cancelled all future interviews to consider new strategies. Two issues were seen as being of critical importance. The questions were too vague, covered too much territory, and were not always seen by managers as being relevant. The staff, however, felt that on the basis of its experience with the ten interviews, it could design an interview shcedule that would avoid these deficiencies. The second issue was that the questions were often charged with emotive value to respondents, and it was not clear that all responses were equally reliable. The staff observed that when managers could discuss a question during the interview if often seemed to result in more considered responses. It was expected that if such discussions were to occur among city managers, as peers, then the purpose and meaning of questions would be clarified and reliable responses would be more likely. Therefore the staff decided the proper strategy would be to conduct group interviews, which would have the additional advantage of being less costly than the individual interviews.

Group City Manager Interviews

In the group interview process four to eight managers were brought together for half a day. At some groups there were only independent city managers; some had only contract city managers; and some included both contract and independent city managers. Although there were response differences between the contract city and independent city managers, none of these differences could be attributed to the kind of group in which they participated.

A senior staff member acted as the principal facilitator, taking the group through each stage of the interview process, explaining the questions and their

---

19. The distance between cities in the metropolitan area contributed to the difficulties of scheduling interviews because of the travel times involved.

purpose, and stimulating the group discussion. Discussion followed the presentation of each question and preceded the responses to each question. Actual responses, however, were recorded on the pre-designed schedules and were not made in the open. A staff member was assigned to each respondent to help in any further clarification that might be needed and to facilitate the process of responding to each of the questions.

A variety of data-collection techniques was used during the group interviews, including Milbrath-like card sorts, matrix entries, and scalar rankings. The group discussions would usually begin with requests for clarification of questions, but would soon become debates over substance. These discussions served to change the pace, to give space for oral expression, and to allow managers to reflect upon the choices they were being asked to make, including hearing others' positions. As the objective was to elicit considered opinions about choices made in a political context of debate and power relationships, such an open interchange seems preferable to the privacy more traditional to individual interviews soliciting unchallenged attitudes and opinions. Indeed it turned out that in a number of cases apparent differences among respondents were resulved through the clarifications that emerged through group discussion. A further advantage of the group discussion was that staff, having heard the discussions, were less likely to misinterpret the responses to the questions and more properly evaluate the results.

The interview began with a card sort in which respondents were given a set of cards identifying 26 specific services and a cardboard sheet containing boxes identifying various service structures. Each respondent was asked to identify how each of the services was currently provided in this city by placing each card with the appropriate box. The respondent was then asked to identify how he expected his city would be providing each service a decade hence. As a third card sort the respondent was asked to indicate his preferences as to how each service should be provided. Finally, the respondent was asked to indicate whether he expected each of the indicated service structures to become more or less important (along a six-point scale) over the coming decade.

After these tallies were made, respondents were asked to write down the reasons for their choices. Then an open discussion of these reasons took place. It had been correctly anticipated that the reasons given for structural selection would fall into four categories: characteristics of the city; attributes of the service and attributes of the provider of the services; measures of performance; and aspects of the decision process. As the group discussion took place a senior staff member wrote the various reasons down on a visible blackboard—separating, but not yet labeling, each category.

After a complete discussion had taken place, including not only an identification of each reason but also a discussion of its validity, each respondent was given a set of five predesigned matrix formatted questions. Each of these questions identified structures in the columns and reasons for selection in the rows.

210 How Cities Provide Services

For the most part staff had properly anticipated the reasons that would be offered by the participants. When this was not the case the unexpected reasons would be added to the questionnaire row in pencil. Respondents were then asked to check the appropriate cells in each of the questions. The first question dealt with service characteristics; the second with service and provider attributes; the third with service performance measures; and the fourth with decision processes.[20] The respondents recorded their choices in private while the staff member assigned to each respondent was available for assistance and any clarification required.

Similar procedures were then used for responses to questions on the effects of contracting in the Los Angeles metropolitan area and the extent of satisfaction with the established relationships between city and county governments.

A final set of questions was concerned with twelve specific services.[21] Respondents were asked to indicate which structures were expected to grow or decline in importance as providers of each service. Then they were asked to check off, in appropriate matrix formatted questions, the structure likely to provide the highest measure of performance for specific performance indicators for each of the twelve services.

There was substantial enthusiasm among city managers to the group interview techniques. They felt part of the creative process rather than being simply subjects. They understood the questions and the relevance of the questions more fully and they participated in the development of the substance of the questions.

20. The wording of the first question is shown below. The other questions were similarly worded.

The group has identified certain *characteristics of a city* as being more or less likely to result in services being provided through one rather than another structure. Some studies have identified still other city characteristics as having this effect. We would now like to obtain and record your perceptions regarding the effects of city characteristics on structures for providing services.

Chart I identifies a list of city characteristics and asks you to indicate whether each characteristic is most likely to lead to most services being provided through

    a city department (col. 1)
or a contract with the county (col. 2)
or a contract with a private firm (col. 3)
or a franchised private firm (col. 4)
or some other structure (col. 5)

You are being asked to identify *only one structure* as being the *most likely* to be associated with each city characteristic by placing a check in the appropriate column. If you believe that the city characteristic has no effect on the selection of a structure for service delivery please indicate that by placing a check in column (6). If you believe there is an effect but it is not the same for most services then check column (7).

21. The twelve services were general law enforcement patrol; residential refuse collection; street cleaning and patching; fire protection; building and safety inspection; planning; traffic signal maintenance; parks; tree planting and trimming; zoning and subdivision; ambulance; and animal control and shelter.

There was little resistance to answering the questions, except for the final question dealing with specific services. This question was the most detailed and came at the end of the day when respondents were both tired and anxious to get away. The advantages of the group interview process as compared to the individual interview which we perceive are as follows:

"Considered" opinions were received. The discussions at various points during the interview encouraged serious reflection about the choices being made. For the purposes of this study, recognition of alternative viewpoints, political forces, and the like was appropriate; additionally, hasty answers appear to be discouraged because of the presence of peers.

"Truthful" opinions were revealed. A problem often encountered in interviewing elites about sensitive, politically relevant topics, is obtaining "truthful" responses. Traditional solutions to this problem emphasize interviewer knowledgeability of the topic in question and promises of confidentiality. Both approaches were used in this study. Although the group interview process in its discussion periods led to sharing of views among those present, this rarely appeared to bother city managers.

The multiple research methods used also provided opportunity for checking elite responses against data systematically gathered in several other ways. As a consequence of the strong convergence of data from several sources and the consistency in responses to similar questions, we are convinced that city managers' evaluations and preferences about service provisions were truthfully provided.

Similarity in the interview process was achieved. Six group sessions were held and the same format was followed in each. Interruptions on "city business' did not occur; no interview was terminated early; only the three senior staff members led the sessions, and they followed identical procedures.

Great numbers of detailed responses were collected. The matrix check-off format used in many questions collects a large amount of detailed information; we had not been able to get city managers to respond to the same questions in the one-on-one pre-tests in their offices.

Interview costs were reduced. The group interview process required only one senior staff member to be present along with one junior interviewer for each respondent. The one-on-one interview required both a senior and junior staff interviewer for each respondent as well as considerable travel time to get to the site of the interview.

Other Interviews
One group interview was held with a sample of independent city police chiefs

from Los Angeles County and another group interview was held with high-level personnel from various Los Angeles County departments providing services to cities. The questions pursued and the format followed were essentially the same as for the city managers.

In the police interview the questions dealt with fourteen specific subservices and were particularly concerned with the performance measures of efficiency, average response time to service calls, and crime rates. In the county department interviews the questions generally separated services into their field and support components, and added some questions on differences between county and city provision of services.

MODES OF SERVICE DELIVERY

Conceptualizing a Typology of Service Delivery Modes

We have seen that the selection of one mode of delivery rather than another is related to the extent of local control a delivery mode provides as well as to the costs of production and the burden of finance associated with the mode of delivery. Thus, if local control is achieved through the activity of planning, we can find a symmetry between this conclusion and the conceptual basis for a typology of structure for delivery of services. This basis is that—although a service mode necessarily involves the three activities of production, finance, and planning—different actors (that is, levels of government or the private sector) can perform each of these three activities in providing a service. Delivery modes, therefore, are defined by the relation between actors and activities. There are four basic service provision modes in the typology:

- *The consolidated mode* occurs when the same actor performs each of the three activities, planning, financing, and producing the service.
- *The contract mode* occurs when the actor who finances and plans the services does not produce it.
- *The regulated mode* occurs when the actor who plans a service does not finance or produce it.
- *The grant mode* occurs when the actor who finances neither plans nor produces the service.

Let us suppose that a service is being produced, financed, and planned by the city government, but that this is believed to be unsatisfactory. How can the provision modes change? If some actor other than a city government can be selected to perform all three activities, a "transfer of service" results, and city government is no longer involved in any of the activities associated with providing the service. This is the traditional approach of those who advocate reform of metropolitan political systems: moving all three activities involved in service provision up ("centralization") or down ("decentralization") the spatial hierarchy of governments.

Alternatively, the city may decide to transfer one of the three activities rather than the entire service. If it transfers only the production of the service, it becomes involved in contracting. If it transfers only financing, it is usually involved with intergovernmental transfers or grants. If it transfers planning then the service probably becomes directly or indirectly regulated. This kind of conceptualization enables further distinctions.

The Consolidated Mode. When the same actor performs each activity, problems of coordination, negotiation, and goal-setting are probably reduced or at least less visible. Perhaps becuase of this the basic consolidated mode—in which the same actor finances, produces, and plans the service—is the most typical. But who is the actor in the consolidated mode?

Most often it is the city government that finances the service through taxes or user charges, produces it through city departments, and plans it through its internal decision-making mechanisms. An important characteristic of the city consolidated market is a lump-sum appropriation of funds to the city departments that are the producers. The resident's role in decisions about these activities is most frequently to act as a constraint upon the decision-makers, and this constraint varies among cities and among services. The resident is usually the source of financing, although an important variant is the subsidized city service in which other governments are responsible for some of the financing through grants. In addition to providing financing, and thus affecting the quality and price of service, these other governments often seek to influence the planning and production of the services they are subsidizing. When these noncity actors are involved, the typology should enable identification of modes that are supplemental to the basic consolidated mode.

Similarly, a county government or a district government can finance, produce, and plan for a service delivered to residents of cities as well as of unincorporated places. Occasionally a state government may perform all three activities for a service.

Division of powers among jurisdictions is likely within a metropolitan area. Jurisdictions are often distinguished by the extent of their spatial boundaries. By this measure, a city government can be considered as decentralized, and a county or regional government can be considered as centralized. The differentiating characteristic is that the centralized government, conventionally encompassing most of a metropolitan area, is larger in scale than any of the decentralized governments that coexist in the same area. Either a centralized or decentralized government can be consolidated, in the sense that it undertakes all three activities (producing, financing, and planning); however, neither centralized nor decentralized governments need be consolidated. The typology thus permits analysis to distinguish between spatial or jurisdictional centralization and service delivery consolidation.

Furthermore, government may not be involved in all, and residents may purchase services directly from private firms. Some of the types of services often provided by local government (such as refuse collection) can be and are provided through the private sector. The distinguishing characteristic of the private consolidated mode is that definable units of service are purchased by city residents (including businesses). Prices in the private mode are set or negotiated between the residents (the consumer) and the firm producing the service. Production and planning are jointly influenced by the residents and private firms, while the residents are also the source of financing, through their price payments. A variant of this mode occurs when the city government imposes some regulation (such as licensing, codes, franchises, utility rates, or health standards) over the production or pricing of a service, in which case we have a city government supplement to the private consolidated mode.

The Contract Mode. A government that accepts responsibility for providing a service to city residents may do so through government finance but not production. For this reason we define the basic contract mode as that in which the actor who finances does not produce but does plan for the service delivery.

A variety of actors exist who might produce a service under contract. The most important of such producers are private firms and county government. The city government usually finances a contract with a private firm or the county. However, as cities increasingly seek innovative forms of contracting, they might select other cities, special districts, or the state government to produce services. The county ordinarily contracts with a private firm; however, it sometimes has the option to finance a contract with district, state, or even city government as a producer. Similarly, if a district government finances a contract, the contract is likely to be with a private firm, but it might be with the county or some other producer.

In the intergovernmental contract mode, then, the government that finances and plans makes a payment, at an agreed price, to another government that produces and delivers service to the city's residents. As is common in most forms of intergovernmental action, decisions are arrived at through negotiation between the organizations involved. Decisions about planning, prices, production level, workload, and even finance are thus the results of interorganizational decision-making processes. The resident is generally the source of financing and acts as a constraint on decision-making elites. Partly because of the difficulty in determining and measuring the service outputs that are purchased, service costs may not match the contract payment. In such a case, a redistribution of income occurs in which taxpayers from some jursidiction are subsidizing residents of other jurisdictions.

Intergovernmental contracting is a particular variant of cooperative action in which there is a formal division of activities among jurisdictions—production by one unit, financing by another, for example. Under contracting, decisions are made through interactions and negotiations among units, and are based on a specification of the rights and duties assigned to each jurisdiction for each activity. Thus, although specific acitivites are performed by different individual governments or firms, the service is provided through interaction among jurisdictions and would not be provided at all if any jurisdiction failed in its own activity responsibility. Such interaction might be considered "vertical." In some other forms of intergovernmental cooperation, such as mutual aid or joint-powers agreements, the interaction is more "horizontal." In this case, several governments and even the private sector could be involved cooperatively with a specific activity or with all activities. Sometimes when this occurs it takes the form of a regional government, which is then identified as a particular governmental actor in the typology. In other cases, however, such cooperation does not occur within a formal governmental framework.

In addition to the intergovernmental contract mode, there is the private producer contract mode that occurs when firms, rather than other governments, produce the service and negotiate its price. It should be noted that governments often contract with firms or other governments for the purchase of items used as inputs in their own production of services. However, since such purchases are not considered as outputs (that is, they are not delivered to final consumers), they would not define a service contract even though a contract exists. In some cases it is difficult to distinguish between a contract for an input and a contract for an output.

Thus, in a contract the responsibility for producing a contract service is assigned by the city government to some other government or firm, usually but not necessarily to a single producer. In order to maintain control over the quality of service provided its citizens, the city government that also finances usually retains some responsibility for planning. The production and planning decisions often result from interactions between the producer on the one hand and the financing government on the other hand. The supply-pricing decision is either made on the basis of negotiation between the producer and the city government or established by formulas. Sometimes, other jurisdictions may become involved in the planning, regulatory, and pricing activities as interested parties.

The Regulated Mode. Another way for government to exercise responsibility for providing a service to its residents is by regulation of the production and finance activities. This regulation may be formal and involve establishment of city ordinances that set rates, control franchises, and so on; or it may be informal, with responsibility and control being exercised through the planning activity. For this reason we define the basic regulated mode as that in which one actor finances and produces the service but a different actor plans it. By this definition the planner is the regulator and the financer-producer is being regulated.

Regulation of the private producer is probably under a franchise, particularly if city government is the regulator. When it is the city government that is being regulated, we would expect the regulator to be a higher level government. When the city government is the regulator, which is the usual case, it may regulate through formal regulations, informal regulatory practices, or planning activities. There is no way of distinguishing between these forms of regulation in this typology.

The Grant Mode. Considerations of equity, externalities, or inadequate tax base may make it desirable for one government to adopt financial responsibility for a service it neither produces nor regulates. The basic grant mode is defined as that in which the financer is not the producer; also in the grant mode, unlike the contract mode, the financer is not the planner and the producer may or may not be the same actor as the planner.

Usually, in the United States, we would expect grants to flow from higher to lower level government. In the typology that has been developed, the city, county, district, and federal governments are seen as potential grantors who can transfer funds to each of the other producer-actors and planner-actors. In California, state aid is not usually in the form of a grant; most state aid to municipalities involves a return of taxes to the taxed jurisdiction. We have treated such a transfer of funds as if it were city-raised revenue.

Implementing the Typology in California

We have already indicated that each of three activities essential to providing a service may be performed by one or several actors. We have used the term basic mode to indicate when there is only one actor, not necessarily the same actor, who dominates in each of the activities—financing, producing, and planning. The actor-activity relationships in the four basic modes are summarized as follows:

Basic consolidated: financer = producer; financer = planner
Basic contract: financer $\neq$ producer; financer = planner
Basic regulated: planner $\neq$ producer; planner $\neq$ financer
Basic grant: financer $\neq$ producer; financer $\neq$ planner

When we identify who the particular actors are, then these basic modes become specific. For example, if the city government is the actor who is producing, financing, and planning, then we have a city-consolidated mode, whereas if it is the county which is performing each of these activities, then we have a county-consolidated mode. Similarly, if the city is engaged in a contract for the county to provide service, we have a county-producer/city-contract mode; but if the county has a contract with a private firm for service delivery, then we have a private-producer/county-contract mode.

But supposing, as is possible, that there is more than one actor involved in a specific activity. Usually, when this occurs, one of the actors is dominant while the other is supplemental. Therefore, in order to take account of such cases, we have included in the typology the possibility for a supplemental mode. For example, if the federal government helps to finance a service that the city also finances, produces, and plans, we have identified a city-consolidated mode supplemented by a federal grant.

The potential number of specific modes and of supplemental modes is an artifact of the number of actors who are separately identified. In the system that we have implemented, there are nine separate actors, including eight levels of government and the private sector.

Precise definitions of these potential service provision modes are possible only when specific combinations of actors and activities are identified. The preceding discussion has identified three activities that are essential for providing a municipal service:

1. Production is the process of combining inputs, ultimately resulting in the delivery of a service to city residents. This includes the creation of the service output, the delivery of service outputs to groups and areas in the community, and the assignment and allocation of workload to groups and areas in the community.

2. Financing is the process by which funds are raised to cover the expenditures required for the costs of producing (including delivery) the services. The major sources of financing are taxes, user charges, and grants.

3. Planning is the process of deciding on the quality and level of service provided to the community. It includes budget decisions and negotiations, formal and informal regulations of service production, monitoring the service production when necessary, and setting the price of a service, whether it is a user charge or contract price.

There are several classes that group the nine key actors that can engage in any one or all of the activities required to provide services to a city:

1. The private sector includes residents and businesses in the city who are recipients of the service, as well as firms located in or outside the city who are actual or potential producers and sellers of the service. Even though residents and firms are different actors, we treat the entire private sector as a single actor.

2. Regional government refers to those governmental organizations that engage in service provision activities on a regionwide basis. In our system this includes as separate actors county government, districts, and regional agencies. Also, for convenience joint-powers agreements among cities are included as a regional government.

3. External government refers to those government organizations that significantly affect city government activities but are not themselves located in the region. In our system, this includes the state and federal governments.

To implement the typology and thereby determine the incidence of the various service modes in California, we used a mailed questionnaire. Responses were received from 84 California cities, of which 42 are in L.A. County and the remaining 42 are located in five other counties as follows: Orange (16), Santa Clara (7), Alameda (7), Contra Costa (8), and Ventura (4).

Data obtained from 84 cities in California enabled us to determine the modes of delivery for 26 municipal services. Table A-3 shows, for each of the 26 services, the proportion of cities that use each mode. For example, only 5 percent of the cities used the city-consolidated mode to provide solid-waste disposal services, while over 95 percent used this mode to provide zoning services. Overall, 48 percent of all the services provided by the sample of cities utilized the city-consolidated mode, while 17 percent utilized the city-contract mode. Table A-4 summarizes the distribution of modes in California cities, cities in L.A. County, and cities in other counties.

As shown in Table A-4 the consolidated mode accounts for about three-quarters of all basic modes; contract modes are one-fifth; and regulated and grant modes together account for less than one-tenth. These percentages hold roughly whether we are talking about cities in L.A. County, cities in other counties, or all cities in California.

In spite of the fact that there are almost 200 conceptually possible specific modes, given the number of factors we have specified, there are relatively few actual modes and they are highly concentrated. Thus, over 80 percent of all provision of services is accounted for by five specific modes: city consolidated, district consolidated, private consolidated, city-financed contract with county producers, and city-financed contract with private producers.

These proportions are based simply on a count of service deliveries by mode. We have given equal weight to those services that require large expenditures and those that do not. Would the results be very different if we were to weigh each service by its average expenditure across cities and then determine the average distribution? This has been done with the service expenditure shares reported in Table A-3 used as weights. The results are shown in Table A-5.

The proportions tend to be about the same whether expenditure weights are used or not. The one possibly important change when expenditure weights are used is that the consolidated mode increases slightly for cities outside L.A. County.

Now that we have seen the distribution of services by basic mode of provision, we can turn to the question of which actors are importantly involved in each basic mode. Table A-6 shows the finance, planning and production actors for each mode.

In the state of California, the city department variant of the consolidated mode accounts for half of all services delivered. The city financed variant of the contracts mode accounts for about 15 percent of all services, and about half of these are contracts with the county. City government regulation accounts for two-thirds of the regulated modes, while city and county governments are each grant recipients in one-third of the grant modes.

Table A-3. Percentage Distribution of Provision Modes for Specific Services Among 84 California Cities

Service	City con-sol. (1)	Other con-sol. (2)	City con-tract (3)	Other con-tract (4)	City regu-lated (5)	Non-city-regu-lated (6)	Grant (7)	Not pro-vided (8)	City fi-nanced (9)[a]	% of total oper-ating expen-ditures[b] (10)
1. General law enforcement	71	2	25	0	0	0	2	0	96	19.0
2. Traffic patrol	70	1	29	0	0	0	0	0	99	8.0
3. Residential refuse	15	48	19	1	0	17	0	0	34	3.0
4. Business refuse	10	59	12	1	0	17	0	1	22	1.5
5. Solid-waste disposal	5	47	19	6	0	16	2	5	26	0.5
6. Sewer maintenance	40	31	12	5	0	5	6	1	52	1.0
7. Street cleaning	76	4	20	0	0	0	0	0	96	2.5
8. Street resurfacing	39	2	51	1	1	1	0	5	91	4.0
9. Street lighting	33	13	26	6	0	14	4	4	59	3.0
10. Traffic signals	35	3	53	2	0	0	4	4	91	1.0
11. Street signs	79	2	19	0	0	0	1	0	98	1.0
12. Parks and recreation	85	6	4	0	0	1	2	2	90	12.0
13. Libraries and museums	30	37	7	11	0	7	6	2	38	6.5
14. Fire protection	56	26	6	6	0	1	6	0	65	14.5
15. Public transportation	6	55	6	2	0	12	10	10	12	0.0[c]
16. Water distribution	45	42	3	3	2	4	4	1	48 }	12.0
17. Water pollution	16	40	5	5	0	10	6	17	24 }	
18. Animal control	20	42	23	3	0	5	6	0	45	1.0
19. Building and safety inspection	68	5	22	2	0	0	2	1	90	2.5
20. Ambulance service	13	53	28	4	0	2	0	0	41	1.0

Table A-3. continued

Service	City consol. (1)	Other consol. (2)	City contract (3)	Other contract (4)	City regulated (5)	Non-city-regulated (6)	Grant (7)	Not provided (8)	City financed (9)[a]	% of total operating expenditures[b] (10)
21. Tree planting and trimming	87	1	10	0	0	0	2	0	97	2.0
22. Noise pollution	50	17	7	0	0	4	0	22	57	0.0[c]
23. Storm drains	55	20	12	6	0	1	6	0	62	0.5
24. Planning	96	0	4	0	0	0	0	0	100 }	1.0
25. Zoning	96	0	4	0	0	0	0	0	100 }	
26. Engineering	74	2	21	0	0	1	2	0	95	2.5
Average	48	22	17	3	0	5	3	3	66	100.0

[a] Includes Columns 1 + 3 + 5.
[b] As estimated from sample of 34 city budgets in Los Angeles County.
[c] Expenditures on these services could not be identified in sample budgets; therefore we have excluded them even though the expenditures are probably substantial.

Table A-4. Summary of Distribution of Provision Modes

Distribution of services, by basic modes

	Average percent for all services			Range of percents across cities		
Basic modes	All Calif. cities	Cities in L.A. County	Cities not in L.A. County	All Calif. cities	Cities in L.A. County	Cities not in L.A. County
Consolidated mode	70%	65%	76%	38-46%	36-93%	38-100%
Contract mode	20	25	15	4-52	0-52	0-50
Regulated mode	5	6	4	0-17	0-21	0-14
Grant mode	3	3	3	0-10	0-7	0-14
Not provided	3	3	3	0-24	0-24	0-29
Total	100	100	100	0-96	0-93	0-100

Table A-5. Expenditure Weighted Distribution of Services by Basic Mode

Basic modes	All California cities	Cities in L.A. County	Cities not in L.A. County
Consolidated mode	73%	65%	81%
Contract mode	19	26	12
Regulated mode	3	4	3
Grant mode	3	3	2
Not provided	3	2	2
Total	100	100	100

City governments finance two-thirds and plan almost three-fourths of all service deliveries. Together, district government and private actors finance one-quarter and plan one-fifth of all services. The city is a relatively more important source of finance and planning in contract modes than in consolidated modes because there are very few privately financed contract modes. In regulated markets, private firms and districts do most of the financing and production, but city governments do most of the planning and, therefore, the regulating.

City government is the producer for only half of all service deliveries. Private firms are producers of one-fifth of the services, and together, county and district governments are the producers of one-fourth. City departments are the producer in over two-thirds of consolidated modes; and district governments and the private sector are each the producer in over one-tenth of the consolidated modes. County government and private firms are about equally important as producers in contract modes.

Table A-6. Finance, Planning, and Producer Actors in Basic Modes for Providing Services (percent distribution)

	Total modes	Basic modes			
		Consolidated mode	Contract mode	Regulated mode	Grant mode
Finance actors					
All California cities					
City finance actor	66%	69%	87%	3%	19%
County finance actor	6	7	3	9	10
District finance actor	13	11	8	43	44
State finance actor	1	1	0	0	0
Private finance actor	11	12	1	46	7
Federal finance actor	0	0	0	0	15
Other city finance actors	0	0	0	0	5
Not provided	3	—	—	—	—
Total	100	100	100	100	100
L.A. County cities					
City finance actor	68	70	87	3	27
County finance actor	6	7	3	7	7
District finance actor	13	11	9	46	47
State finance actor	1	1	0	0	0
Private finance actor	9	11	1	44	3
Federal finance actor	0	0	0	0	17
Other city finance actors	0	1	0	0	0
Not provided	3	—	—	—	—
Total	100	100	100	100	100
Cities not in L.A. County					
City finance actor	65	69	88	3	10
County finance actor	7	7	4	13	14
District finance actor	12	10	6	38	41
State finance actor	1	1	0	7	0
Private finance actor	12	13	1	48	10
Federal finance actor	0	0	0	0	14
Other city finance actors	0	0	0	0	10
Not provided	3	—	—	—	—
Total	100	100	100	100	100
Planning actors					
All California cities					
City planning actor	70	69	87	65	51
County planning actor	8	7	3	19	34
District planning actor	10	11	8	6	12
State planning actor	1	1	0	3	0
Private planning actor	8	12	1	3	3
Agency planning actor	0	0	0	4	0
Not provided	3	—	—	—	—
Total	100	100	100	100	100

Table A-6. continued

	Basic modes				
	Total modes	Consolidated mode	Contract mode	Regulated mode	Grant Grant mode
L.A. County cities					
City planning actor	71	70	87	59	50
County planning actor	8	7	3	23	40
District planning actor	9	11	9	5	10
State planning actor	1	1	0	5	0
Private planning actor	7	11	1	2	0
Agency planning actor	0	0	0	5	0
Not provided	3	–	–	–	–
Total	100	100	100	100	100
Cities not in L.A. County					
City planning actor	70	69	88	80	51
County planning actor	7	7	4	8	28
District planning actor	9	10	6	8	14
State planning actor	1	1	0	3	0
Private planning actor	10	13	1	0	7
Agency planning actor	0	0	0	3	0
Not provided	3	–	–	–	–
Total	100	100	100	100	100
Producer actors					
All California cities					
City producing actor	50	69	1	3	37
County producing actor	16	7	46	9	36
District producing actor	11	11	8	43	17
State producing actor	1	1	1	0	0
Private producing actor	19	12	41	46	10
Other city producing actors	1	0	3	0	0
Joint producing actors	0	0	0	0	0
Not provided	3	–	–	–	–
Total	100	100	100	100	100
L.A. County cities					
City producing actor	46	70	1	3	33
County producing actor	20	7	57	7	47
District producing actor	12	11	8	46	7
State producing actor	0	1	0	0	0
Private producing actor	18	11	33	44	13
Other city producing actors	0	1	1	0	0
Joint producing actors	0	0	0	0	0
Not provided	3	–	–	–	–
Total	100	100	100	100	100
Cities not in L.A. County					
City producing actor	54	69	2	3	45
County producing actor	11	7	27	13	28

Table A-6. continued

	Total modes	Basic modes			
		Consolidated mode	Contract mode	Regulated mode	Grant Grant mode
District producing actor	10	10	8	38	17
State producing actor	1	1	3	7	10
Private producing actor	20	13	54	48	0
Other city producing actors	1	0	8	0	0
Joint producing actors	0	0	1	0	0
Not provided	3	–	–	–	–
Total	100	100	100	100	100

Although the percentages cited relate to all cities in California, the indicated distributions are about the same whether applied to cities in L.A. County or other California cities. About the only important regional differences are that among L.A. County cities, the county is a relatively large producer under contract, while among other cities the private producers have a relatively large share of the contracts. Also, it appears that cities in L.A. County are more involved than other cities in regulating services that they do not produce.

So far we have described the distribution of service modes in terms of the dominant actors involved in each activity. We have earlier noted that the same activity might involve several actors, and the question arises whether the distribution would change if the supplemental actors were taken into account.

The supplemental mode indicates the additional actors involved in providing a service. For example, if a city contracts with the county for the police service and finances the service partly with a federal grant, this is identified in the typology as a city contract mode supplemented by a federal grant; or if a city department maintains the city streets but also contracts for some additional maintenance with the county, this is a city consolidated market supplemented by a contract mode.

Supplemental provision modes are most likely to occur when there are subservices whose delivery can be spun off from the primary service. For example, a city police department might decide to contract its laboratory work or to let the state maintain its records. In the former case, police service would be a city consolidated mode with a contract supplement; in the latter case it would be a city consolidated mode with a state consolidated supplement. This suggests that, as cities seek to make changes in their modes for providing services, they can potentially benefit by supplementing the existing modes as well as replacing them. Indeed, there is some evidence that this is what cities are actually doing.

Table A-7 shows the distribution of supplemental modes. Seventy percent of all services did not have any supplemental mode. Proportionately, slightly fewer

Table A-7. Supplemental Modes of Service Provision (percent distribution)

		Basic modes			
Type of supplement	Total modes	Consolidated mode	Contract mode	Regulated mode	Grant mode
All California cities					
Total	100	100	100	100	100
No supplement	70	70	62	83	54
Consolidated supplement	9	11	5	7	14
Contract supplement	5	4	12	1	5
Regulated supplement	9	9	12	7	20
Grant supplement	2	1	4	2	3
Combination supplement	5	5	6	0	3
Cities in L.A. County					
Total	100	100	100	100	100
No supplement	72	74	62	85	47
Consolidated supplement	8	9	4	5	20
Contract supplement	7	5	15	0	7
Regulated supplement	10	9	13	10	20
Grant supplement	1	1	2	0	3
Combination supplement	3	3	4	0	3
Cities not in L.A. County					
Total	100	100	100	100	100
No supplement	68	67	63	80	62
Consolidated supplement	11	14	5	10	7
Contract supplement	4	3	8	3	3
Regulated supplement	9	9	1	3	21
Grant supplement	3	2	6	5	3
Combination supplement	6	6	7	0	3

supplements are found in the basic contract and basic grant modes, with slightly more found in the basic regulated mode. Of the 30 percent of services that had supplements, about 10 percent were consolidated supplements, another 10 percent were regulated supplements, and 5 percent were contract supplements. These proportions are about the same for cities in L.A. County and for cities in other counties.

In order to determine whether including supplemental modes yields a distribution different from that obtained when they are not included, we have had to decide the relative importance of a supplemental mode. We have arbitrarily considered a supplemental mode to be one-fourth as important as a basic mode; weighting supplemental markets by 20 percent and basic markets by 80 percent then shows the distribution of services among modes, including supplemental modes. Table A-8 compares this distribution for all California cities with that of the unweighted and expenditure-weighted distribution previously shown.

We expected that including consideration of supplemental modes would increase the relative importance of contract, regulated, and grant modes of pro-

Table A-8. Comparison of Weighted and Unweighted Basic Modes of Provision

Distribution of Services by Mode

Modes	Unweighted(%)	Expenditure, Weighted(%)	Weighted by Supplemental Mode(%)
Consolidated	70%	73%	69%
Contract	20	19	19
Regulated	5	3	6
Grant	3	3	3
Not provided	3	3	3

viding services. For the adoption of a particular mode for providing a subservice that differs from the mode for providing the major components of the service would, we thought, generally involve a movement away from city departments. However, this was not the case. The distribution of supplements by mode is the same as the distribution of basic modes. There are proportionately as many city departments acting as supplements to other basic modes as there are city departments providing the major components of services. This indicates that when structural diversity and new opportunities for service provision are being considered, the city department should not be excluded.

City Types in California

Modes describe the provision of services by distinguishing which actors perform what activities, and different services tend to be provided through different modes. Since cities may generally favor one over another mode irrespective of the service, it is possible that cities can be grouped on the basis of criteria that specify such preferences. If this is so, a classification of city types can be designed in which each type is based on particular combinations of service modes. Such a classification, which consists of five city types based on mode combinations into which cities can be grouped, has been developed.

Our survey showed that there is a wide range in choices of modes for service provision in the eighty-four cities in our sample. Two cities provide all of their services through consolidated modes, while two other cities provided only 35 percent of their services through consolidated modes. As shown in Table A-9, other cities fall within these extremes and also provide varying proportions of their services through contract, regulated, and grant modes.

We have analyzed the distribution of services according to the service clusters used in earlier analyses. The results are summarized in Table A-10, which shows the grouping of modes into their city core and optional clusters and the actors that tend to be associated with each cluster.

The city core services are financed primarily by the city for both contract and consolidated modes. However, a much larger proportion of cities financed

Appendix 227

Table A-9. Percentage Distribution of Modes for All Services, by Cities in Los Angeles County and Other Counties (percent of all services)

	Cities in L.A. County						Cities not in L.A. County				
City Code	No mode	Consolidated	Contract	Regulated	Grant	City Code	No mode	Consolidated	Contract	Regulated	Grant
656	0%	100%	0%	0%	0%	214	0%	100%	0%	0%	0%
663	0	96	0	4	0	314	4	96	0	0	0
666	0	92	0	4	4	107	0	96	4	0	4
612	4	92	4	0	0	411	0	92	8	0	4
673	0	81	15	0	4	324	0	92	8	0	0
654	0	85	12	4	0	308	4	92	4	0	0
634	0	85	15	0	0	208	8	92	0	0	0
607	8	85	0	8	0	401	0	88	12	0	0
601	0	85	12	4	0	201	4	88	8	0	0
645	4	77	15	4	0	112	0	88	0	12	0
626	0	77	23	0	0	109	0	88	8	4	0
677	4	73	4	19	0	301	0	85	15	0	0
668	4	73	23	0	0	415	0	81	19	0	0
661	0	73	27	0	0	311	4	81	12	4	0
655	8	73	12	0	8	213	4	81	15	0	0
632	4	73	12	8	4	205	0	81	8	0	12
629	0	73	15	0	12	113	8	81	12	0	0
618	0	73	23	4	0	107	4	81	12	4	0
605	0	69	27	4	0	319	0	77	12	8	0
676	15	65	4	15	0	315	0	77	19	4	0
665	0	65	23	8	4	211	0	77	4	8	12
649	4	65	19	12	0	108	4	77	19	0	0
633	4	65	27	0	4	508	0	73	15	0	12
621	0	62	12	15	12	505	0	73	19	0	8
619	4	62	35	0	0	409	4	73	15	8	0
657	4	58	23	4	12	403	0	73	23	0	4
640	0	58	35	0	8	316	4	73	19	4	0
675	0	54	46	0	0	110	0	73	15	12	0

228 How Cities Provide Services

Table A-9. continued

	Cities in L.A. County						Cities not in L.A. County				
City Code	No Mode	Consolidated	Contract	Regulated	Grant	City Code	No mode	Consolidated	Contract	Regulated	Grant
637	4	50	35	8	4	322	8	69	15	4	4
636	4	50	35	4	8	306	0	69	15	4	12
622	0	50	31	12	8	304	0	69	15	4	12
616	4	50	46	0	0	303	4	69	12	12	4
609	0	50	42	8	0	506	0	65	12	23	0
669	9	46	50	0	0	407	8	65	19	0	8
613	0	46	23	15	15	318	0	65	35	0	0
608	8	46	31	12	4	509	12	62	23	4	0
660	0	42	38	19	0	408	15	62	15	4	4
638	0	42	46	12	0	313	23	62	0	4	12
672	12	38	38	8	4	320	4	58	31	8	0
641	8	38	54	0	0	207	4	54	42	0	0
628	4	38	54	4	0	326	0	54	54	4	0
653	0	35	46	19	0	203	15	35	31	19	0

Table A-10. Service Clusters, by Actor (percent of service categories)

	Finance actors				Producer actors				Planner actors			
	Total	City	County	Dist.	Private	Total	City	County	Dist.	Private	Total	City	County	Dist.	Private

All basic modes
Total	100%	65%	7%	13%	11%	100%	50%	16%	11%	19%	100%	62%	13%	10%	11%
City core services	100	94	2	1	1	100	71	15	1	11	100	86	9	1	2
City production core	100	96	1	2	1	100	84	7	1	7	100	92	4	1	2
Contract competition core	100	92	3	1	0	100	57	24	0	16	100	80	15	—	3
City optional services	100	42	10	22	27	100	30	17	20	27	100	42	17	17	19
District competition	100	47	10	30	9	100	39	16	27	9	100	48	16	22	5
Private competition	100	34	11	7	58	100	14	19	8	58	100	32	17	7	43

Consolidated basic modes
Total	100	69	7	11	12	100	69	7	11	12	100	69	7	11	12
City core services	100	96	3	1	0	100	96	3	1	0	100	96	3	1	0
City production core	100	97	1	2	0	100	97	1	2	0	100	97	1	2	0
Contract competition core	100	95	4	0	1	100	95	4	0	1	100	95	4	—	1
City optional services	100	41	15	19	24	100	41	15	19	24	100	41	15	19	24
District competition	100	53	15	25	5	100	53	15	25	5	100	53	15	25	5
Private competition	100	20	14	8	58	100	20	14	8	58	100	20	14	8	58

Contract basic modes
Total	100	87	3	8	1	100	1	46	8	41	100	87	3	8	1
City core services	100	99	1	—	—	100	—	53	4	40	100	99	1	—	—
City production core	100	100	—	—	—	100	—	42	7	51	100	100	—	—	—
Contract competition core	100	97	2	1	—	100	—	66	1	27	100	97	2	1	—
City optional services	100	73	5	18	4	100	1	41	19	34	100	73	5	18	4
District competition	100	65	6	25	4	100	—	48	24	19	100	65	6	25	4
Private competition	100	87	4	5	4	100	1	28	10	59	100	87	4	5	4

Appendix 229

optional services (particularly private competition optional services) for contract modes than for consolidated modes. This is offset by the relatively more private and county government financing of optional services under consolidated than under contract modes.

City governments finance three-fifths of the cities' services, but produce only half. County government and the private sector are relatively more important as producers than as financers of municipal services. This is primarily because city-financed contract modes, whether for core or optional services, are not city-produced services but tend to be produced by county government and private firms. On an overall basis it is clear that city government is more important than any other actor, whether in financing, producing, or planning. However, city government is relatively more important as financer-planner than as producer. County government is relatively more important as producer-planner than as financer. District government has about the same degree of relative importance, whether as financer, producer, or planner. The private sector has relatively more importance as producer than as financer-planner.

We also sought to determine whether specific clusters are associated with particular community characteristics. We ran a simple correlation analysis for each basic mode between pairs of community characteristics and service clusters and between community characteristics and specific services. The statistical analysis indicates that cities with a high average educational level, a large population size, and a small proportion of Spanish-surname population provide a significantly greater number of their services through consolidated modes and a smaller number through contract modes. These results are essentially consistent with the results of the Chapter 4 regression analyses.

THE ECONOMETRIC ANALYSIS

In testing any model, questions arise that have no solid empirical answers. Often a blending of theoretical and empirical principles becomes the basis for decisions on these issues. In the contracting model, which was discussed in Chapter 4, several key questions had to be answered. The primary purpose of this discussion is to describe these queries, the principles used in resolving the dilemmas, and the results.

Several empirical issues are addressed. Data issues are extensively discussed. A complete glossary of variables and variable descriptors for different sample groups are provided. The functional forms of certain variables, intercorrelations or multicollinearity problems for sets of right-hand variables in the model, and data sampling procedures are examined. Pooling (that is, the combining of contract and self-provision cities) and its effect on interpretations of coefficients for the all-cities equations are focused on in the second section. Finally, the nature of the recursive modeling process and, in particular, interpretations of coefficients for right-hand dependent variables in the model are discussed.

Data Issues

The data used in the estimation of the contracting model was cross-sectional information on cities in Los Angeles County for 1970. As shown in Table A-11, each row of observation is information on a specific city. As described in Chapter 4, each self-provision city in the sample (44 cities) spent less than 10 percent of its budget expenditures for contracting services in 1970. The highest recorded percentage for a self-provision city was Bell Gardens with 3.06 percent. Similarly, no self-provision city spent 4 percent or more of its police expenditures for contracting. Among the contracting cities sample (28 cities), a minimum of 11.96 percent was recorded for contracting expenditures on the city budget level and a minimum of 24.97 percent on the police expenditure level.

In all the remaining variables, overlapping values were recorded for the two groups of cities. One variable which stands out however, is the city budget property tax rate. Over half of the contract cities had a zero property tax rate recorded in 1970. The use of this measure as a left-hand or dependent variable in the model may therefore be questionable because of empirical problems resulting from the clustering of its data values around zero. In particular, if the expected value of the error term is not random, the ordinary least squares (OLS) procedure is not useful.

Table A-12 describes variables used in the contracting model as well as sources of the data. However, it can be seen that community variables were not logged in the model, while the tax bases, contracting, city expenditures, and service expenditures were logged. Tax rates and total city employment variables were similarly not logged. The functional form of each variable was determined on the basis of three criteria: (1) Did a logged variable have meaning? (2) Were similar types of variables consistently logged in the model? (3) What empirical advantages could be associated with choosing a particular form?

In the ($PERCON70$) case, the data was clearly separated into two subgroups on the basis of the contracting city definition. Comparing the natural and logged values for this variable, the logged values were clearly more normally distributed than the unlogged values. Therefore, in the regression model, much better explanatory results were shown in the log-linear form. Similarly, where elasticity measures were useful (that is, for sales and expenditures and property base values), logged forms were chosen. However, since little sense could be placed in statistical descriptions of logged community variables and tax rates, this form was not used.

Overall, while no conclusive testing was done to determine if the "best" equation (that is, the most highly significant, explanatory relationship) was chosen, the choice process relied heavily on consistency of form and elimination of common empirical problems such as multicollinearity. For the descriptive statistics, unlogged means were preferred where theoretical and regression issues allowed for a choice.

In determining which data sample to use for the descriptive statistics versus

Table A-11. Selected Data for Cities in Los Angeles County

	County contracting share of budget exp. (percent)	County contracting share of budget police exp. (percent)	1970 pop.	No. city employees per 1,000 pop.	City budget expend. per capita	Municiapl services expend. per capita	Commercial tax base per capita	Property tax base per capita	City budget property tax rate
Self-Provision Cities (44)									
Beverly Hills	0.00%	0.00%	33,396	18.48	$354	$489	$ 8,202	$ 9,658	0.9829
Glendale	0.01	0.03	132,774	10.42	153	179	2,773	2,582	1.1777
Montebello	0.01	0.00	42,851	6.95	129	131	2,373	2,826	1.4065
San Gabriel	0.01	0.00	29,136	5.39	96	122	2,743	2,275	1.1237
San Marino	0.01	0.00	14,242	7.72	127	189	867	4,471	1.7562
South Pasadena	0.01	0.00	22,979	7.53	110	126	1,134	2,323	1.8433
Alhambra	0.02	0.00	62,149	7.19	113	147	2,351	2,446	1.5028
Arcadia	0.02	0.00	44,602	6.39	112	142	2,177	3,178	1.0027
Inglewood	0.02	0.00	90,014	5.82	163	189	2,446	2,160	1.5634
Manhattan Beach	0.04	0.00	35,302	5.64	111	133	1,433	2,883	1.4952
Claremont	0.05	0.00	23,480	5.11	93	117	863	2,053	1.9281
El Monte	0.05	0.00	69,665	4.05	76	104	2,810	1,911	0.8510
El Segundo	0.05	0.00	15,618	14.73	289	403	7,123	15,910	0.8340
Sierra Madre	0.07	0.00	12,140	8.32	105	137	440	2,163	2.0292
Glendora	0.08	0.00	31,285	5.18	95	117	1,697	2,090	1.1841
Torrance	0.08	0.00	134,507	6.67	144	197	2,941	3,492	1.0860
Hawthorne	0.10	0.00	53,221	4.11	106	178	2,024	3,292	0.7411
Burbank	0.11	0.00	88,894	13.63	181	197	2,361	3,761	1.5706
Monterey Park	0.13	0.00	49,146	5.27	98	124	1,493	2,213	1.6982
Santa Monica	0.14	0.01	88,289	11.67	177	208	3,088	3,572	1.2094
Gardena	0.16	0.00	41,090	5.87	125	148	3,144	2,634	0.6443
Hermosa Beach	0.16	0.12	17,418	5.34	127	169	1,714	2,630	1.5067
Monrovia	0.16	0.00	30,072	6.55	128	164	2,359	2,413	1.5777
West Covina	0.17	0.00	67,929	4.56	108	139	2,090	1,887	1.0157

Table A-11. continued

	County contracting share of budget exp. (percent)	County contracting share of budget police exp. (percent)	1970 pop.	No. city employees per 1,000 pop.	City budget expend. per capita	Municipal services expend. per capita	Commercial tax base per capita	Property tax base per capita	City budget property tax rate
South Gate	0.18	0.00	56,881	5.73	109	138	2,750	2,593	0.6386
Pomona	0.19	0.14	87,418	7.85	140	163	2,630	2,043	2.2572
Palos Verdes Estates	0.21	0.00	13,946	5.31	82	136	313	4,289	0.9824
Signal Hill	0.21	0.00	5,575	14.35	280	332	9,816	5,654	0.6583
Redondo Beach	0.22	0.60	56,014	5.70	135	165	1,921	3,366	1.4622
Lynwood	0.29	0.00	43,386	4.01	72	93	1,508	1,813	0.9026
San Fernando	0.31	0.00	16,502	8.79	143	143	3,105	1,561	2.3746
Huntington Park	0.35	0.00	33,796	6.42	125	146	3,272	2,130	1.0463
Baldwin Park	0.36	0.00	47,122	2.89	59	90	770	1,247	0.9994
Culver City	0.37	0.00	31,350	10.97	202	159	5,138	4,615	1.1820
Bell	0.45	0.00	22,005	3.45	68	88	1,831	1,602	1.3340
Pasadena	0.45	3.17	113,254	14.71	227	205	3,182	4,003	1.4338
Covina	0.55	0.00	30,405	6.87	138	157	4,392	2,735	1.3910
Compton	0.63	0.00	78,493	4.65	101	100	1,705	1,513	1.4571
Maywood	0.66	0.00	16,990	3.77	51	65	1,189	1,175	1.2263
Azusa	0.67	0.00	25,296	8.30	146	168	2,052	2,291	1.4202
Whittier	0.89	3.58	72,629	5.92	102	128	2,720	2,478	0.8043
Downey	1.05	3.66	89,012	4.49	95	115	3,007	2,503	0.5396
La Verne	2.11	0.00	12,931	4.64	93	117	766	1,733	1.8620
Bell Gardens	3.06	0.03	29,315	.72	53	94	942	1,173	0
Contracting Cities (28)									
San Dimas	11.96	100.00	15,639	2.30	87	129	469	1,896	0.5828
Sante Fe Springs	14.22	99.72	14,620	8.21	299	407	12,484	10,025	0.4644
Commerce	17.12	100.00	10,590	10.39	724	925	43,844	27,029	0

Appendix 233

Table A-11. continued

	County contracting share of budget exp. (percent)	County contracting share of budget police exp. (percent)	1970 pop.	No. city employees per 1,000 pop.	City budget expend. per capita	Municiapl services expend. per capita	Commercial tax base per capita	Property tax base per capita	City budget property tax rate
Avalon	17.52	82.27	1,572	12.72	339	351	3,532	5,511	2.2162
Cerritos	19.35	90.96	15,967	1.25	168	268	4,313	5,407	0
Bradbury	19.48	82.53	1,371	1.46	70	120	9	2,482	0.5808
Duarte	21.66	100.00	15,099	1.13	57	93	653	1,618	0
Rolling Hills	22.49	24.97	2,026	0.99	90	223	69	7,070	0.9767
Norwalk	23.92	98.07	91,860	0.95	50	73	1,157	1,299	0
Bellflower	28.12	93.11	50,624	1.01	59	96	1,912	1,843	0
Lakewood	28.61	100.00	82,928	1.81	64	111	2,028	1,819	0.0786
South El Monte	29.75	100.00	13,643	0.95	95	127	4,435	3,184	0
Rolling Hills Estates	36.99	100.00	6,015	2.00	105	222	4,045	5,900	0.0014
Artesia	37.98	100.00	14,737	2.04	49	77	1,049	1,461	0.6108
Pico Rivera	38.33	99.25	54,224	1.12	47	87	1,699	2,009	0
Cudahy	39.04	100.00	17,000	0.29	39	60	719	1,056	0
Rosemead	39.91	100.00	40,802	0.74	48	78	1,397	1,551	0
Paramount	42.40	100.00	34,808	0.52	49	97	2,111	2,114	0
Temple City	44.38	90.25	29,700	0.81	44	94	818	1,847	0
Lomita	46.26	100.00	19,927	0.60	42	81	1,377	1,609	0
Carson	46.71	100.00	71,626	0.80	44	125	1,890	4,011	0.0005
La Puente	48.19	100.00	31,225	0.64	41	69	1,373	1,255	0
La Mirada	49.21	98.60	30,972	0.45	40	112	1,985	2,634	0
Lawndale	52.31	92.33	24,915	0.64	42	68	1,340	1,394	0
Walnut	53.54	100.00	5,992	1.00	55	123	217	2,551	0.8378
Hawaiian Gardens	54.35	100.00	8,798	0.68	37	74	1,735	1,183	0
Palmdale	59.65	100.00	8,511	0.59	83	247	2,753	6,845	0
Hidden Hills	100.00	100.00	4,204	0.71	12	60	14	1,539	0.5109

Appendix 235

Table A-12. Glossary of Variables

Variable Mnemonic	Description	Key to city sample	N	Mean	Std. Dev.	Data source
Contracting Variables						
PERCON 70	Percentage of city budget expenditures contracted with L.A. County	A	72	14.7%	21.4	1, 2
		B	28	37.3%	18.5	1, 2
LPER70	Log of PERCON70	A	72	0.074	3.046	1, 2
Revenue Variables						
TAXRATE	City Budget Property Tax Revenues as percentage of assessed property value	A	72	0.869%	0.692	1
		B	28	0.245%	0.488	1
		C	42	1.270%	0.712	1
		D	114	1.017%	0.723	1
PROPTX	City budget property tax revenues per capita	A	72	$26.65	27.44	1
		B	28	$10.82	26.88	1
LPROPTX	Log of PROPTX	A	72	1.648	3.520	1
		B	28	-1.123	4.325	1
REBATE	Intergovernmental transfers to city budget per capita	A	72	$25.29	7.81	1
		B	28	$24.58	10.98	1
LREBATE	Log of REBATE	A	72	3.185	0.329	1
		B	28	3.111	0.475	1
SPDISTRT	Aggregate of special districts' property tax rates (%)	A	72	1.443%	0.837	7
		B	28	2.037%	0.654	7
MUNIRATE	Aggregate of property tax rates within cities for municipal types of services	A	72	2.312%	0.682	7
		B	28	2.282%	0.639	7
Expenditure Variables						
EXPTOT	Total city budget expenditures per capita	A	72	$119.73	100.88	1
		B	28	$102.76	142.36	1
		C	42	$124.05	50.64	1
		D	114	$121.32	85.61	1

Table A-12. continued

Variable Mnemonic	Description	Key to city sample	N	Mean	Std. Dev.	Data Source
LEXPTDT	Log of EXPTOT	A	72	4.562	0.654	1
		B	28	4.212	0.805	1
		C	42	4.749	0.381	1
		D	114	4.631	0.574	1
MUNIEXP	Aggregate of expenditures per capita within cities for municipal types of services*	A	72	$161.82	122.94	1, 7
		B	28	$164.22	173.70	1, 7
LMUNIEXP	Log of MUNIEXP	A	72	4.932	0.506	1, 7
		B	28	4.828	0.657	1, 7
EXPOL	City budget police expenditures per capita	A	72	$24.91	15.04	1
		B	28	$19.92	18.81	
		C	42	$23.01	6.97	
		D	114	$24.21	12.68	
LEXPOL	Log of EXPOL	A	72	3.068	0.542	
		B	28	2.736	0.650	
		C	42	3.086	0.346	
		D	114	3.074	0.477	
EXFIRE	City budget fire expenditures per capita	A	72	$15.46	24.29	1
		B	28	$10.35	35.58	
		C	42	$15.07	8.75	
		D	114	$15.32	19.97	
LEXFIRE	Log of EXFIRE	A	72	1.808	1.595	
		B	28	0.381	1.508	
		C	42	2.369	1.114	
		D	114	2.015	1.457	
EXHIGH	City budget street expenditures per capita	A	72	$21.72	11.82	1
		B	28	$23.06	16.43	
		C	42	$21.35	6.51	
		D	114	$21.59	10.16	

Table A-12. continued

Variable Mnemonic	Description	Key to city sample	N	Mean	Std. Dev.	Data Source
LEXHIGH	Log of EXHIGH	A	72	2.876	0.832	
		B	28	2.741	1.229	
		C	42	3.017	0.303	
		D	114	2.928	0.688	
EXGARB	City budget garbage expenditures per capita	A	72	$3.84	4.74	1
		B	28	$0.67	1.88	
		C	42	$3.09	3.83	
		D	114	$3.56	4.55	
LEXGARB	Log of EXGARB	A	72	0.844	1.233	
		B	28	0.179	0.572	
		C	42	0.627	1.288	
		D	114	0.764	1.252	
EXPARK	City budget parks & recreation expenditures per capita	A	72	$13.87	24.40	1
		B	28	$15.06	38.09	
		C	42	$14.14	11.20	
		D	114	$13.97	20.48	
LEXPARK	Log of EXPARK	A	72	2.192	0.912	1
		B	28	1.841	1.218	
		C	42	2.329	0.926	
		D	114	2.242	0.916	
EXLIB	City budget library expenditures per capita	A	72	$3.07	4.85	1
		B	28	$1.49	5.46	
		C	42	$3.11	4.16	
		D	114	$3.09	4.59	
LEXLIB	Log of EXLIB	A	72	0.621	1.365	
		B	28	0.260	0.765	
		C	42	0.536	1.611	
		D	114	0.590	1.454	

Table A-12. continued

Variable Mnemonic	Description	Key to city sample	N	Mean	Std. Dev.	Data Source
Employment Variables						
TOTPC	Total city government employees per 1,000 population	A C D	72 42 114	5.124 5.352 5.208	4.207 2.382 3.632	4
COPSPC	Total police employees per 1,000 population	A C	72 42	1.058 1.318	0.990 0.537	4
FIREPC	Total fire employees per 1,000 population	A C D	72 42 114	0.819 0.915 0.854	0.877 0.577 0.778	4
HIGHPC	Total street employees per 1,000 population	A C D	72 42 114	0.495 0.559 0.519	0.475 0.327 0.426	4
GARBPC	Total garbage employees per 1,000 population	A C D	72 42 114	0.228 0.173 0.207	0.413 0.257 0.363	4
PARPC	Total parks & recreation employees per 1,000 population	A C D	72 42 114	0.715 0.609 0.676	0.871 0.480 0.751	4
LIBPC	Total library employees per 1,000 population	A C D	72 42 114	0.208 0.193 0.202	0.358 0.223 0.314	4
Community Characteristic Variables						
VALUE	Total assessed property value per capita	A B C D	72 28 42 114	$3382. $3862. $2992. $3238.	3677. 5064. 1147. 3001.	1

Table A-12. continued

Variable Mnemonic	Description	Key to city sample	N	Mean	Std. Dev.	Data Source
LVALUE	Log of VALUE	A	72	7.877	0.612	
		B	28	7.878	0.769	
		C	42	7.944	0.341	
		D	114	7.902	0.528	
OUTLET	Taxable sales of retail and other outlets per capita	A	72	$2959.	5317.	5
		B	28	$3551	8249.	
		C	42	$2267.	994.	
		D	114	$2704.	4270.	
LOUTLET	Log of OUTLET	A	72	7.409	1.243	
		B	28	7.049	1.759	
		C	42	7.584	0.651	
		D	114	7.474	1.064	
EDUC	Median educational level attained by population 25 years old and over	A	72	11.8 yrs.	1.1	3
		B	28	11.6 yrs.	1.1	
		C	42	12.7 yrs.	.9	
		D	114	12.2 yrs.	1.1	

Table A-12. continued

Variable Mnemonic	Description	Key to city sample	N	Mean	Std. Dev.	Data Source
SPAN	Percentage of Spanish-surname population	A	72	19.0%	14.6	3
		B	28	22.9%	18.1	
		C	42	12.9%	7.7	
		D	114	16.8%	12.8	
AGE	Median age of population	A	72	28.9 yrs	5.5	3
		B	28	26.1 yrs.	5.0	
		C	42	27.3 yrs	3.9	
		D	114	28.3 yrs.	5.0	
DISTANCE	Miles to center of city	A	71	14.4 miles	6.5	6
		B	28	16.1 miles	6.4	
		C	42	9.7 miles	7.9	
		D	114	12.6 miles	7.4	

Note: A = 72 cities from L.A. County which are in the sample.
B = 28 contracting cities from L.A. County which are in the sample.
C = 42 cities outside L.A. County which are in the sample. Includes 9 cities from Alameda County; 7 from Contra Costa; 12 from Orange; 8 from Santa Clara; and 6 from Ventura.
D = 114 California cities in the sample; including 72 from L.A. County and 42 from other counties.

which sample to use for the OLS regressions, a consistent conclusion was not reached. Rather, the number of contract cities was different in the two testing modes. For the descriptive statistics, a 24-city sample was used, while a 28-city sample was employed in the OLS regression analysis. As shown in Table A-13, the descriptive statistics for the larger grouping exhibit fewer significant differences than those recorded in Table 4-1.

Although using two samples is technically inconsistent, one reason such a distinction may be useful is that the descriptive statistics focus on single variables and are therefore much more susceptible to extreme values than the regression or multivariate analysis. Using this argument, the results showed that four cities could reasonably be excluded from the descriptive statistics because of extreme values for certain variables. Although the multivariate analysis accounted for a significant amount of the variation for the larger contracting sample, there is no reason to believe that equivalent results would have been recorded for a smaller sample group. While the criterion used for excluding variable values was at best a careful visual examination of the data, it clearly showed how a few extreme cases can alter descriptive statistics.

Multicollinearity is a common empirical problem in cross-sectional, recursive models. The nature of this process in recursive models like the contracting system was examined in detail earlier in this appendix.[22] Here we deal with the general problem of multicollinearity as applied to specific equations.

Where "perfect" collinearity between variables is not present, but two or more right-hand variables are "closely related" (that is, they have simple correlations close to but not equal to 1), the $(X'X)^{-1}$ matrix exists, but biased coefficients will result for the collinear variables. Solutions to the imperfect multicollinear case are not clear-cut.

The literature on imperfect multicollinearity is also unclear on how to interpret coefficients in an equation where this bias is present. Many econometricians, including Goldberger, Theil, Wannocott and others, indicate that the predictability of the equation is not affected even though the coefficients of the collinear variables are biased and therefore meaningless. Dhrymes contends that an equation with collinear variables would be entirely unreliable because of the statistical ties between biasedness and inconsistency. At this stage of development, then, no theoretical solutions to imperfect collinearity are evident. The effects are serious but often interpreted differently.

A matrix of simple correlations between variables in the contracting model was developed. High correlations between dependent and independent variables are associated with potentially high explanatory relations, and are therefore preferred. It is the entries that show high correlations between sets of independent variables which suggest a concern over bias.

For the all-cities sample, the correlations between (*LPER70/TAXRATE*) and

---

22. See the section "Modes of Service Delivery," above.

Table A-13. Mean Values for Selected Variables in Los Angeles County Cities: An Alternative Sample

Variables	Units of measure	Selected cities in L.A. County (72)	Contracting cities (28)	Self-provision cities less contracting cities
Degree of contracting in budget	%	14.7	37.3	-37.0
City budget property tax rate	%	.87	0.25	1.01[a]
Special district property tax rate	%	1.44	2.04	-0.97[a]
Municipal services property tax rate	%	2.31	2.28	.05
Property taxes per capita	$	27	11	26[a]
Intergovernmental transfers per capita	$	25	25	1
City budget expenditures per capita	$	120	103	28
Municipal service expenditures per capita	$	162	164	-4
Special district expenditures per capita	$	42	61	-31[a]
Sales tax base per capita	$	2,959	3,551	-969
Property tax base per capita	$	3,381	3,862	-786
City government employees per 1,000 persons	no.	5.1	2.0	5.1[a]
Median age	year	28.9	26.1	4.6[a]
Distance from central city	miles	14.4	16.1	-2.8[b]
Spanish-surname share of population	%	19.0	22.9	-6.4[b]
Median education	years	11.8	11.6	0.4
Service expenditures per capita				
Police	$	25	20	8[a]
Fire	$	15	10	8
Streets	$	22	23	-2
Refuse	$	4	1	5[a]
Parks & recreation	$	14	15	-2
Library	$	3	1	3[a]
Service employees per 1,000 persons				
Police	no.	1.1	0.0	1.7[a]
Fire	no.	0.8	0.2	1.0[a]
Streets	no.	0.5	0.2	0.5[a]
Refuse	no.	0.2	0.1	0.2[a]
Parks & recreation	no.	0.7	0.6	0.2
Library	no.	0.2	0.1	0.2[a]

[a] Statistically significant difference of means at 0.05 level using a two-tailed test.
[b] Statistically significant difference of means at 0.10 level using a two-tailed test.

(*MUNIRATE/SPDISTRT*) are above 0.70 but well below 0.90. In the first three stages of the model, then, only (*LPER70/TAXRATE*) and (*MUNIRATE/ SPDISTRT*) could possibly create a serious bias. In the contracting cities sample, (*LPER70/TAXRATE*), (*MUNIRATE/LOUTLET*), and (*MUNIRATE/ SPDISTRT*) exhibit high levels of correlation in the first three stages. For the self-provision cities, only (*MUNIRATE/SPDISTRT*) has a high simple correlation. In the fourth stage of the model the correlation between (*LEXPTOT/ LVALUE*) for both the contracting cities sample and the self-provision cities sample is high. Examining the regression results, the estimated coefficients are not of the same magnitude and do not have opposite signs. This is a good indication that the bias is not critical, because severe cases exhibit opposite signs for approximately equal coefficients.

When interpreting the coefficients of the affected variables, the reader should be aware that biased coefficients are to some small degree present, although the degree of biasedness is not calculated. However, since the bias is not large, adjustments in the model—such as excluding a collinear variable—have not been made.

Pooling Issues

For some time, econometricians have experimented with combining different populations of data. This can be generally termed pooling. The types of pooling done in the contracting mode combine defined sets of cross-sectional observations for a single period of time, and therefore do not have to be examined for dynamic issues. The primary pooling issue addressed here is, Under what conditions can samples be combined to yield information on the decision to become a contracting or self-provision city?

From the text the reader is aware that the decision to become a contracting (self-provision) city is different from the decision to increase the extent of contracting (self-provision). To answer the structural selection question, it is necessary that the estimated equations incorporate similarities in explaining the data. In particular, given the observations for self-provision cities, it is necessary to test whether the observations for the contract cities, in the context of the contracting model, can be viewed as additional observations from the initial population. The statistical test used was the Chow F-Test.

It should be noted that data on all cities in the Los Angeles County area (that is, both self-provision and contract cities) may be discussed on the aggregate level if the estimated regression relationships are statistically significant. However, the use of the total sample for interpretations of major structural decisions (such as why a city becomes a contracting city), requires that the model be more properly specific, (that is, variables designed to reflect such factors must be included). In the contracting model, the specification of the system was not sufficient to make such interpretations at any of the four stages. Only in the comparison between cities in Los Angeles County and cities in other California counties did the model specification and data lend itself to these threshold decision statements.

Using the all-cities equations to interpret structural selection or threshold decisions must be done with great care. A more complete specification of variables could make stronger interpretations possible. The text has suggested that attitudes toward city and county police departments are likely variables to improve the specification.

Also, segmentations of data may be meaningful where heteroscedasticity problems are present. Although homoscedasticity testing did not yield conclusive results, segmentation of data into smaller groups would affect the regression results and therefore the pooling issues.

Recursive Modeling Issues

The contracting model, as stated, is a recursive system. In stipulating the contracting equations, certain assumptions are crucial. The sequence of equations in any recursive model is mathematically described by:

$$Y_1 = a_{11} + b_{11}X_1 + b_{12}X_2 + \ldots + b_{1n}X_n + e_1$$

$$Y_2 = -b_1 Y_1 + a_{21} + b_{21}X_1 + b_{22}X_2 + \ldots + b_{2n}X_n + e_2$$

According to Dhrymes, the classification of variables as endogenous or predetermined is not important, as the real issue is determining if the regressors are independent with the error terms. This statement acknowledges that the use of OLS may be inappropriate where Y_1 is not independent (that is, is more than minimally correlated) with the error term or other right-hand variables in the second equation.

In empirical terms, biasedness and consistency can be expected where either of the above conditions hold, since it is a required assumption of OLS that the error terms be "independent" of all regressors in an equation. In terms of the recursive model, this means that each X_1 is "independent" of e_1 and e_2. Where the regressors and the error term are related, inconsistency and biasedness can be examined using covariance operators:

$$\frac{S_{xy}}{S_{xx}} = \beta + \left(\frac{S_{xe}}{S_{xx}} = \text{bias}\right)$$

If, for example (Y_1, e_2) were positively correlated, we would find a positive S_{Xe_2} and the coefficient of Y_1 would be biased upward.

In the contracting model, tests between Y_1-type variables and the residuals in Y_2-type equations were done. The first and second stages of the contracting model were not tested because the simple correlations of regressors exhibited minimal values. In the third and fourth stages, however, the probability of bias is higher, and therefore the correlations between certain right-hand variables and the error term were calculated.

The correlations tested the association between appropriate error terms and two variables (*LPER70, TOTPC*) in both the fourth-stage police service equation and in the third-stage equations. In the sample of all cities (N = 72), the highest recorded correlation (0.026) was between *LPER70* and the residual terms in the *LEXPOL*. For the self-provision cities (n = 44), similar insignificant results were found. Only in the contracting sample (n = 28), did the correlations rise above a minimal level in a single instance. In the *LEXPTOT* equation, the correlation between the error terms and *TOTPC* was (-0.48). On this basis, the coefficient of *TOTPC* is negatively biased and the equation may be inconsistent. As shown in Table 4-5, the estimated coefficient is (-0.09). Because of the described bias, this coefficient need not reflect a negative relationship.

Since the regressors and residuals were not more than minimally correlated in all but one case, it can be asserted that bias and inconsistency problems resulting from the use of a recursive format generally were not evident.

Summary

The contracting model designed to identify relationships between relevant contracting variables yielded interesting results about the nature of this process. The equations in this system were interpreted in the text on the basis of their overall explanatory power (that is, R^2), on the significance of the equation (F = statistic), and on the signs and significance of the individual variables. In some cases the R^2 and F = statistics were low, but each equation was statistically significant. The stipulated equations were found to contain little bias or inconsistency, although the system was recursive and was therefore susceptible to these problems. Data issues were reviewed and were found to be relevant in several areas. The most important empirical issue was the specification of individual relationships, which was often less than adequate for purposes of determining reasons for structural selection, even though adequate for purposes of determining the extent of contracting or self-provision.

Bibliography

OTHER REPORTS OF THIS STUDY

1. Cadei, Phyllis. *Equity and Responsiveness in Local Government Performance.* Institute of Government and Public Affairs. Los Angeles: University of California, 1974 (mimeo)
2. Clayton, Reva, and Stevens, Anne. *Municipal Expenditures and Revenues Under Contracting.* Institute of Government and Public Affairs Publication no. 191. Los Angeles: University of California, 1974.
3. Kirlin, John, and Ries, John C. *The Future of Service Provision Structures: Evaluations, Preferences, and Expectations of California City Managers.* Institute of Government and Public Affairs Publication no. 195. Los Angeles: University of California, 1974.
4. Mehay, Stephen L. *Evaluating the Performance of Governmental Structure: The Case of Contract Law Enforcement.* Institute of Government and Public Affairs Publication no. 193. Los Angeles: University of California, 1974.
5. ———. *Economic Evaluation of Alternative Delivery Systems.* Institute of Government and Public Affairs. Los Angeles: University of California, 1974 (mimeo)
6. Newhouse, Margaret. *Citizen Orientation Toward Local Government: A Review of the Literature.* Institute of Government and Public Affairs. Los Angeles: University of California, 1974 (mimeo)
7. Scott, Douglas. *Citizen Evaluation of Local Government Services: Some Measurement Questions.* Institute of Government and Public Affairs Publication no. 192. Los Angeles: University of California, 1974.
8. ———. *Contracting Project Survey: Some Methodological Considerations.* Institute of Government and Public Affairs. Los Angeles: University of California, 1974 (mimeo)

9. Sonenblum, Sidney. *Ways to Provide Municipal Services: A Market Typology.* Institute of Government and Public Affairs Publication no. 196. Los Angeles: University of California, 1974.
10. Stipak, Brian. *Citizen Evaluations of Municipal Services in Los Angeles County.* Institute of Government and Public Affairs Publication no. 194. Los Angeles: University of California, 1974.
11. Sonenblum, Sidney; Ries, John.; and Kirlin, John J. *Selecting Structures for Providing Municipal Services.* Institute of Government and Public Affairs Publication no. 198. Los Angeles: University of California, 1974.
12. *Providing Municipal Services: The Effects of Alternative Structures.* Institute of Government and Public Affairs. Los Angeles: University of California, 1975.

GOVERNMENT STRUCTURE

1. Advisory Commission on Intergovernmental Relations. *Substate Regionalism and the Federal System.* Vols. 1, 2 ACIR, 1973.
2. Bish, Robert L. *The Public Economy of Metropolitan Areas.* Chicago: Markham, 1971.
3. Bish, Robert L., and Ostrom, Vincent. *Understanding Urban Government: Metropolitan Reform Reconsidered.* Washington, D.C.: American Enterprise Institute for Public Policy Research, 1973.
4. Break, George F. "Changing Roles in Different Levels of Government," in *The Analysis of Public Output.* Universities National Bureau Committee for Economic Research. New York: Columbia University Press, 1970.
5. Cook, Gail C.A. "Effect of Metropolitan Government on Resource Allocation: The Case of Education in Toronto," *National Tax Journal* 26 (1973):585-90.
6. Crouch, Winston, and Dinerman, Beatrice. *Southern California Metropolis.* Berkeley and Los Angeles: University of California Press, 1963.
7. Erie, S.; Kirlin, J.; and Rabinovitz, F. "Can Something Be Done? Propositions on the Performance of Metropolitan Institutions," in *Reform of Metropolitan Governments.* Washington, D.C.: Resources for the Future, 1972.
8. Fitch, Lyle. "Increasing the Role of the Private Sector in Providing Public Services," in *Improving the Quality of Urban Management,* ed. Hawley, Willis O. and Rogers, David, (Beverly Hills: Sage Publications, 1974).
9. Greene, K.V.; Neenan, W.; and Scott, C.D. *Fiscal Interactions in a Metropolitan Area.* Lexington, Mass.: Lexington Books, D.C. Health, 1974.
10. Kirlin, John, and Erie, Steven. "The Study of Governance and Public Policy Making: A Critical Appraisal," *Public Administration Review,* March 1972.
11. Olson, Mancur. "Strategic Theory and Its Application to the Principle of Fiscal Equivalence: The Division of Responsibilities among Different Levels of Government," *American Economic Review* 59 (1969).
12. Ostrom, Vincent, and Ostrom, Elinor. "Public Choice: A Different Approach to the Study of Public Administration," *Public Administration Review,* March 1971.
13. Ostrom, V.; Tiebout, C.M.; and Warren, R. "The Organization of Government in Metropolitan Areas: A Theoretical Inquiry," *American Political Science Review* 55 (1961):831-42.

14. Warren, Robert. "A Municipal Services Market Model of Metropolitan Organization," *Journal of the American Institute of Planners.* Volume 30, Number 3, August 1964.

15. Young, Dennis. "Institutional Change and the Delivery of Urban Public Services," *Policy Sciences* 2 (1971):425-38.

16. Zimmerman, Joseph. "Meeting Service Needs Through Intergovernmental Agreements," *Municipal Yearbook,* 1973.

17. March, James G., and Simon, Herbert A. *Organizations* (New York: Wiley, 1958)

GOVERNMENT PERFORMANCE

1. Bradford, D.; Malt, R.; and Oates, W. "The Rising Cost of Local Public Services: Some Evidence and Reflections," *National Tax Journal* 22 (1969): 185ff.

2. Davies, David G. "The Efficiency of Public Versus Private Firms; The Case of Australia's Two Airlines," *Journal of Law and Economics* 14 (1971):149-67.

3. Hatry, Harry P., and Fisk, Donald M. *Improving Productivity and Productivity Measurement in Local Governments.* Washington, D.C.: National Commission on Productivity, 1971.

4. Hatry, Harry. "Issues in Productivity Measurement for Local Government," *Public Administration Review* 32 (1972).

5. ———. "Measuring Productivity," *Public Administration Review* 32 (1972).

6. ———. "Criteria for Evaluation in Planning State and Local Programs," in *Program Budgeting and Benefit-Cost Analysis,* H. Hinrichs and G. Taylor. Pacific Palisades, Calif.: Goodyear, 1969.

7. National Commission on Productivity. *Opportunities for Improving Productivity in Police Services.* Washington, D.C.: Government Printing Office, 1973.

8. Urban Institute and International City Management Association. *Measuring the Effectiveness of Basic Municipal Services.* Washington, D.C.: Urban Institute, 1974.

9. U.S. Congress. Joint Economic Committee. *Measuring and Enhancing Productivity in the Federal Sector.* 92nd Cong., 2nd Sess., 1972.

10. Young, Dennis. *How Shall We Collect the Garbage? A Study in Economic Organization.* Washington, D.C.: Urban Institute, 1972.

CONTRACTING IN LOS ANGELES

1. Assembly Interim Committee on Municipal and County Government. *Transcript of Proccedings: Incorporations.* Vol. I. 1958.

2. ———. *Transcript of Proceedings: Subcommittee on Annexation and Related Problems.* 1954.

3. ———. *Transcript of Proceedings: Workshop Discussion on "Administrative Problems in Contractual Public Services."* Long Beach, 1957.

4. ———. *Final Report: Annexation and Related Incorporation Problems in the State of California.* 1961.

5. Governor's Commission on Metropolitan Area Problems. *Metropolitan California,* ed. E.A. Engelbert. Sacramento, 1961.

250 Bibliography

6. Assembly Interim Committee on Municipal and County Government. *Transcript of Proceedings: Annexation and Related Incorporation Problems.* Palm Springs, November 17, 1960.

7. ———. *Transcript of Proceedings: Multi-Purpose Metropolitan Districts.* Los Angeles, November 16, 1961.

8. ———. *Transcript of Proceedings: Subcommittee on Functional Consolidation.* Los Angeles, February 27, 1958.

9. ———. Letter from John Todd to Subcommittee on Functional Consolidation of Local Government, 1957.

10. California Contract Cities Association. *Analysis of California Contract Cities Services Information Log Survey,* Prepared by Joseph Leach, mimeo, no date.

11. ———. *Municipal Seminar Proccedings.* 1960–1963.

12. Cion, Richard M. "Accommodation Par Excellence: The Lakewood Plan," in *Metropolitan Politics,* ed. Michael Danielson. Boston: Little, Brown, 1966.

13. Crouch, Winston. "Expanding the Role of the Urban County: The Los Angeles Experiment," in *Metropolitan Analysis,* ed. Sweeney and Blair. Philadelphia: University of Pennsylvania Press, 1958.

14. Greenberg, Bernard, and Dicker, Robert. "Municipal Incorporation and Annexation in California," *UCLA Law Review* 4 (1957).

15. Hollinger, L.S. "Report on County-City Consolidation." Los Angeles County Chief Administrative Officer, 1964 (Mimeo.)

16. ———. "Tax Inequity Study." Los Angeles County Chief Administrative Officer, 1970. (Mimeo.)

17. Hulpke, John, "The Lakewood, or Contract, Plan of Municipal Government." San Francisco State University, 1962. (Mimeo.)

18. ———. "The Lakewood, or Contract, Plan of Municipal Government: An Annotated Bibliography." San Francisco State University, 1962 (Mimeo.)

19. Jamison, Judith, and Bigger, Richard. "Metropolitan Coordination in Los Angeles," *Public Administration Review* 17 (1967).

20. Kennedy, Harold. "County Viewpoints on Metropolitan Government—The Lakewood Plan the Answer?" 1958.

21. Los Angeles County Chief Administrative Officer. "The Lakewood Plan." 1955

22. Los Angeles County Auditor-Controller. "Explanation and Computation of General County Overhead." 1960.

23. Los Angeles County Chief Administrative Officer. "Report on the Proposed City of ———." (See City History for the list of approximately 120 proposed incorporation reports.)

24. ———. "Los Angeles County's Contract Services Program (The Lakewood Plan)." 1964.

25. ———. "Report re City Administrative Officer's Study Alleging City Tax Subsidies to Unincorporated Areas." 1961.

26. ———. "Los Angeles County Contract Services Program: Municipal Services Provided to Cities." 1972 (Mimeo.)

27. Los Angeles County Grand Jury. "Report Upon Examination of County Departments Relative to Services Rendered to Cities." 1958.

28. Los Angeles County Road Department. "County Road Department Contract Serivces." (Mimeo.) n.d.
29. Los Angeles County Department of Engineers. "Municipal Services." (Mimeo.) n.d.
30. Letter from John Leach to Bill Milton, January 13, 1956. n.d.
31. Little, Richard. "The Politics of Overlapping Government in Los Angeles." Falk Foundation Program of Political Training and Research Seminar Series, UCLA Department of Political Science.
32. Ries, John C., and Kirlin, J. "Government in the Los Angeles Area: The Issue of Centralization and Decentralization." Los Angeles, 1970. (Mimeo.)
33. Trygg, C.E. "Police and Fire Departments Re-Established after Signal Hill Tries Contract Services," *Western City* 37 (1961).
34. Warren, Robert. *Government in Metropolitan Regions: A Reappraisal of Fractionated Political Organization.* Davis: Institute of Governmental Affairs, University of California, Davis, 1966.
35. Will, Arthur, Jr. "Another Look at Lakewood." 1962.
36. ———. "Report Concerning the County Contract Services Program." Los Angeles County Chief Administrative Officer, 1974. (Mimeo.)
37. Voight, George. "Survey of Contract Services." Contract Cities Association, August 1972. (Mimeo.)
38. Interview transcripts on file at University Research Library, UCLA.

LAW ENFORCEMENT CONTRACTING

1. Booz, Allen and Hamilton. "Determination of Law Enforcement Contractual Costs." 1971. Los Angeles.
2. ———. "Performance and Cost Decisionmaking System for the Field Policing Function." November 1972. Los Angeles.
3. City Council of Carson City. "Municipal Law Enforcement Department." Carson City, 1970. (Mimeo.)
4. Earle, Howard. *Contracting Law Enforcement Services by the Los Angeles County Sheriff's Department.* John W. Donner Publication Number 9. Los Angeles: School of Public Administration, University of Southern California, 1960.
5. Holston, Billie. *Proposed Police Department For City of Bell Gardens.* 1970. (Mimeo.)
6. Kirlin, John J. "Impact of Contract Service Arrangements Upon the Los Angeles Sheriff's Department and Law Enforcement Services in Los Angeles County," *Public Policy* 21 (1973).
7. Los Angeles County Sheriff's Department. *Statistical Summary FY 1968/69.*
8. Los Angeles County Sheriff's Department. *Contract Patrol Services, 1968/69.* (Mimeo.)
9. Los Angeles County Sheriff's Department. "A Proposal For Law Enforcement Service: Lakewood Sheriff's Station Area." 1970. (Mimeo.)
10. McDowell, R.D. "Law Enforcement Alternatives." Contract Cities Association, 1970. (Mimeo.) Los Angeles.
11. Pitchess, Peter. *Law Enforcement For Los Angeles County: A Blueprint for the Future.* Los Angeles County Sheriff's Department, 1971.

12. Santa Clara County. Office of the County Executive. "Contract Law Enforcement: A Survey of California Counties." June 1970. (Mimeo.)
13. Shoup, Donald, and Rosett, Arthur. "Fiscal Exploitation of Central Cities by Overlapping Governments." Institute of Government and Public Affairs Publication no. 135. Los Angeles: University of California, 1969.
14. "Temple City Law Enforcement Alternatives for Municipal Police Service." Temple City, 1970. (Mimeo.)
15. Will, Arthur. "Recommendations Regarding Changes to Contract Cities for Law Enforcement Services." Los Angeles County Chief Administrative Officer, 1973. (Mimeo.)
16. Peat, Marmick, Mitchell, "Examination and Reviews For the Grand Jury of the County of Los Angeles," 1969.

THE POLICE SERVICE

1. Bloch, Peter. *Equality of Distribution of Police Services—A Case Study of Washington, D.C.* Washington, D.C.: Urban Institute, 1974.
2. Chapman, Jeffrey. "The Demand for Policemen in California." Paper presented at Western Economic Association Meetings, Claremont, Calif., 1973.
3. Kakalik, James, and Wildhorn, Sorrel. *Aids to Decisionmaking in Police Patrol.* R-593-HUD/RC. Santa Monica: Rand Corp., 1971.
4. Mehay, Stephen L. "The Production of Crime Prevention by Urban Police Departments." Paper presented at Western Economic Association Meetings, Las Vegas, Nevada, 1974.
5. Ostrom, E. "On the Meaning and Measurement of Output and Efficiency in the Provision of Urban Police Services," *Journal of Criminal Research* 1 (1973):93-112.
6. Shoup, Donald, and Mehay, Stephen. *Program Budgeting for Urban Police Departments.* New York: Praeger, 1972.
7. Maltz, Michael E. *Evaluation of Crime Control Programs.* U.S. Department of Justice, LEAA. Washington, D.C.: Government Printing Office, 1972.
8. Weicher, John C. "The Allocation of Police Protection by Income Class," *Urban Studies* 8 (1971):207-20.

CITIZEN SURVEY METHODOLOGY

1. Asher, Herbert. "Some Problems in the Use of Multiple Indicators." Paper presented at the conference on "Design and Measurement Standards for Research in Political Science," Delevan, Wisconsin, May 13-15, 1974.
2. Beardsley, Philip L., et al. *Measuring Public Opinion on National Priorities.* Beverly Hills: Sage Professional Papers in American Politics 04-104, 1974.
3. Belson, William A. "The Effects of Reversing the Presentation Order of Verbal Rating Scales," *Journal of Advertising Research* 6, no. 4 (1966):1-11.
4. Blalock, Hubert M., Jr. "The Measurement Problem: A Gap Between the Language of Theory and Research," in *Methodology in Social Research*, ed. Hubert M. Blalock, Jr. and Ann Blalock, pp. 5-27. New York: McGraw-Hill, 1968.
5. ———. "Causal Inferences, Closed Populations, and Measures of Association," *American Political Science Review* 61 (1967):130-36.

6. Cannell, Charles, and Oksenberg, Lois. "Some Factors Underlying the Validity of Response in Self Report." Paper prepared for the Conference on "Design and Measurement Standards for Research in Political Science," Delevan, Wisconsin, May 13-15, 1974.

7. Cannell, Charles et al. *Reporting of Hospitalization in the Health Interview Survey.* Vital and Health Statistics Series 2, no. 6. Washington, D.C.: U.S. Public Health Service, July 1965.

8. Cataldo, E.F., et al. "Card Sorting as a Technique for Survey Interviewing," *Public Opinion Quarterly* 34 (1970):202-15.

9. Clark, Terry Nichols. "Can You Cut a Budget Pie?" Research Report no. 50 of the Comparative Study of Community Decision-Making, University of Chicago, 1974.

10. ———. "Citizen Values, Power, and Policy Outputs: A Model of Community Decision-Making," *Journal of Comparative Administration*, February 1973, pp. 385-427.

11. Cobb, Sidney, and Cannell, Charles. "Some Thoughts About Interview Data," *International Epidemiological Association Bulletin* 13 (1966):43-54.

12. Coleman, James S. *Policy Research in the Social Sciences.* Morristown, N.J.: General Learning Press, 1972.

13. Converse, Philip E. "The Nature of Belief Systems in Mass Publics," in *Ideology and Discontent,* ed. David Apter, pp. 206-61. New York: Free Press, 1964.

14. Cook, Stuart W., and Selltiz, Claire. "A Multiple Indicator Approach to Attitude Measurement," *Psychological Bulletin* 62 (1964):36-55.

15. Cronbach, L.J. "Coefficient Alpha and the Internal Structure of Tests," *Psychometrika* 16 (1951):297-334.

16. Fishbein, M., ed. *Attitude Theory and Measurement.* New York: Wiley, 1967.

17. Grigsby, J. Eugene, III, et al. *Prototype State-of-the-Region Report for Los Angeles County.* Los Angeles: School of Architecture and Urban Planning, University of California, 1973.

18. Hamblin, Robert L. "Mathematical Experimentation and Sociological Theory," *Sociometry* 50 (1971):423-52.

19. ———. "Ratio Measurement for the Social Sciences," *Social Forces* 50 (1971):191-206.

20. Hennessey, Bernard C. *Public Opinion.* 2nd ed. Belmont, Calif.: Wadsworth, 1970.

21. Hensler, Carl. *The Structure of Orientations Toward Government,* Ph.D. dissertation, Massachusetts Institute of Technology, Cambridge, 1971.

22. Hoinville, G., and Berthoud, R. "Identifying Preference Values: A Report on Development Work." London: Social and Community Planning Research, 1970.

23. Katona, George. "The Human Factor in Economic Affairs," in *The Human Meaning of Social Change,* ed. Angus Campbell and Philip Converse, pp. 229-62. New York: Russell Sage Foundation, 1972.

24. Laurent, Andre. "Effects of Question Length on Reporting Behavior in the Survey Interview," *Journal of the American Statistical Association* 67 (1972).

25. Leege, David, D., and Francis, Wayne L. *Political Research*. New York: Basic Books, 1973.

26. Maynes, E. Scott. "An Appraisal of Consumer Anticipations Approaches to Forecasting," in *1967 Proceedings of Business and Economic Statistics Section*, American Statistical Association, pp. 114-20.

27. Marquis, Kent H., and Cannell, Charles. *A Study of Interviewer-Respondent Interaction in the Urban Employment Survey*. Ann Arbor: Survey Research Center, 1969.

28. Marquis, Kent, et al. *Reporting of Health Events in Household Interviews: Effects of Reinforcement, Question Length, and Re-interviews*. Vital and Health Statistics Series 2, no. 45. Washington, D.C.: U.S. Public Health Service, 1972.

29. McGuire, W.J. "The Nature of Attitudes and Attitude Change," in *Handbook of Social Psychology*, 2nd ed., ed. Gardner Lindzey and Elliot Aronson, pp. 136-314. Reading, Mass.: Addison-Wesley, 1968.

30. Milbrath, Lester. "The Nature of Beliefs and the Relationship of the Individual to the Government," *American Behavioral Scientist* 12, no. 2 (1968):28-36.

31. Mueller, Eva. "Ten Years of Consumer Attitude Surveys: Their Forecasting Record," *Journal of the American Statistical Association* 58 (1963): 899-917.

32. Ostrom, Elinor. "The Need for Multiple Indicators in Measuring the Output of Public Agencies," *Policy Studies Journal* 2, no. 2 (1968):87-92.

33. Payne, Stanley. *The Art of Asking Questions*. Princeton: Princeton University Press, 1951.

34. Robinson, John P., et al. *Measures of Political Attitudes*. Ann Arbor: Institute for Social Research, University of Michigan, 1968.

35. Rokeach, Milton. *Beliefs, Attitudes, and Values*. San Francisco: Jossey-Bass, 1966.

36. ———. *The Nature of Human Values*. New York: Basic Books, 1973.

37. ———. *The Open and Closed Mind*. New York: Basic Books, 1960.

38. Scott, William A. "Attitude Measurement," in *Handbook of Social Psychology*, 2nd ed., ed. Gardner Lindzey and Elliot Aronson, pp. 204-73. Reading, Mass.: Addison-Wesley, 1968.

39. Sellin, Thorsten, and Wolfgang, Marvin. *Measuring Delinquency*. New York: Wiley, 1964.

40. Shinn, Allen M. Jr., "An Application of Psychophysical Scaling Techniques to the Measurement of National Power," *Journal of Politics* 31 (1969): 932-51.

41. ———. *The Application of Psychophysical Scaling Techniques to Measurement of Political Variables*. Chapel Hill: Institute for Research in Social Science, 1969.

42. ———. "Magnitude Estimation: Some Applications to Social Indicators." Paper presented at the Annual Meeting of the American Political Science Association, Chicago, 1971.

43. ———. "Measuring the Utility of Housing: Demonstrating a Methodological Approach," *Social Science Quarterly* 52 (1971):88-102.

44. ———. "Relations Between Scales," in *Measurement in the Social*

Sciences: Theories and Strategies, ed. Hubert M. Blalock, Jr. Chicago: Aldine, forthcoming.

45. ———. "Towards a Policy-Oriented Urban Transportation Demand Model: A Psychometric Approach to Modal Split." Paper presented to the Urban Regional Information Systems Association, San Francsico, 1972.

46. Sudman, Seymour, and Bradburn, Norman M. *Response Effects in Surveys* Chicago: Aldine, 1974.

47. Summers, Gene F., ed. *Attitude Measurement.* Chicago: Rand-McNally, 1970.

48. Torgerson, Warren S. *Theory and Methods of Scaling.* New York: Wiley, 1958.

49. Tryon, Robert C., and Bailey, Daniel E. *Cluster Analysis.* New York: McGraw-Hill, 1970.

50. Upshaw, Harry S. "Attitude Measurement," in *Methodology in Social Research,* ed. Hubert M. Blalock, Jr. and Ann Blalock, pp. 60–111. New York: McGraw-Hill, 1968.

51. Webb, Eugene J., et al. *Unobstrusive Measures: Non-Reactive Research in the Social Sciences.* Chicago: Rand-McNally, 1966.

52. Webb, Kenneth, and Hatry, Harry P. *Obtaining Citizen Feedback: The Application of Citizen Surveys to Local Government.* Washington, D.C.: Urban Institute, 1973.

53. Wilson, R.L. "Livability of the City: Attitudes and Urban Development," in *Urban Growth Dynamics,* ed. F.S. Chapin, Jr. and S.R. Weiss. New York: Wiley, 1962.

CITIZEN EVALUATIONS

1. Abelson, Robert. "Are Attitudes Necessary?" in *Attitudes, Conflict, and Social Change,* ed. Bert King and Elliot McGinnies. New York: Academic Press, 1972.

2. Aberbach, Joel D. "Alienation and Political Behavior," *American Political Science Review* 63 (1969):86–89.

3. Aberbach, Joel D., and Walker, Jack L. "The Attitudes of Black and Whites Toward City Sources: Implications for Public Policy," in *Financing the Metropolis: Public Policy in Urban Economics,* ed. J.P. Crecine, pp. 519–38. Vol. 4, Urban Affairs Annual Reviews. Beverly Hills: Sage Publications, 1970.

4. ———. "Political Trust and Racial Ideology," *American Political Science Review* 64 (1970:1199–1219.

5. Agger, Robert; Goldstein, Marshall N.; and Pearl, Stanley A. "Political Cynicism: Measurement and Meaning," *Journal of Politics* 23 (1961):447–507.

6. Alford, Robert A. *Bureaucracy and Participation.* Chicago: Rand-McNally, 1969. Esp. Chs. 1, 2, 7, 8, 9 and *passim.*

7. Alford, Robert A., and Scoble, Harry M. "Political and Socioeconomic Characteristics of American Cities," in *Municipal Year Book, 1965,* pp. 82–97. Chicago: International City Managers Association, 1965.

8. ———. "Sources of Local Political Involvement," *American Political Science Review* 62 (1968):1192–1206.

9. Almond, Gabriel A., and Verba, Sidney. *The Civil Culture.* Princeton, N.J.: Princeton University Press, 1963.

10. Andrews, Frank, N.; Morgan, James N.; and Sonquist, John A. *Multiple Classification Analysis: Report on a Computer Program for Multiple Regression Using Categorical Predictors.* Ann Arbor: Institute for Social Research, 1967.

11. Andrews, Frank N., and Withey, Stephen B. "Developing Measures of Perceived Life Quality: Results from Several National Surveys." Paper presented at the Annual Convention of the American Sociological Association, New York City, August 1973.

12. Bayley, David H., and Mendelsohn, Harold. *Minorities and the Police.* New York: Free Press, 1969.

13. Bloomberg, Warner, Jr., and Rosenstock, Florence J. "Who Can Activate the Poor? One Assessment of Maximum Feasible Participation," in *Power, Poverty and Urban Policy,* ed. W. Bloomberg and H. Schmandt, pp. 313-54. Vol. 2, Urban Affairs Annual Reviews. Beverly Hills: Sage Publications, 1968.

14. Bockman, Sheldon, and Hahn, Harlan. "Networks of Information and Influence in the Community." in *People and Politics in Urban Society,* ed. H. Hahn, pp. 71-94. Beverly Hills: Sage Publications, 1972.

15. Bordua, David, J., and Tifft, Larry L. "Citizen Interviews, Organizational Feedback, and Police Community Relations Decisions," *Law and Society Review* 6 (1971):155-82.

16. Bosworth, Claud A. "A Study of the Development and the Validation of a Measure of Citizens' Attitudes Toward Progress and Game Variables Related Thereto." Ph.D. dissertation, University of Michigan, 1954. Community Attitude Scale is taken from Robinson et al., *Measures of Political Attitudes.* Ann Arbor: Survey Research Center, Institute for Social Research, 1968, pp. 392-96.

17. Bowman, Lewis; Ippolito, Dennis S.,; and Levin, Martin L. "Self Interest and Referendum Support: The Case of a Rapid Transit Vote in Atlanta," in *People and Politics in Urban Society,* ed. H. Hahn, pp. 71-94. Beverly Hills: Sage Publications, 1972.

18. Boynton, G.R.; Patterson, Samuel; and Hedland, Ronald D. "The Structure of Public Support for Legislative Institutions," *Midwest Journal of Political Science* 12 (1968):163-80.

19. Cadei, Phyllis E. "Conceptualization and Measurement of Outputs for Police Services." Los Angeles: Institute of Government and Public Affairs, UCLA, 1973. (Mimeo.)

20. Campbell, Angus; Converse, Philip E.; Miller, Warren E.; and Stokes, Donald E. *The American Voter.* New York: Wiley, 1960.

21. Campbell, Angus, and Schuman, Howard. "Racial Attitudes in Fifteen American Cities," in *Supplemental Studies for the National Advisory Commission on Civil Disorders,* pp. 1-67. Washington, D.C.: Government Printing Office, 1968.

22. Caplan, Nathan. "The New Ghetto Man: A Review of Recent Empirical Studies," *Journal of Social Issues* 26 (1970):59-74.

23. Cherlin, Andrew. "Results of the Analysis of the Impact of Contracting in the LAMAS IV Sample." Memo to John C. Ries and John J. Kirlin regarding the Lakewood project, UCLA, 1973.

24. Clark, Terry N. "Community Structure, Decision-Making, Budget Expenditures and Urban Renewal," in *Community Politics: A Behavioral Approach,* ed. C. Bonjean, T. Clark, and R. Lineberry. New York: Free Press, 1971.

25. ———. "Please Cut the Budget Pie." Paper no. 37 of the Comparative Study of Community Decision-Making Project, University of Chicago, 1972. (Mimeo.)

26. ———. "The Structure of Community Influence," in *People and Politics in Urban Society,* ed. H. Hahn, pp. 283-314. Vol. 4, Urban Affairs Annual Reviews. Beverly Hills: Sage Publications, 1972.

27. ———. "Community Social Indicators: From Analytical Models to Policy Applications," *Urban Affairs Quarterly* 9 (1973):3-36.

28. Clark, Terry N., and Nanda, Krishan. "Citizen Demands and Public Policy: A Preliminary Report." Paper prepared for the Annual Meeting of the American Political Science Association, Washginton, D.C. 1972.

29. Clubb, Jerome M., and Traugott, Michael W. "National Patterns of Referenda Voting: The 1968 Election," in *People and Politics in Urban Society,* ed. H. Hahn, pp. 137-69. Vol. 6, Urban Affairs Annual Reviews. Beverly Hills: Sage Publications, 1972.

30. Cole, Richard. "Toward a Model of Political Trust," *American Journal of Political Science* 17 (1973):809-17.

31. Coleman, James, *Introduction to Mathematical Sociology.* New York: Free Press, 1964. Esp. pp. 189-203.

32. Comer, John; Steinman, Michael; and Welch, Susan. "Satisfaction of Governmental Services: Implications for Political Behavior," *Politics* 73 (1973).

33. Converse, Philip E. "The Nature of Belief Systems in Mass Publics," in *Ideology and Discontent,* ed. David Apter, pp. 206-261. New York: Free Press, 1964.

34. ———. "Attitudes and Non-Attitudes: Continuation of a Dialogue," in *The Quantitative Analysis of Social Problems,* ed. E.R. Tufte, pp. 168-89. Reading, Mass.: Addison-Wesley, 1970.

35. Conway, M. Margaret. "Political Participation in a Non-Partisan Local Election," *Public Opinion Quarterly* 33 (1969):425-30.

36. Crespi, Irving. "What Kinds of Attitudes Are Predictive of Behavior?" *Public Opinion Quarterly* 35 (1971):325-34.

37. Czudnowski, Moshe M. "A Salience Dimension of Politics for the Study of Political Culture," *American Political Science Review* 62 (1968):878-88.

38. Dahl, Robert A. *Who Governs? Democracy and Power in an American City.* New Haven: Yale University Press, 1961.

39. ———. "The City in the Future of Democracy," *American Political Science Review* 61 (1967):953-70.

40. Downes, Bryan T. "Introduction: The Policy-Making Approach to the Study of Local Municipalities," in *Cities and Suburbs: Selected Readings in Local Politics and Public Policy,* ed. B. Downes. Belmont, Calif.: Wadsworth, 1971.

41. Dye, Thomas R. "The Local Cosmopolitan Dimension and the Study of Urban Politics," *Social Forces* 41 (1966):239-46.

42. Easton, David. *A Systems Analysis of Political Life.* New York: Wiley, 1965.

43. Edelman, Murray. *The Symbolic Uses of Politics.* Urbana: University of Illinois Press, 1964.

44. Ehrlich, Howard J. "Attitudes, Behavior, and the Intervening Variables," *American Sociologist* 4 (1969):29-34.

45. Eisinger, Peter K. "Protest Behavior and the Integration of Urban Political Systems," *Journal of Politics* 33 (1971):980-1007.

46. ———. "The Pattern of Citizen Contacts with Urban Officials," in *People and Politics in Urban Society*, ed. H. Hahn, pp. 43-69. Vol. 6, Urban Affairs Annual Reviews. Beverly Hills: Sage Publications, 1972.

47. ———. "Racial Differences in Protest Participation," *American Political Science Review*, forthcoming.

48. Engstrom, Richard L., and Giles, Michael. "Expectations and Images: A Note on Diffuse Support for Legal Institutions," *Law and Society Review* 6 (1972):631-36.

48a. Finifter, Ada W. "Dimensions of Political Alienation," *American Political Science Review* 64 (1970):389-410.

49. Fishbein, Martin. "The Relationships Between Beliefs, Attitudes and Behavior," in *Cognitive Consistency: Motivational Antecedents and Behavioral Consequences*, ed. Shel Feldman. New York: Academic Press, 1966.

50. ———. "Attitude and the Prediction of Behavior," in *Attitude Theory and Measurement*, ed. M. Fishbein, pp. 477-92. New York: Wiley 1967.

51. Forward, John R. and Williams, Jay R. "Internal-External Control and Black Militancy," *Journal of Social Issues* 26 (1970):75-92.

52. Frazer, John. "The Impact of Community and Regime Orientations on Choice of Political System," *Midwest Journal of Political Science* 14 (1970): 413-33.

53. ———. "The Mistrust-Efficacious Hypothesis and Political Participation," *Journal of Politics* 32 (1970):444-49.

54. Furstenberg, Frank F., Jr., and Wellford, Charles F. "Calling the Police: The Evaluation of Police Service," *Law and Society Review* 7 (1973):393-406.

55. Gamson, William A. *Power and Discontent.* Homewood, Ill.: Dorsey Press, 1968.

56. Garn, Harvey A.; Flax, Michael J.; Springer, Michael; and Taylor, Jeremy B. "Social Indicator Models for Urban Policy—Five Specific Applications." Working Paper 1206-1211. Washington, D.C.: Urban Institute, 1973.

57. Gilbert, Charles E. *Governing the Suburbs.* Bloomington: Indiana University Press, 1967. Esp. parts V and VI.

58. Gilbert, Claire. "Community Power and Decision Making: A Quantitative Examination of Previous Research," in *Community Structure and Decision Making*, ed. T.N. Clark, pp. 139-58. San Francisco: Chandler, 1968.

59. Gurin, Patricia; Gurin, Gerlad; Lao, Rosina; and Beattie, Muriel. "Internal-External Control in the Motivational Dynamics of Negro Youths," *Journal of Social Issues* 25 (1969):29-54.

60. Hahn, Harlan. "The Political Impact of Shifting Attitudes," *Southwestern Social Science Quarterly* 51 (1970):730-42.

61. ———. "Ghetto Assessments of Police Protection and Authority," *Law and Society Review* 6 (1971):183-94.

62. Hamilton, Howard D. "Direct Legislation: Some Implications of Open Housing Referenda," *American Political Science Review* 64 (1970):124-37.

63. ———. "Voting Behavior in Open Housing Referenda," *Southwestern Social Science Quarterly* 51 (1970):715-29.

64. Hatry, Harry. "Issues in Productivity Measurement for Local Governments," *Public Administration Review* 32 (1972).

65. Hauser, Robert M. "Context and Consex: A Cautionary Tale," *American Journal of Sociology* 75 (1970):645-64.

66. Hawley, Amos H., and Zimmer, Basil G. *The Metropolitan Community: Its People and Government.* Beverly Hills: Sage Publications, 1970.

67. Hawkins, Brett; Marando, Vincent L.; and Taylor, George A. "Efficacy, Mistrust, and Political Participation: Findings from Additional Data and Indicators." Research Note, *Journal of Politics* 33 (1971):1130.

68. Henderson, James, and Quandt, Richard. *Microeconomic Theory.* New York: McGraw-Hill, 1957. Esp. Ch. 2.

69. Hennessy, Bernard. "A Headnote on the Existence and Study of Political Attitudes," *Southwestern Social Science Quarterly* 51 (1970):463-75.

70. Hensler, Carl P. "The Structure of Orientations Toward Government, Involvement, Efficacy, and Evaluation." Paper presented at the Annual Meeting of the American Political Science Association, Chicago, September 7-11, 1971.

71. ———. "Effects of Fallacies: Inference Problems in Contextual Analysis." Los Angeles: University of California, forthcoming.

72. Hensler, Deborah R. "The Impact of Suburban Residence on Political Attitudes and Behavior: A Contextual Analysis." Ph.D dissertation, Massachusetts Institute of Technology, Cambridge, 1972.

73. Hirschman, Albert O. *Exit, Voice, and Loyalty: Response to Decline in Firms, Organizations and States.* Cambridge: Harvard University Press, 1970.

74. Hoinville, G. "Evaluating Community Preferences," *Environment and Planning* 3 (1971):33-50.

75. Jackson, John L., III, and Shade, William L. "Citizen Participation, Democratic Representation and Survey Research," *Urban Affairs Quarterly* 9 (1973):57-90.

76. Jacob, Herbert. *Debtors in Court: The Consumption of Government Services.* Chicago: Rand-McNally, 1969.

77. ———. "Black and White Perceptions of Justice in the City," *Law and Society Review* 6 (1971):69-90.

78. ———. "Contact with Governmental Agencies: A Preliminary Analysis of the Distribution of Government Services," *American Journal of Political Science* 16 (1972):123-46.

79. Jacob, Herbert, and Lipsky, Michael. "Outputs, Structure, and Power: An Assessment of Changes in the Study of State and Local Politics," *Journal of Politics* 30 (1968):510-38.

80. Jennings, M. Kent. "Pre-Adult Orientations to Multiple Systems of Governments," *Midwest Journal of Political Science* 11 (1967):291-317.

81. ———. "Parental Grievances and School Politics," *Public Opinion Quarterly* 32 1968):363-78.

82. Jennings, M. Kent, and Niemi, Richard G. "Patterns of Political Learning," *Harvard Educational Review* 38 (1968):443-46.

83. Jennings, M. Kent, and Zeigler, Harmon. "The Salience of American State Politics," *American Political Science Review* 64 (1970):523-35.

84. ———. "The Salience of American State Politics," revised version, in *Political Opinion and Behavior*, ed. E. Breyer and W. Rosenbaum, pp. 257-285. 2nd ed. Belmont, Calif.: Wadsworth, 1970.

85. Johnson, Richard. "Introduction: Propensity for Change in an Urban Setting," in *Final Report on a Study of Change in Processes in Buffalo, New York*, ed. L.W. Milbrath et al. Submitted to the Office of Research, Plans, Programs, and Evaluation of the U.S. Office of Economic Opportunity, 1969.

86. Johnson, James. *Econometric Methods*. New York: McGraw-Hill, 1963.

87. Kasl, Stanislar, and Harburg, Ernest. "Perceptions of the Neighborhood and the Desire to Move Out," *Journal of American Institute of Planners* 38 (1972):318-24.

88. Kellstedt, Lyman A. "Riot Propensity and System Disaffection," and "Dimensions of Political Participation," in *Final Report on a Study of Change Processes in Buffalo, New York*, ed. L.W. Milbrath et al., Chaps. 8, and 7. Submitted to the Office of Research, Plans, Programs, and Evaluation of the U.S. Office of Economic Opportunity, 1969.

89. Kirlin, John J., personal communication with the author, work in progress.

90. Kirlin, John J. and Erie, Steven. "The Study of Urban Governance and Public Policy Making: A Critical Appraisal," *Public Administration Review* 32 (1972):173-84.

91. Kraut, Robert E., and McConahay, John B. "How Being Interviewed Affects Voting: An Experiment," *Public Opinion Quarterly* 37 (1973):398-406.

92. Lane, Robert E. *Political Life: Why and How People Get Involved in Politics*. New York: Free Press, 1959.

93. Levy, Sheldon G. "The Psychology of Political Activity," *Annals of the American Academy of Political and Social Sciences* 391 (1970):83-96.

94. Lineberry, Robert, and Sharkansky, Ira. *Urban Politics and Public Policy*. 2nd ed. New York: Harper and Row, 1974. Esp. Chap. 1.

95. Lipskey, Michael. "Protest as a Political Resource," *American Political Science Review* 62 (1968):1144-58.

96. Litt, Edgar, "Political Cynicism and Political Futility," *Journal of Politics* 23 (1963):312-23.

97. ———. *The Political Cultures of Massachusetts*. Cambridge: Massachusetts Institute of Technology Press, 1965. Esp. Chs. 1 and 3.

98. Luttbeg, Norman R. "Awareness on the Part of the Unrepresented Citizen," in *Public Opinion and Public Policy: Models of Political Linkage*, ed. Normal R. Luttbeg, pp. 446-52. Homewood, Ill.: Dorsey Press, 1968.

99. ———. "The Structure of Beliefs Among Leaders and the Public," *Public Opinion Quarterly* 32 (1968):398-409.

100. ———. "The Structure of Public Beliefs on State Politics: A Comparison with Local and National Findings," *Public Opinion Quarterly* 35 (1971):114-16.

101. Lyons, W.E., and Engstrom, Richard L. "Life Style and Fringe Attitudes Toward the Political Integration of Urban Governments," *Midwest Journal of Political Science* 15 (1971):475-94.

102. ———. "Socio-Political Cross Pressures and Attitudes Toward Political Integration of Urban Governments," *Journal of Politics* 35 (1973):682-711.

103. Marshall, Dale R. "Who Participates in What?" *Urban Affairs Quarterly* 4 (1968):201-23.

104. ———. "Public Participation and the Politics of Poverty," in *Race, Change and Urban Society*, ed. P. Orleans and W.R. Ellis, Jr., pp. 451-82. Vol. 5, Urban Affairs Annual Reviews. Beverly Hills: Sage Publications, 1971.

105. McDill, Edward L., and Ridley, Jeanne C. "Status, Anomia, Political Alienation, and Political Participation," *American Journal of Sociology* 68 (1962):205-13.

106. McMurray, Carl D., and Parson, Malcolm B. "Public Attitudes Toward the Representational Role of Legislators and Judges," *Midwest Journal of Political Science* (1965):167-85.

107. McPhail, Clark, "Civil Disorder Participation: A Critical Examination of Recent Research," *American Sociological Review* 36 (1971):1058-73.

108. Milbrath, Lester, W. *Political Participation*. Chicago: Rand-McNally, 1965.

109. ———. "The Nature of Political Beliefs and the Relationship of the Individual to the Government," *American Behavioral Scientist* 12 (1968):28-36.

110. ———. "Satisfactions and Dissatisfactions with Governmental Performance," in *Final Report on A Study of Change Processes in Buffalo, New York*, ed. L.W. Milbrath. Submitted to the Office of Research, Plans, Programs, and Evaluation of the U.S. Office of Economic Opportunity, 1969.

111. ———. "Individuals and Government," in *Politics in the American States*, ed. H. Jacob and K. Vines, pp. 27-82. 2nd ed. Boston: Little Brown, 1971.

112. ———. "A Paradigm for the Comparative Study of Local Politics," *Ill Politico* 36 [University of Paris] (1971):5-35.

113. ———. "People and Government," Unpublished manuscript, State University of New York at Buffalo, 1971.

114. Muller, Edward N. "Correlates and Consequences of Beliefs in the Legitimacy of Regime Structures," *Midwest Journal of Political Science* 14 (1970): 397-412.

115. ———. "Cross-National Dimensions of Political Competence." *American Political Science Review* 64 (1970):792-809.

116. ———. "The Representation of Citizens by Political Authorities: Consequences for Regime Support," *American Political Science Review* 64 (1970): 1149-66.

117. ———. "A Test of a Partial Theory of Potential for Political Violence," *American Political Science Review* 66 (1972):928-59.

118. Newhouse, Margaret L. "The Performance of Performance: A Critical Appraisal of Research on the Outcomes of Local Political and Educational Systems." Unpublished paper, UCLA, 1972.

119. ———. "When Attitudes Are Necessary: A Consideration of Conditions Under Which Attitudes Affect Behavior," Unpublished paper, UCLA, 1972.

120. Olson, Marvin. "Two Categories of Political Alienation," *Social Forces* 47 (1969):288-99.

121. Orbell, John. "Impact of Metropolitan Residence on Social and Political Orientations," *Social Science Quarterly* 51 (1970):634-48.

122. Orbell John, and Uno, Toro. "A Theory of Neighborhood Problem Solving: Political Action vs. Residential Mobility," *American Political Science Review* 66 (1972):471-89.

123. Ostrom, Elinor; Baugh, William H.; Guarasci, Richard; Parks, Roger B.; and Whitaker, Gordon P. *Community Organization and the Provision of Police Services.* Beverly Hills: Sage Publications, 1973.

124. Ostrom, Elinor, and Parks, Roger B. "Surburban Police Departments: Too Many and Too Small?" in *The Urbanization of the Suburbs,* ed. L.H. Masotti and J.K. Hadden, pp. 367-402. Vol. 7, Urban Affairs Annual Reviews. Beverly Hills: Sage Publications, 1973.

125. Ostrom, Elinor, and Whitaker, Gordon P. "Black Citizens and the Police: Some Effects of Community Control." Paper prepared for the Annual Meeting of the American Political Science Association, 1971.

126. ———. "Does Local Community Control of Police Make a Difference? Some Preliminary Findings," *American Journal of Political Science* 17 (1973): 48-76.

127. Ostrom, Vincent, and Ostrom, Elinor. "Public Choice: A Different Approach to the Study of Public Administration," *Public Administration Review* 31 (1971):203-16.

128. Paige, Jeffrey. "Political Orientation and Riot Participation," *American Sociological Review* 36 (1971):810-20.

129. Patterson, Samuel D., and Boynton, G.R. "Perceptions and Expectations of the Legislature and Support for It," *American Journal of Sociology* 75 (1969):62-76.

130. Reiss, Albert J., Jr. "Monitoring the Quality of the Criminal Justice System," in *The Human Meaning of Social Change,* ed. A. Campbell and P.E. Converse, pp. 391-441. New York: Russell Sage Foundation, 1972.

131. Richard, Robert. *Subjective Social Indicators.* Chicago: NORC, University of Chicago, 1969.

132. Robinson, John P., Rusk, Jerrold G.; and Head, Kendra B. *Measures of Political Attitudes.* Ann Arbor: Institute for Social Research, University of Michigan, 1968.

133. Rossi, Peter. "Community Social Indicators," in *The Human Meaning to Social Change,* ed. A. Campbell and P.E. Converse, pp. 87-126. New York: Russell Sage Foundation, 1972.

134. Rossi, Peter, and Berk, Richard. "Local Political Leadership and Popular Discontent in the Ghetto," *Annals of the Academy of Political and Social Sciences* 391 (1970):111-27. (Rossi, Beck, and Edison, *Roots of Urban Discontent,* which is based on the same data, has just been published by Wiley Interscience.)

135. Roth, M., and Boynton, G.R. "Communal Ideology and Political Support," *Journal of Politics* 31 (1969):167-85.

136. Schuman, Howard. "Attitudes vs. Actions vs. Attitudes vs. Attitudes," *Public Opinion Quarterly* 36 (1972):347-54.

137. Schuman, Howard, and Gruenberg, Barry. "The Impact of City on Racial Attitudes," *American Journal of Sociology* 76 (1970):213–61.

138. ———. "Dissatisfaction with City Services: Is Race an Important Factor?" in *People and Politics in Urban Society,* ed. H. Hahn, pp. 369–92. Vol. 6, Urban Affairs Annual Reviews. Beverly Hills: Sage Publications, 1972.

139. Schwartz, David C. *Political Alienation and Political Behavior.* Chicago: Aldine, 1973.

140. Scott, Douglas, "Contracting Project Survey: Some Methodological Considerations." Los Angeles: Institute of Government and Public Affairs, UCLA, 1974. (Mimeo.)

141. Sears, David O. "Black Attitudes Toward the Political System in the Aftermath of the Watts Insurrection," *Midwest Journal of Political Science* 13 (1969):515–44.

142. ———. "Political Socialization," in *Handbook of Political Science,* ed. F.I. Greenstein and N.W. Polsby. Vol. 3, *Theoretical Aspects of Micro-Politics.* Reading, Mass.: Addison-Wesley, forthcoming.

143. Sears, David, O., and McConahay, Robert. *The Politics of Violence: The New Urban Blacks and the Watts Riot.* Boston: Houghton-Mifflin, 1973.

144. Sharkansky, Ira. "Environment, Policy, Output, and Impact: Problem of Theory and Method in the Analysis of Public Policy," in *Policy Analysis in Political Science,* ed. I. Sharkansky, pp. 61–79. Chicago: Markham 1970.

145. Stagner, Ross. "Perceptions, Aspirations, Frustrations, and Satisfactions: An Approach to Urban Indicators," *Annals of the American Academy of Political and Social Sciences* 388 (1970):59–68.

146. Stokes, Donald E. "Popular Evaluations of Government: An Empirical Assessment," in *Ethics and Bigness: Scientific, Academic, Religious, Political, and Military,* ed. H. Cleveland and H. Tasswell, pp. 61–72. New York: Conference on Science, Philosophy, and Religion in Their Relationship to the Democratic Way of Life, 1962.

147. Stone, Clarence. "Local Referenda: Alternative to the Alienated Voter Model," *Public Opinion Quarterly* 29 (1965):212–22.

148. "Symposium on Urban Observatories," *Urban Affairs Quarterly* 8 (September 1972):3–54.

Index

Adaptation, 64-65
Adaptive motivated behavior, 15-18, 68
Advisory Commisssion on Intergovernmental Relations, 3
Age, and contract vs. self-provision, 118-20, 124
Allocation efficiency, defined, 76
Alternative service structures. *See also* Consolidated mode; Contract mode; Grant mode; Regulated mode
  availability of, 18-21, 62-69
  vs. departments, 7-11, 16-22, 22-27, 42-43, 212
A-95 review procedures, 3
Annexation, vs. incorporation, 82-84
Attitudes, and service structure
  of citizens, 13, 15-16, 39-42, 188-94
  of city managers, 16, 46-48, 66, 84, 194-212
  defined, 191

Back-up forces. *See also* Capacity utilization
  and city managers, 34-35
  and cost of service, 25-26
  and county contracts, 43
Blalock, Hubert M., 186
Booz, Allen, and Hamilton report, 92-94, 110, 112, 161, 166
Bradley-Burns Tax Act, 84
Budget, city. *See also* Expenditures, city
  and contracts, 51-52, 117-28, 138-41
  and departments, 21-22, 39-41, 130-31, 139-41, 148-49
  and police service, 143, 153, 177-79
  and private franchise, 147
  and special districts, 128-30
Budget pies, 188, 193-94
Buffalo Metropolitan Area research, 189n

Capacity utilization, 25-26
Card-sorting technique, 188-91, 194, 209
Cataldo, Everett, 189, 191n
Citizen survey
  attitudinal analysis method, 184, 188-94
  and departments, 29-42, 213
  and service structure selection, 13, 15-16
City classification system, 12-14, 53-54, 226-30
City consolidated mode, 8, 213, 218-20
City control group, 13-14
City core services, 9-10, 18-21, 43-45, 67, 226-30
City councils, 3, 21, 39-42
City-County Coordinator's Office, 99
City departments. *See* Departments, city
City-financed contract mode, 8, 214, 218-21, 230

265

266 Index

City government, role in service
  delivery, 230. *See also* Local control
City managers survey
  attitudinal analysis method, 184,
    194-212
  consensus index of, 46-48
  departments vs. contracts, 30-39,
    43-45, 139, 153-55
  and expenditures, 21
  and performance contracting, 155-
    56
  and private contracts, 56n-59n
  and service structure selection, 16,
    66
City optional services, 9-10, 18-21,
  67, 226-30
City production core services, 18-23
  and city managers, 43-45
  and consolidated mode, 9-10, 229
  and local control, 67-68
  and service attributes, 27
Clark, Terry, 185
Cluster analysis, 189-91
Cognitive filter questions, 191-93
Coleman, James, 183
Collective bargaining, and departments, 39
Commercial sales value, and contracts,
  51n, 122-24, 136-37
Community wealth
  and contract mode, 119, 122
  and patrol personnel, 166-69, 171
  and police expenditures, 171
Competition
  and contracts, 77-78
  district, 19-23, 67-68
  private, 19-21, 43-45, 67-68
Consensus index of managers, 46-48
Consolidated mode. *See also* Departments, city
  in California, 7-11, 218-21
  and city type, 226-30
  and contracts, 73-74
  defined, 6-7, 212-14
  and law enforcement, 110-14, 155
  and supplemental mode, 224-26
Contract cities
  and budgets, 117-28, 136
  and contracting model, 231-34
  and crime rates, 162-63, 175-77,
    179-81
  vs. departments, 20-21, 49-52, 138-
    41
  and fire protection, 143-46
  and government employees, 130-31
  and libraries, 147

and local control, 49-52, 136-37
and parks and recreation, 147
and patrol personnel, 162, 165-71,
  177-79
and police expenditures, 162, 171-
  74, 177-79
and police service, 137, 142-43,
  156-60, 162-65, 174-77
and refuse collection, 147
and special districts, 132-34, 136
and street maintenance, 146-47
and tax rates, 49-52, 117, 124-25,
  137
Contract Cities Association study, 55
Contract competition core service,
  9-10, 18-21, 23, 67-68
  and city managers, 43-45
Contract mode (service)
  and back-up forces, 26
  in California, 7-11, 218-21
  and citizens, 16, 191-93
  and city-county relationship, 79-87
  and city managers, 37-39, 42, 204-
    206
  and city type, 226-30
  and cost of service, 23-25
  vs. departments, 20-21, 49-52, 138-
    41
  and efficiency, 72, 76-79
  and finance stage, 8, 214, 218-21,
    230
  and intergovernmental cooperation,
    72-76
  model for, 231-45
  and performance, 72
  and police chiefs, 59-63, 75
  and production stage, 213
  and property crime, 174-77
  and service delivery, 7, 19-21, 67-
    68, 212, 214-15
  and service disaggregation, 55
  and supplemental mode, 224-26
Contract pricing, 87-95, 106, 153
Contract service plan, 71, 86-87, 95-
  99, 105-15
Cost of service
  analysis method, 183
  department vs. alternative, 22-27,
    42-43
  of police, 60-62, 90-91, 156-60
  of structure change, 53-59, 64
County Contract Program, 95-115
County government. *See also* District
  government
  and city managers, 33-35, 37-39
  and consolidated mode, 213, 218
  and contract mode, 42-43, 71-76,

Index 267

80-87, 99-115, 214, 218
  and cost of service, 25-26, 42-43, 93
  and finance stage, 72-73, 80-82, 213, 221-24
  and production stage, 55-59, 212-13, 221-24
  role of, 230
  and service disaggregation, 55-59
  and service quality, 27
County Supervisors Association, 81
Crime rates
  and contracts, 162, 175-77, 179-81
  and patrol personnel, 165-71
  and service quality, 164

Data
  for econometric model, 231-43
  quality, techniques for, 189-91
Decision-making process
  and alternative service structures, 16-21
  and city managers, 206
  and multiple data collection techniques, 185-88
  and type of service structures, 15-17, 34-42, 64-69
Delivery modes, defined 7-11, 212
Departmental county costing, 91
Departments, city
  vs. alternative structures, 16-21, 22-27, 27-33
  as consolidated mode, 6, 213, 218-19, 221-23
  vs. contracts, 138-41, 148-52, 153
  and cost of service, 22-27
  and expenditures, 22, 179
  and law enforcement, 114
  and local control, 136-37, 138-39, 179
  and police chiefs, 60-62
  and property tax base, 137
  and property tax rate, 148
  reasons for, 63-69
  and service delivery, 5, 7-9, 11-13, 19-21, 128-32, 148-52
  and service disaggregation, 55
  and service needs, 119-20
  and supplemental mode, 226
Departments, county, and contracts, 72-76, 99-115
Departments, police, and service quality, 161
District consolidated mode, 8, 213, 218. *See also* County government
District competition optional services, 19-23, 26, 67-68
  and city managers, 43-45

District government. *See also* County government; Regionalization concept
  and consolidated mode, 8, 213, 218
  and contract mode, 8, 214, 221
  and cost of service, 6, 23
  role of, 230

Econometric analysis method, 183, 230-45
Economies of scale, and service production, 22-27
  and city managers, 34-35
  and county contracts, 42-43, 107
  and efficiency, 77-79
  and intergovernmental cooperation, 74
  and police chiefs, 62
  and police contracts, 153
Education, and contracts vs. self-provision, 119
Efficiency
  and contracts, 72, 76-79, 81
  and performance, 65-66
  types of, 76
  and police chiefs, 62-63
Employees, and service structure
  city, 54-55
  county, 54-55
  government, 24, 118-20, 130-31, 147
Engineers, County Department of, 95, 98-107
Expenditures, city
  and contracts, 21-22, 49-52, 125-28, 136, 138-41, 148-52
  and county contracts, 117, 125-28, 136, 138-41, 153
  and departments, 21-22, 62-63, 130-31, 139-41, 148-49
  and police contracts, 143, 153, 177-79
  and street maintenance, 146
Expenditures, police, and contracts, 143, 156-60, 162, 171-74, 177-79
External government, defined, 217

Federal government, programs, of, 2-6. *See also* Grant mode
Feedback process, 188
"Field Unit Requirement" formula, 161
Finance stage
  in California, 8, 15, 53-54, 218-23, 226-30
  and city managers, 43-48, 52, 205-206

and county contracts, 72-73, 80-82, 213, 221-24
defined, 217
and intergovernmental cooperation, 74
and performance, 65-67
and service clusters, 18-19, 226-30
and service delivery, 4-7, 212-16, 218-23, 226-30
and start-up costs, 25
and structure change, 53-59, 64
and type of service, 21n
Fire protection
and city managers, 38, 48
and contracts, 143-46
and district competition core, 22-23
and intergovernmental cooperation, 74
Fiscal policy, and alternative structures, 17, 64-69, 73-74. *See also* Budgets, city
Fiscal equivalence principle, 77
Fitch, Lyle, 76, 79
Franchise, 147, 216
Full-service contracts, 71, 82-87, 95

General law enforcement. *See* Law enforcement
Goerlick, Harry, 83
Gonsalvez, Bill, 94-95
Government, 3-5. *See also* City government; County government; District government; Local government
Government employees, 24, 118-20, 130-31, 147
Grant mode, and service delivery, 3, 6, 7, 212, 216
in California, 7-11, 218-21
and city type, 11-12, 53-54, 226-30
and supplemental modes, 224-26
Group interviews, and city managers, 194, 208-12

Hatry, Harry, 184-86
Health services
and county contracts, 73-74, 95
and intergovernmental cooperation, 74
Historical analysis method, 183
Hollinger, L.S., 73, 83
Hollopeter, Lee, 83
Homogeneous multiple measures strategy, 186
Hospitals, and county contracts, 95

Income, family. *See also* Community wealth
and contracts vs. self-provision, 119-20, 122
and crime rate, 175-77
Incorporation stage
and contracts, 79-87, 98, 119, 137
and county contracts, 95
and police service, 85-87, 112, 153
and service structure selection, 15-16, 64
and start-up costs, 25
Independent cities. *See also* Self-provision cities
and contracts, 33, 72, 76, 95, 98
and crime rates, 162-65, 175-77, 179-81
and patrol personnel, 162, 165-71, 177-79
and police expenditures, 162, 171-74
and police service, 110-11, 114-15, 156-60, 162-65
and service quality, 27, 161-65
and service structure, 33-34, 37
Individual interviews, and city managers, 194, 207-208
Intergovernmental contract mode, 214-15
and cooperation, 71-76
and Lakewood Plan, 82-87
Intergovernmental transfers
and contracts, 72-76, 124, 138, 214
and finance stage, 213
International City Management Association, 2

Johnson, President Lyndon, 2-3
Joint agreements, 60-62

Kennedy, Harold, 83
Kirlin, John, 75-76, 88
Klinger, Keith, 83

Labor costs, 24-26. *See also* Wage rates
Lakewood Plan, 15n-16n
and contracts, 71, 82-85
and incorporation stage, 82-87
Lakewood Taxpayers Association report, 83
Lakewood Water and Power Company, 83
LASD. *See* Los Angeles County Sheriffs Department

Law enforcement
  and city managers, 37
  and contract pricing, 87-95
  and contracts, 22-23, 85-87, 177-79
  and county contracts, 111-15, 153-56
  and intergovernmental cooperation, 74
Law Enforcement for Los Angeles County: A Blueprint for the Future, 93
Leach, John, 83, 88
League of California Cities, 73-74, 81-82
Leege, David D., and Wayne L. Francis, 186-87
Legg, County Supervisor, 83
Libraries
  and contracts, 147
  and district competition core, 22-23
  and intergovernmental cooperation, 74
Literature review method, 184
Local Agency Formation Commission, 84
Local control
  in California, 7-11, 53-54
  and city managers, 39-48, 52-53, 59
  and contracts, 49-52, 124, 130, 136-41
  and departments, 33-34, 42, 51, 130, 136-37, 139-41, 177
  and expenditures, 128
  and incorporation stage, 84, 119
  and law enforcement, 114
  and performance contracting, 155-56
  and police chiefs, 62
  and property tax rate, 125
  and service structure selection, 1-2, 5-11, 15-16, 62-69, 212
Local government, role of, 12-14, 230
Los Angeles County
  and contracts, 17, 24-26, 42, 49-52, 71-115
  and Lakewood Plan, 15n-16n
  and service disaggregation, 55-62
  and wage scale, 24
Los Angeles County Sheriffs Department, 153-81. *See also* Crime rates; Expenditures, police
  and contract pricing, 88-95
  and contracts, 72, 75-76
  and performance contracting, 155-56
  and police protection, 85-87
  and regional police, 154-55
Los Angeles County Board of Supervisors, 99, 106
Los Angeles Metropolitan Area Survey (LAMAS VII), 188-89
Los Angeles Police Department, 110-12

March, James, and Herbert Simon, 16-17
Marginal city costing, 90-93
Maturation stage, and contracts, 86-87, 95-98
Milbrath, Lester, 187
Multicollinearity problems, 231, 241-43
Multiple data collection techniques, 184-88
Multiple heterogeneous measures strategy, 187-88
  and citizens survey, 188-94
  and city managers survey, 194-212
Multiple homogeneous indicators, 187
Multiple operational strategy, 187
Municipal property-tax rate, 132, 138. *See also* Property-tax rate

National Conference of Mayors, 2
National League of Cities, 2
National Municipal League study, 2
Newhouse, Margaret, 187
Non-city-control group, 13-14
Non-city department cities, 52. *See also* Contract cities
No opinion categories, and citizens survey, 192-93

Officials, city, and role of, 16-18. *See also* City managers
Optional district competition services, 9-10. *See also* optional services
Optional private competition services, 10
Ordinal scale techniques, 188-91, 193
Ostram, Eleanor, 185, 187

Parks and recreation service
  and city managers, 38-39, 205
  and city production core, 22-23
  and consolidated mode, 9-10
  and contracts, 147
Peeat, Marwick, and Mitchell report, 90-92
Performance characteristics
  and contracts, 72, 77

of local government, 184
and planning stage, 65-66
of police, 155-56, 160-65
and service structure selection, 35-39, 43-52, 64-65
Performance contracting, 155-56
Pitchess, Peter, 83
Planning stage
in California, 53-54
defined, 217
and departments, 9-10
and federal government, 3, 5
and intergovernmental cooperation, 74
and performance, 65-66
and service delivery, 5-7, 212-16, 218-23
Police chiefs
and alternative service structures, 59-62
and group interview, 194, 211-12
and questionnaire, 194, 206-207
Police patrol personnel, and contracts, 162, 165-71, 177
Police services. *See also* LASD
and city managers, 37, 204-205
and contract vs. independent cities, 156-60, 177-79
and contracts, 23, 118n, 137, 142-43, 152-56, 162-65, 174-77
and county contracts, 85-87
and district back-up, 26
in LA county, 73-76, 110-15, 153-81
and regionalization plan, 93-95, 154-55
and service disaggregation, 55-62
and service quality, 160-64
Politics, and service structure, 4-5, 21, 59
Pooling, and population diversity, 169, 243-44
Population density
and patrol personnel, 167-71
and pooling, 243-44
Population distribution, and crime rate, 165
Private consolidated mode, 8, 214
Private contracts
and budgets, 147
and city managers, 34, 37-39
and efficiency, 78-79
and labor costs, 24
and service disaggregation, 55-59
Private producer contract mode, 215

Private sector
and city managers, 43-45
and city staff, 57-59
defined, 217
and franchises, 147
and police chiefs, 60-62
role of, 19-21, 67-68, 230
Production efficiency, 65-68
defined, 76
Production stage
in California, 8, 12-13, 53-54, 212-13
and city managers, 43-48, 52
and cost of service, 23
defined, 217
and service delivery, 4-7, 18-21, 212-16, 218-23
Production transfer of core services, defined, 53n
Production transfer of optional services, defined, 53n
Procurement contracting, 77
Property crimes, 163-65, 179-81
Property-tax base
and budget, 128
and contracts, 49-52, 118-25, 136-37, 141
and incorporation stage, 84
and police expenditures, 143
and self-provision cities, 118-25, 137
and street maintenance, 146
Property-tax rates
and alternative service structures, 16-18
and budget, 128
and city type, 14
and contract cities, 117-18, 124-25, 136, 137-38, 177
and departments, 130, 148-49
and fire protection, 146
and police expenditures, 143
and self-provision cities, 118-25, 137-38
and special districts, 49-52, 132-33
and street maintenance, 146
Property tax revenues, 124-25, 137
Psychometric theory, 185-86
Public services, and homogeneous needs, 119, 160

Quality of service, 26-27, 160-64, 179
and city type, 14
Questionnaires, research, 194, 204, 206-207

Index 271

Refuse collection service, 23-24, 147
   and city managers, 37, 205
Regional Allocation of Police Services (RAPS), 154
Regional government, defined, 217
Regionalization concept
   and contract pricing, 91, 93-95
   and County Department of Engineers, 106-107
   and police service, 154-55
Regional Planning Commission of Los Angeles County, 80
Registrar/Recorder, and county contracts, 95
Regression analysis method, 184
Regulated modes, 212, 215-16
   in California, 7-11, 218-21
   and city type, 226-30
   and planning stage, 213
   and supplemental mode, 224-26
Residential vs. nonresidential cities, and contracts, 122-24, 136-37
Retail sales, and property crimes, 175-77. *See also* Commercial sales value
Roads
   and county contracts, 80, 95, 107-10
   and service disaggregation, 55-58
Roads, County Department of, 107-10

Sales base, commercial
   and budget, 128
   and contracts, 119-24, 139-41
   and departments, 139-41
   and property tax revenues, 125-26
Satisfaction, and service structure, 16, 34-42, 68
Scott, William A., 186-89
Self-anchoring scales, 188, 190, 194
Self-provision cities, 12-13, 204, 218-21, 226-30. *See also* Independent cities
   and budget, 21, 118, 125-28, 136, 138
   and contracting model, 231-34
   vs. contracts, 49-50, 73-74
   and government employees, 130-31
   and local control, 119, 136-37
   and police service, 142-43
   and property taxes, 118-25, 136-37
   and service quality, 27, 161-65
   and special districts, 133
   and street maintenance, 146
   and supplemental mode, 224-26

Service clusters, 18-27, 43-48, 55-58, 226-30
   and local control, 66-68
Service disaggregation, 55-62, 64, 66, 77
Service structure, defined, 66
Service transfer cities, 12-13, 53-54, 212
Sheriff, in LA county, 72, 75-76. *See also* LASD; Police chiefs
   and contract pricing, 88-95
   and county contracts, 85-87, 95, 98, 110-15
   and wage rates, 179
Shoup-Rosett study, 90
Single indicator/multiple-method strategy, 186
Single indicator/single method strategy, 186
Size of area, effects of, 42, 77
Sky Knight program, 111
Southern California Gas Company, 83
Special districts, 6, 19-21, 34, 67
   and contracts, 74, 130, 132-34, 137-38, 141, 214
   and tax rates, 51-52
Start-up costs, 24-25, 34-35, 42-43
Stationhouse costing, 91-92
Street and Highways Code 2106-2107, 109
Street maintenance, 9-10, 146-47
   and city managers, 37-38, 205
Structural analysis method, 183, 212-30
Studenski, Paul, 2
Subservices, 224-26
Subsidy issue, 80-82, 86-87, 153
Suburban stage, 79-82
Supplemental mode, 9, 224-26

Tax base. *See* Property-tax base
Tax rates. *See* Property-tax rates
Tax revenues, and special districts, 132-33
Total Transfer of Core Services, defined, 53n
Total Transfer of Optional Services, defined, 53n
Traffic accidents, 167-71
Traffic patrol, 9-10, 22-23
Traffic signal maintenance, 38
Transaction costs, 78-79
Types of cities, 11-14, 52-54, 226-30
Types of service structures, 9-11, 18-21, 35-43

Urban governance, and contracts, 71, 76-79
Urban Institute, 184
Urbanizing stage, 80

Values, property, 122, 138
Violent crimes, 163-65, 179-81

Wage rates
  and city managers, 34-35
  and patrol personnel, 166-71, 179
  and service structure, 24
Webb, Eugene, 184, 186
Will, Arthur, 72, 80, 83, 85, 95
Workload, and patrol personnel, 167-71

Zimmerman, Joseph, 74
Zoning, 9-10, 39

About The Authors

Sidney Sonenblum was research professor at UCLA during the preparation of this report. His particular research interests have related to economic development, urban policy, government finance, information systems, and energy and the economy. He has pursued these interests in government agencies, at Universities, in the private sector and is now an economic research consultant. His publications have included *Local Government Porgram Budgeting: Theory and Practice; Governing Urban America in the 1970's; Selecting Regional Information for Government Planning and Decision Making;* and *Energy and Economic Growth.*

John J. Kirlin is Associate Professor of Public Administration at the University of Southern California in Los Angeles. He is author or co-author of several articles and monographs on Urban and Metropolitan Government.

John C. Ries is Associate Vice Chancellor, Undergraduate Affairs and Professor of Political Science at UCLA.